Entrepreneurship
and
Innovation
MANAGEMENT
An Industry Perspective

Edited By
R GOPAL
PRADIP MANJREKAR

EXCEL BOOKS

ISBN: 978-81-7446-787-4

First Edition: New Delhi, 2010

EXCEL BOOKS
A-45, Naraina, Phase I,
New Delhi-110 028

Published by Anurag Jain for Excel Books, A-45, Naraina, Phase I, New Delhi-110 028
and printed by him at Excel Printers, C-205, Naraina, Phase I, New Delhi-110 028

Contents

Preface

Entrepreneurship is one of the most meaningful movements of our time. Peter Drucker, the eminent author of numerous books on management, calls this revival the most significant economic event of our time. Entrepreneurs are the ones who make economic gains from innovative ideas and creative efforts. Thus,

Entrepreneurs:

(i) create

(ii) innovate

(iii) employ

(iv) are vital to the success of every economy

(v) facilitate change as facilitating change is at the core of entrepreneurial action.

Rapid growth in entrepreneurship is seen because of the influx of small industries and the growth of technologies like Information Technology and Biotech and new enterprises like BPOs and KPOs, R&D Centres, Call Centres, etc. Many institutions world over now offer education and training programmes in the field of entrepreneurship. Entrepreneurship and Small Business Management is one of the popular programmes in business schools worldwide today.

While entrepreneurship's importance to the business and economic landscape seems abundantly clear (i.e., responsibility for new products and services, job creation and economic vitality, it is often taken for granted. Indian economy faces many challenges in the years ahead in the context of globalisation, intense competition, rapid product obsolescence, technological development and increasing the pace of innovation. Since entrepreneurs have been critical to the commercialization of major innovations in the past, it is only natural to ask 'What can be done to maximize the chance that innovations of greater importance will be initiated in this century?'

By nature, research is designed to produce answers to what we do not know. Researchers have provided many answers to questions such as who is an entrepreneur, with a variety of definitions used. Considerable exploratory studies are done on entrepreneurial motivations also. But we have limited information about issues like nature of business, regional spread and the demographic compositions of existing entrepreneurs and networks of researchers, innovation incubators, venture capitalists and angel financiers, etc. In particular, we lack data on high impact/high growth entrepreneurs who are starting and growing firms that generates benefits to the economy and society beyond the monetary benefits given by the entrepreneurs. Further research is necessary to better understand the apparent link between new business formation and productivity growth.

Variation in entrepreneurial success across the world suggests that entrepreneurial environment including educational levels of local population, prior industry concentration and regional income growth may play a significant role in entrepreneurship development. Entrepreneurship is a central ingredient in the economic growth. It serves as a vehicle for the commercial introduction of new goods and services as well as opening of new markets to innovations. Academic researchers are also working on the fundamental questions about exactly why the entrepreneurship process plays such a fundamental role in emerging economies and how policy and institutions can be designed to ensure long-term prosperity.

The last decade has seen a growing interest in entrepreneurship research. There have been an increasing number of practitioners, academic centers and journals in the areas of entrepreneurship and small business as well as a significant increase in the number of entrepreneurship centres. The contributions and shortcomings of past entrepreneurship research can be viewed within the context of six research design specifics: purpose, theoretical perspective, focus, level of analysis, time frame and methodology. The recent trend towards theory driven research, that is contextual and process-oriented, is encouraging. But it is time for entrepreneurship researchers to pursue causality more aggressively.

This book is compilation of papers drawn from the pool of papers received for the 1st & 2nd International Research Conference on Entrepreneurship held in November, 2007 & November, 2008, in association with Maharashtra Centre for Entrepreneurship Development (MCED) & National Entrepreneurship Network (NEN). We hope that this book will provide a good platform for dissemination of additional knowledge generated in this field by various investigators. We trust that this book will make a good beginning for a chain of academic activities in this field by our institution as well as other institutions for economic growth and higher productivity. Padmashree Dr. D.Y. Patil University's Department of Business Management organized the Conferences on Entrepreneurship to provide a podium to researchers and practitioners to deliberate upon some of the current issues, to draw viable solutions and to suggest the ways to fortify entrepreneurship for win-win outcomes.

DR R GOPAL
DR PRADIP MANJREKAR

Acknowledgements

We are thankful to all the contributors who have helped us in giving a final shape to the Book. Every effort in this direction had to pass through various phases where it was facilitated by many people either directly or indirectly. It is not possible to put on record the support of each and every person by name. We are grateful to all who have assisted us in the process of giving this book a tangible form.

However, in spite of the above generic statement, we would like to put on record our whole hearted sincere thanks to Dr. Ajeenkya Patil, President, Ramrao Adik Education Society; Mr. Vijay Patil, President, Padmashree Dr. D. Y. Patil Sports Academy; Dr. James Thomas, Vice-Chancellor, Padmashree Dr. D.Y. Patil University, Navi Mumbai and Dr. F.A. Fernandez, Registrar, Padmashree Dr. D.Y. Patil University, Navi Mumbai, for their wholehearted support in researching this nascent but yet a very important industry.

We would be failing in our duty if we did not acknowledge the guiding spirit in this venture viz., Founder Chancellor Padmashree Dr. D. Y. Patil, without whose guidance, this conference could not have taken place.

We are grateful to the unstinting efforts of our International Co-Conveners, Prof (Ms) Rashmi Gopinathan and Prof Krishna Shetty and also to the students of Department of Business Management, Padmashree Dr. D.Y. Patil University, Navi Mumbai, without whose co-operation this research conference could not have been a great success. We are also grateful to all our sponsors and associates.

About the Editors

Dr R Gopal is currently working as Director in the Department of Business Management at Padmashree Dr. D. Y. Patil University, Navi Mumbai. He has more than 27 years of Corporate experience. He has worked in organizations like Larsen and Toubro, Bush India Ltd., Tata Economic Consultancy Services and Siemens. At Siemens, he was actively involved in evolving and implementing strategies including launching of new products. Prior to this, he was also deputed to Siemens AG, Germany, where he was involved in the preparation of the strategic plan for various European Subsidiaries of Siemens AG.

He has extensive teaching experience as a visiting faculty in several B Schools in Mumbai, in the areas of Marketing, Market Research, Direct Marketing and Strategic Management/ Business Policy, etc. He has also conducted several programs in the USA on topics like "How to do Business in India", "Competitive Scenario in India", etc. He has published more than 100 research papers both in Indian and foreign journals. His research paper got the 'Best Outstanding Research Paper Award' at the 2nd Asia Pacific Marketing Conference, held in Malaysia, in October 2007. He is a member of the Editorial Board of a book titled *A Panorama of Research Work*.

Dr Pradip Manjrekar is presently working as Professor, Head, Research and Extension Centre and Head, Industry Institute Interaction Centre (inclusive of Placement Activities), Department of Business Management at Padmashree Dr. D.Y. Patil University, Navi Mumbai. He holds a Ph.D. (1985) from Mumbai University and MBA from Jamnalal Bajaj Institute of Management Studies, Mumbai. He holds two Postgraduate Diplomas in Sales and Marketing Management and Journalism & Mass Communication. He is a Fellow of Indian Chemical Society and Ex-Research Fellow of University Grants Commission (UGC), Govt. of India. He has work experience of more than 23 years in senior positions

in both the private as well as the public sector organizations like M/s Hindustan Organic Chemicals (HOC), M/s Blue Circle, M/s Classic Solvents, etc. He has been a Consultant to several industries in areas like Marketing Strategy, International Business, MIS, etc., and especially in areas related to ISO 9001: 2000 QMS Certification. He has wide teaching experience as visiting management faculty at several leading Management Educational Institutions in Mumbai. He has published more than 150 research papers in National and International Conferences/Journals in different areas of Chemical Sciences & Management. He has received "Outstanding Research Paper Award" for his research paper during the Asia Pacific Marketing Research Conference, 2007, held in Malaysia. He chaired various prestigious Research Conferences, like Asia Pacific Marketing Conference (2007), Malaysia; Strategic Management Research Conference (2008), IIT Kanpur, etc. He is the Editor of *DYPIMS Research Review* and Former Editor of *SFIMAR Research Review*. He is the Co-Editor of the book *Pathh : A Research Base for Entrepreneurial Excellence*.

An Empirical Attempt to Understand the Motivational Profile of Indian Women Entrepreneurs

Shailaja Karve*

Motivation is a phenomenon, which is increasingly having an impact on the working life of all professionals. The type of motivation and the kind of motives affect entrepreneurs and influence their work lives. The present study was undertaken to identify the motivational profile among women entrepreneurs.

Motivational Analysis of Organizational Behaviour (MAOB) incorporated 60 women entrepreneurs of Maharashtra and Karnataka in India. Responses were analyzed by using t-test (p<0.05). The findings reveal the nature and type of motives of women entrepreneurs.

INTRODUCTION

Motivation is one of the important facets of modern management. Motivational analysis helps in understanding the motivational profile, which can be used for increased effectiveness. Women are increasingly becoming an integral part of the modern managerial workforce. It is imperative to understand the motives of women and what motives set women entrepreneurs apart. Women can use their motivational analysis to increase their operating effectiveness.

In this paper, it is the endeavour of the researcher to examine the motivation amongst women.

Objectives of this Study

To assess the motivational style amongst women entrepreneurs and compare it with women managers/executives.

CONCEPTS

Motivation: A person's basic behaviour is the result of several factors or motives. Knowledge of the typical, primary motivators of behaviour in a work setting can help managers and consultants to deal more effectively with people. Thus, six primary needs or motives, which

---

* Faculty HR & OB, Somaiya Institute of Management and Research, Vidyavihar, Mumbai.

are relevant for understanding the behaviours of people in organizations, have been identified. These are as follows:

1. *Achievement:* Characterized by concern for excellence, competition with the standards of excellence set by others or by oneself, the setting of challenging goals for oneself, awareness of the hurdles in the way of achieving goals, and persistence in trying alternative path to reach one's goals.

2. *Affiliation:* Characterized by a concern for establishing and maintaining close personal relationships, by value on friendships, and a tendency to express one's emotions.

3. *Influence:* Characterized by a concern to make an impact on others, a desire to make people do what one thinks to be right, and an urge to change matters and (develop) people.

4. *Control:* Characterized by a concern for orderliness, a desire to remain informed, and an urge to be relevant and take corrective action when needed.

5. *Extension:* Characterized by a concern for others, interest in superordinate goals, and an urge to be useful and relevant to larger groups including society.

6. *Dependence:* Characterized by a desire for help from others in one's own self-development, checking with significant others (experts, associates, knowledgeable persons, etc.), submitting ideas or proposals for approval, having an urge to maintain an approval relationship.

The six motives of achievement, affiliation, influence, control, extension and dependence can be used to study behavior of people in industries. Each of these motives can have two dimensions: Approach and avoidance. An individual's effectiveness may result from the extent of the approach or avoidance dimension of a particular motivation.

MOTIVATIONAL BEHAVIOUR

McClelland (1975), demonstrated the importance of achievement motivation for entrepreneurship and power motivation in management. Pareek (1968), suggested extension motivation as use of power motivation for the benefit of others. Birney and Burdick (1969), Heckhawsen (1967), found "fear of failure" and "hope of success" as an important component of achievement motivation. Mathur (1993), found positive correlation between motivational aspects and job satisfaction.

McNeese-Smith and Donna-K. (1999), in their ex-post facto/correlational study examined the relationships among the following variables: Nurse, manager motivation for power, achievement and affiliation (N = 19), managerial leadership behaviours, staff nurse outcomes of job satisfaction, productivity and organizational commitment (N = 221), and patient satisfaction with nursing care (N = 299). Results show that managerial motivation for power is negatively correlated with managerial use of leadership behaviours and staff nurse job satisfaction, but positively correlated with patient satisfaction. Managerial motivation for achievement is positively correlated with use of leadership behaviours as well as nurse job satisfaction, productivity and organizational commitment, and generally to patient satisfaction. Managerial motivation for affiliation reveals few significant positive or negative relationships with other variables. The researcher concludes that both power and achievement motivation of the manager influence staff and patient outcomes in healthcare in the 1990s.

Shukla (1995), examined the relationship of entrepreneurial behaviour with verbal creativity and achievement motivation. *The Comprehensive Scale of Entrepreneurial Behaviour* (V. P. Sharma, 1978), *Verbal Test of Creative Thinking* (B. Mehdi, 1973) and *Achievement Motive Scale* (P. Mehta, 1969) was completed by 100 managers working in medium size industries in the public (N = 50) as well as private (N = 50) sectors. Pearson's coefficients of correlation were computed between them. Results indicate that: (1) Except for Personality Maturity (PM) and Human Relations (HR), the other four components of entrepreneurial behaviour have been found highly significantly related with achievement motivation; however, a moderately significant relationship has been obtained between global entrepreneurial behaviour and achievement motivation; (2) Achievement motivation has been found highly significantly related with fluency, flexibility and originality as well as with composite verbal creativity; and (3) All six components of entrepreneurial behaviour as well as global entrepreneurial behaviour have shown highly significant relationships with composite verbal creativity as well as its various components.

Amabile (1997), defines and gives specific examples of entrepreneurial creativity, which is the generation and implementation of novel, appropriate ideas to establish a new venture. Entrepreneurial creativity can be exhibited in established organizations as well as in start-up firms. The central thesis of this paper is that entrepreneurial creativity requires a combination of intrinsic motivation and certain kinds of extrinsic motivation—a motivational synergy that results when strong levels of personal interest and involvement are combined with the promise of rewards that confirm competence, support skill development, and enable future achievement.

Ghosh (1998), explored potential perceived differences in Need Satisfaction (NS) of 22 middle and 34 lower executives (aged 25-58 yrs) of two public sector organizations in eastern India. Service Sector completed measures of NS and managerial success. Deficiency in need fulfillment was more pronounced in lower level executives than in middle-level executives, especially in need areas of esteem, autonomy, and self-actualization. Areas of greatest importance were a higher-order need (self-actualization) and a lower-order need (security). In general, in both lower and middle-management positions, the most critical need hierarchy area was the area of self-actualization with respect to both prime importance and deficiency in need fulfillment. Also, there was only a trend toward psychological needs predicting managerial success of an executive.

Silverthorne (1996), investigated motivation and managerial styles in the private and public sectors in Taiwan (Republic of China) 120 service sectors in public service and 120 service sectors in private industry were selected. Each of these samples included 40 managers and 80 non-managers. Service sectors completed a survey with their demographic data, reasons for taking their particular job, and managerial inventory opinion data. Results indicate that there is little difference between the motivational needs of public and private-sector employees, and managers and non-managers. Compared to normative data for the US, motivational levels are much higher in Taiwan. A strong positive perception of public sector work exists in Taiwan, as well as a greater understanding and commitment to participate in motivationally based managerial styles in all types of organizations. A greater respect for public-sector employees seems to translate into effective motivational and managerial approaches.

Karwowska and Strelau (1990), investigated preferences for managerial styles differing in stimulative value as a function of individual reactivity in 168 male managers (aged 39-62 yrs) of large companies. The stimulative value of these styles was described in terms of a discrepancy between the individual's capacity for coping with professional tasks and the demands of the environment. The discrepancy was manipulated by lowering the service sector's social or task self-competences. Results show that: (1) the level of the managers' reactivity is significantly lower than in a standardization sample, (2) managers prefer managerial styles of high stimulative value, whether production or people-oriented, (3) high reactive managers prefer managerial styles of low stimulative value whereas in low reactives an opposite tendency was noted, and (4) under stress, an increase of preference for less stimulating managerial styles was noted, this being especially evident in the more reactive managers.

Kool and Saksena (1989), explored prevalent managerial styles and their effectiveness in 1 private and 1 public sector organization by surveying 220 executives in top, middle, and lower level management. Four management styles were examined: (1) high task/low relationship, (2) high task/high relationship, (3) high relationship/low task, and (4) low task/low relationship. The majority of managers (87%) adopted Style 2 as their primary or secondary leadership style followed by Style 3. Top and middle level managers preferred Style 2 more than lower level managers. Ownership also affected the leadership preference. The private sector organization was found slightly task-oriented. 74% of the managers were effective. Public sector managers differed significantly. Level of management did not affect the leadership effectiveness

Klein, Kossek, Astrachan and Fleming (1998), explored gender and level differences in work experiences, their study examined the actual work experiences reported by women and men leaders. Case material was collected from 5 female executives and 12 female managers from major companies and public organizations attending a series of training seminars. A sample of 5 male executives and 12 male managers, matched for attendance at the same seminar and age, were chosen for comparison. Each participant was asked to submit a 2-page typed case involving unresolved organizational issues to be reviewed in the discussion group at the seminar. Cases were reviewed for whether the problem was with a superior, peer, or subordinate; whether the specific problems involved authority, motivation, reorganization, psychological contract violation, conflict or legitimacy; and whether the reported managerial style differences were due to age, gender, and race. Men, more frequently than women, tended to experience problems with subordinates and focused on changes in authority, difficulties in motivating others, reorganization, and violation of the psychological contract. Women tended to report more problems with superiors, their own legitimacy, and issues of age and gender.

Orpen (1997), formulated the hypothesis that job involvement moderates the relationship between the quality of communication and employee job satisfaction and work motivation was examined among a sample of 135 managers from 21 different firms (4 to 7 managers from each firm) in a variety of industries. The quality of communication for each manager was measured on a scale of Organizational Communication Effectiveness (Frone & Major, 1988); the average scores of other managers (never less than 3) from the same firm were used to remove response bias from the communication-outcome correlation. In a hierarchical regression analysis, the involvement communication interaction added significantly to the explained variance in both satisfaction and motivation. Managers who were more involved were more affected by the quality of communication.

Johnson, Schneider and Oswald (1997), applied a typological approach to the performance domain by investigating the profile similarity of managers across a number of managerial performance dimensions. Service sectors where 346 managers (mean age 39.9 yrs) employed in a variety of organizations, who had been given feedback on their management skills via the Management Skills Profile. Inverse principal components analysis identified 3 types of managers, which were defined by examining correlations between person-component loadings and scores on performance, ability, and personality variables. Task-oriented Technicians were technically skilled but interpersonally ineffective; Amiable Underachievers were interpersonally sensitive, but were lacking in motivation and many managerial skills; and People-oriented Leaders excelled in leadership and supervision aspects of the job, but had relatively poor financial and quantitative skills. Despite the differences in their profiles, mean scores for Task-oriented Technicians and People-oriented Leaders did not differ on a measure of overall performance.

Chen, Yu and Miner (1997), assessed 82 Chinese women's motivation to manage using projective methods and the relationship of motivation to managerial success in Chinese state-owned enterprises. Information on job level, education, sex, age, and work unit were gathered. Data were compared with that of 121 male workers. Results show that overall managerial motivation of Chinese women was as high as that of Chinese men. Overall managerial motivation, imposing wishes, and standing out from the group were positively related to the hierarchical job level. Female workers/clerks scored lower but female professionals/managers scored higher than their male counterparts on the variable of standing out from the group. Of the various component motives, the desires to exercise power and to stand out from the group were the significant predictors.

Adamiec and Kozusznik (1996), from diagnostic research of 600 people in middle and top level management in Poland yielded a basic procedural-sequential model of managerial characteristics. The model suggests that the effective manager is composed of 6 characteristics: Assertiveness, motivation, creativity, criticism, extraversion, and lack of pathological deformations. The authors use the term meta-trait to emphasize that effective managerial behaviour consists of two hierarchical layers: The first is personality equipped with a special set of properties, and the second is the skill of using these properties as tools during action.

On examining the above studies the present investigator found that there is a lacunae in research on women entrepreneurs and women executives on motivation. To bridge this gap the investigator proposed to study motivation among women entrepreneurs and women executives.

PURPOSE

To assess the motivational behaviour of women entrepreneurs.

Sample

In the present study, the sample will consist of two groups of adult working women namely "entrepreneur". It was proposed to have 60 respondents in the age range of 25-60 years. This age group has been selected because individuals have settled in their chosen vocation and career path.

Primary source for women entrepreneurs will be collected from National Small Industries Corporation (NSIC), Maharashtra Industrial Developmental Corporation (MIDC), Association of Women Entrepreneurs Karnataka (AWAKE), Women Entrepreneurs of Maharashtra Association (WIMA), etc. Randomised sampling techniques and snowball technique were used.

Description of the Instrument

The Motivational Analysis of Organizational Behavior (MAOB) scale used in the study is a questionnaire developed by Pareek (1997), which is prepared in English language. The Gutman split-half reliability is 0.62 of MAOB (Pareek, 1997). Motivational Analysis of Organizations Behavior (MAOB) was developed to study manager or employee behaviour in an organization. MAOB contains sixty items, five for each dimension (approach and avoidance) of each of the six motives: achievement, affiliation, extension, influence, control and dependency.

Administration

The investigator contacted all the respondents personally and administered the test. The MAOB scale was administered in a predetermined order in individual or group set-up. Clear instructions were given and doubts, if any, were clarified. Importance of giving honest answers rather than ideal answers was emphasized. Total confidentiality was assured and cooperation solicited. Approximate time required to complete the scale was 25 minutes.

Scoring

The scoring procedure followed by Pareek (1997), was adopted in scoring the MAOB. In scoring the responses of the respondents on the scale and its subscales, the response indicating 'if you never/rarely feel or behave this way' is given a score of 1, the response indicating 'if you sometimes/occassionally never feel or behave this way' is given a score of 2, the response indicating 'if you often/frequently never feel or behave this way' is given a score of 3 and the response indicating' if you usually/always never feel or behave this way ' is given a score of 4. MAOB has twelve sub-scales six for approach mode and six for avoidance mode of motivational behavior. The following are the six sub-scales of the MAOB on approach mode with their respective items: Achievement (items 1, 13, 25, 37, 49), Influence (items 3, 15, 27,39, 51), Control (items 5, 17, 29, 41, 53), Affiliation (items 8, 20, 32, 44, 56), Dependence (items 10, 22, 34, 46, 58), Extension (items 12, 24, 36, 48, 60), and the six sub-scales of the MAOB on avoidance mode with their respective items are as follows: Achievement (items 7, 19, 31, 43, 55), Influence (items 9, 21, 33, 45, 57), Control (items 11, 23, 35, 47, 59, 52), Affiliation (items 2, 14, 26, 38, 50), Dependence (items 4, 16, 28, 40, 52), Extension (items 6, 18, 30, 42, 54). The respondent's Operating Effectiveness Quotient (OEQ) for each of the six motive-specific aspects of behaviour can be obtained by using the formula

$$OEQ = \frac{P-5}{P+V-10} \times 100$$

(where "P" and "V" represent total scores for approach and avoidance dimensions respectively of a motive-specific behaviour). Thus, by using the formula the Operating Effectiveness Quotient (OEQ) of achievement (A), influence (B), control (C), affiliation (F), dependence (D), extension (E) can be found. The total score for each dimension (approach and avoidance) of the six motives can range from 5 to 20. To obtain the OEQ for each motive the total score thus obtained by the formula is then referred to in the following operating effectiveness quotient matrix.

Operating Effectiveness Quotient Matrix

Avoidance Scores	Approach scores															
	5	6	7	8	9	10	11	12	13	14	15	16	17	18	19	20
5	0	100	100	100	100	100	100	100	100	100	100	100	100	100	100	100
6	0	50	67	75	80	83	85	87	89	90	91	92	92	93	93	99
7	0	33	50	60	67	71	75	78	80	82	83	85	86	87	87	89
8	0	25	40	50	52	62	67	70	73	75	77	78	80	81	82	83

Contd...

9	0	20	33	43	50	55	60	64	67	69	71	73	75	76	78	79
10	0	17	28	37	44	50	54	58	61	64	67	69	70	72	74	75
11	0	14	25	33	40	45	50	54	59	60	62	65	67	68	70	71
12	0	12	22	30	36	42	46	50	53	56	59	61	63	65	67	68
13	0	11	20	27	33	38	43	47	50	53	55	58	60	62	64	65
14	0	10	18	25	31	36	40	44	47	50	53	55	57	59	61	62
15	0	9	17	23	28	33	37	41	44	47	50	52	54	56	58	60
16	0	8	15	21	27	31	35	39	42	45	48	50	52	54	56	58
17	0	8	14	20	25	29	33	37	40	43	45	48	50	52	54	56
18	0	7	13	19	23	28	32	35	38	41	43	46	48	50	52	54
19	0	7	12	18	22	26	30	33	36	39	41	44	46	48	50	52
20	0	6	12	17	21	25	29	32	35	37	40	42	44	46	48	50

Norms

The mean value for the OEQ of MAOB scores, in a sample of 500 employees from four banks in India (Sen, 1982) and 200 health managers in Indonesia, are shown. Standard deviation values are also given for the Indonesian sample. These can tentatively be used as cut-off points for interpretation of scores. For example, for the Indonesian group, the mean plus 0.5 SD will be regarded as a high score, and mean minus 0.5 SD will be regarded as a low score. However, norms should be developed for different groups.

Dimensions	India Mean	Indonesia		Executives (20)	
	500 bankers	Mean	SD	Mean	SD
Achievement	68	58	10	63	11
Affiliation	65	67	10	71	14
Influence	56	55	8	58	7
Control	63	59	6	55	6
Extension	64	59	9	66	13
Dependence	65	56	10	65	6

Variables

The focus of this research is on some aspects of women entrepreneur and women executives. Specifically Motivational analysis of behaviour, Conflict management style (approach and avoidance), Role efficacy, Role stress and Coping with role stress (proactive and reactive).

OPERATIONAL DEFINITIONS OF TERMS USED IN THIS STUDY

1. *Entrepreneur:* One, who is engaged in her own venture for at least 5 years, is not a figurehead only.

2. *Motivation:* In the present study motivation is the operational effectiveness quotient based on the scores on Achievement, Affiliation, Influence, Control, Extension and Dependent motives on Motivational Analysis of Organization Behaviour (MAOB) scale. (Pareek)

Statistical Analysis of Data

With the help of the statistical software, SPSS/Statistical, the data were analyzed. Further, reliability analyses on each item/dimension with respect to the instrument used in this study were attempted.

Reliability Analysis

The reliability coefficients of different items on measures used in the study were obtained by correlating the scores of the subjects on the different items with the scores on their respective scales. So far as, the item total correlation are concerned, these are the measures of item analysis used for selecting the critical item for a given scale. On the other hand, to judge the internal consistency or compositeness of the scale, Cronbach alpha coefficients (1951), were calculated. It may be noted that alpha coefficient ranges from 0 to 1.0. The higher the coefficients, the greater the internal consistency of composite scales. The cut-off point generally accepted is 0.60. Since the scales used in this study have yielded alpha coefficients as shown below which are above the cut off point of 0.60, it was concluded that, the instruments selected in these studies are capable of providing the reliable measures of the variables being investigated.

After completing the data collection, the responses on MAOB scale were scored and the data tabulated for women entrepreneur. The data collected in the investigation as described earlier were statistically analyzed.

Table 1: Reliability Analysis of Motivational Analysis of Organizations-Behavior (MAO-B)

Motivational Analysis of Organizations-Behavior (MAO-B) Scale Items	Item Total Correlation Entrepreneur	Motivational Analysis of Organizations-Behavior (MAO-B) Scale Items	Item Total Correlation Entrepreneur
1. Achievement (app)1	.417*	31. Achievement (avd)3	.286
2. Affiliation (avd)1	.141	32. Affiliation (app)3	.353*
3. Influence (app)1	-.091	33. Influence (avd)3	-.076
4. Dependence (avd)1	-.046	34. Dependence (app)3	.225
5. Control (app)1	.154	35. Control (avd)3	.047
6. Extension (avd)1	.527*	36. Extension (app)3	.271
7. Achievement (avd)1	.337*	37. Achievement (app)4	.192
8. Affiliation (app)1	.228	38. Affiliation (avd)4	.547*
9. Influence (avd)1	-.350*	39. Influence (app)4	.450*
10. Dependence (app)1	-.115	40. Dependence (avd)4	.432*
11. Control (avd)1	.088	41. Control (app)4	.456*
12. Extension (app)1	.278	42. Extension (avd)4	.144
13. Achievement (app)2	.094	43. Achievement (avd)4	.312*
14. Affiliation (avd)2	.283	44. Affiliation (app)4	.603*
15. Influence (app)2	.335*	45. Influence (avd)4	.173
16. Dependence (avd)2	.388*	46. Dependence (app)4	.069
17. Control (app)2	.494*	47. Control (avd)4	.341*
18. Extension (avd)2	.406*	48. Extension (app)4	.338*
19. Achievement (avd)2	.376*	49. Achievement (app)5	.037
20. Affiliation (app)2	.161	50. Affiliation (avd)5	-.029
21. Influence (avd)2	-.217	51. Influence (app)5	.363
22. Dependence (app)2	.395*	52. Dependence (avd)5	-.060
23. Control (avd)2	-.032	53. Control (app)5	.010
24. Extension (app)2	.448*	54. Extension (avd)5	.422*
25. Achievement (app)3	.385*	55. Achievement (avd)5	-.470
26. Affiliation (avd)3	-.047	56. Affiliation (app)5	.615*
27. Influence (app)3	.294	57. Influence (avd)5	-.258
28. Dependence (avd)3	.278	58. Dependence (app)5	.662*
29. Control (app)3	.063	59. Control (avd)5	.111
30. Extension (avd)3	.354*	60. Extension (app)5	-.028

The reliability analysis on the scale of Motivational Analysis of Organizations-Behaviour (MAOB) Scale was done by using the responses of 60 subjects included in the sample. There are sixty items in the scale and inter-item correlation on all sixty items for Entrepreneur are presented in Table 1. From the table, it can be seen that the items 1,6,7,15,16,17,18,19, 22,24,25,30,32,38,39,40,41,43,44,47,54, 56,58 of Motivational Analysis of Organizations-Behaviour (MAO-B) Scale has yielded high correlation coefficients for entrepreneurs.

Table 2: Reliability Analysis of Sub-scales of Motivational Analysis of Organisations-Behaviour (MAO-B)

Subscales of Motivation (MAO-B)	Mean	SD	Inter item Total correlation	Cronbach alpha coefficient
Achievement (app)	16.76	2.42	.287	.647*
Affiliation (app)	11.79	2.38	.058	.238
Influence (app)	14.26	2.31	.051	.192
Dependence (app)	11.96	2.92	.151	.460
Control (app)	16.47	2.31	.151	.448
Extension (app)	13.61	3.09	.285	.658*
Achievement (avd)	10.93	2.69	.175	.511
Affiliation (avd)	14.89	2.77	.206	.562
Influence (avd)	10.75	2.94	.107	.362
Dependence (avd)	16.54	2.23	.178	.497
Control (avd)	14.94	2.05	.025	.099
Extension (avd)	16.86	2.12	.152	.501

Table 2 shows the reliability coefficient of the twelve dimensions of Motivational Analysis of Organizations-Behavior (MAO-B) scale. This was obtained by inter-item correlation of five items on each dimension. There are sixty items in the scale and the correlation coefficient pertaining to the reliability of all the twelve dimensions were worked out by using Cronbach alpha coefficient method for each sub-scale. The reliability coefficient for the following subscales is significant Achievement (app) and Extension (app) for women entrepreneurs. The overall Cronbach alpha coefficient is 0.768 for women entrepreneurs. It was concluded that the scale on Motivational Analysis of Organizations-Behavior (MAO-B) used in the present study is capable of providing valid and reliable information on entrepreneurial motivation and its dimensions.

t- test to compare the mean score of entrepreneur and executives

Table 3: Means of Scores on Dimensions of Motivation for Women Entrepreneurs and Women Executives and Results of t-test

Dimensions of Motivation	Group	Mean	SD	t-value
Achievement (APP)	Entrepreneur	16.48	3.23	3.04*
	Executive	14.81	2.43	
Affiliation (APP)	Entrepreneur	14.65	3.35	0.726
	Executive	14.23	2.90	
Influence (APP)	Entrepreneur	13.91	2.95	0.497
	Executive	13.65	2.91	
Control (APP)	Entrepreneur	16.20	3.12	3.25*
	Executive	14.46	2.69	

Contd...

Extension (APP)	Entrepreneur	16.56	3.01	2.76*
	Executive	15.08	2.84	
Dependence (APP)	Entrepreneur	16.26	3.07	1.93
	Executive	15.23	2.78	
Total Approach	Entrepreneur	94.08	15.85	2.47*
	Executive	87.48	13.23	
Achievement (AVD)	Entrepreneur	10.75	3.01	-1.79
	Executive	11.75	3.08	
Affiliation (AVD)	Entrepreneur	11.55	2.81	-1.75
	Executive	12.45	2.78	
Influence (AVD)	Entrepreneur	10.58	3.09	-.852
	Executive	11.08	3.32	
Control (AVD)	Entrepreneur	14.05	3.13	2.75*
	Executive	12.51	2.96	
Extension (AVD)	Entrepreneur	13.38	3.53	.328
	Executive	13.18	3.11	
Dependence (AVD)	Entrepreneur	11.33	3.43	-3.00*
	Executive	13.06	2.86	
Total Avoidance	Entrepreneur	71.65	13.51	-.949
	Executive	74.05	14.16	

Table 3 contains means of scores on all the dimensions motivation for both entrepreneur and executive and the results of the t-test. Mean scores of entrepreneur are higher than the executives on all dimensions of motivation on the approach mode; control and extension dimensions of motivation on the avoidance mode. Mean scores of executives are higher than the entrepreneur on achievement, affiliation, influence, dependence and total avoidance, on avoidance mode of motivation. The significant t-values indicate that the mean differences are statistically significant in the case of on Achievement (app), Control (app), Extension (app), and total Approach mode; on Control (avd) and Dependence (avd) of avoidance mode. It appears that these dimensions of motivation are the most defining dimensions in differentiating motivation among entrepreneurs and executives.

Table 4: Means of Operational Effectiveness Quotient Scores on Dimensions of Motivation for Women Entrepreneurs and Women Executives and Results of t-test

Dimensions of Motivation	Group	Mean	SD	t-value
Achievement (OEQ)	Entrepreneur	66.93	12.86	2.52*
	Executive	60.57	14.65	
Affiliation (OEQ)	Entrepreneur	59.48	9.41	1.95
	Executive	53.12	23.38	
Influence (OEQ)	Entrepreneur	62.38	14.48	.945
	Executive	59.93	13.82	
Control (OEQ)	Entrepreneur	55.39	9.61	-.570
	Executive	56.43	10.29	

Contd...

Extension (OEQ)	Entrepreneur	59.48	10.52	1.47
	Executive	56.48	11.79	
Dependence (OEQ)	Entrepreneur	65.11	13.68	3.89*
	Executive	55.96	11.98	
Operational Effectiveness Quotient (OEQ)	Entrepreneur	57.11	4.56	2.98*
	Executive	54.51	4.96	

Significant at .05 level.

Table 4 contains means of operational effectiveness quotient scores on all the dimensions of motivation for both entrepreneur and executive and the results of the t-test. Mean scores of entrepreneur are higher than the executives on all dimensions of motivation of operational effectiveness quotient except extension dimension. Mean scores of executives are higher than the entrepreneur on extension dimension of operational effectiveness quotient. The significant t-values indicate that the mean differences are statistically significant in the case of Achievement (OEQ), Dependence (OEQ) and total Operational Effectiveness Quotient of the six dimensions of motivation. It appears that these dimensions of motivation are the most defining dimensions in differentiating motivation among entrepreneurs and executives.

The finding of the present study is that the entrepreneurs and the executives systematically distinguish between themselves on motivation. Motivational behaviour appears to be a crucial factor in differentiating between an entrepreneur and executives.

In discussing the dimensions of motivation, of the six dimensions of motivational behaviour, it appears that Achievement (characterized by concern for excellence, competition with the standards of excellence set by others or by oneself, the setting of challenging goals for oneself, awareness of the hurdles in the way of achieving goals, and persistence in trying alternative path to reach one's goals), Dependence (characterized by a desire for help from others in one's own self development, checking with significant others, submitting ideas or proposals for approval, having an urge to maintain an approval relationship) and overall Operational Effectiveness Quotient are the most defining dimensions in differentiating motivational behaviour among entrepreneurs and executives.

References

Amabile, Teresa M. (1997), *Journal of Creative Behavior*, Vol 31(1), 18-26.

Chen, Chao C., Yu, K. C., Miner, J. B. (1997), "Motivation to Manage: A study of women in Chinese state-owned enterprises", *Journal of Applied Behavioral Science*, June, Vol 33(2), 160-173.

Ghosh, Anjali (1998), *Journal of the Indian Academy of Applied Psychology*, Jan-Jul, Vol 24(1-2), 33-36.

Johnson, Jeff W., Schneider, Robert J., Oswald, Frederick L. (1997), "Toward a Taxonomy of Managerial Performance Profiles, *Human Performance*, Vol 10(3), 227-250.

Karwowska Szulkin, Renata, Strelau, Jan (1990), "Reactivity and the stimulative value of managerial styles", *Polish Psychological Bulletin*, Vol 21(1), 49-60.

Klein, Edward B. (Ed), Gabelnick, Faith G. (Ed), *et al.* (1998), *The Psychodynamics of Leadership*, pp. 279-295, Madison, CT, USA, Psychosocial Press/International Universities Press, Inc. xvi, 371 pp.

Klein, Edward B., Kossek, Ellen E., Astrachan, Joseph H., Fleming, Claudia H. (1998), The Organization woman: Reflections of society in the workplace.

Kool, Reeta, Saksena, N. K. (1989), "Leadership styles and its effectiveness among Indian executives", *Indian Journal of Applied Psychology*, Jan, Vol 26(1), 9-15.

Orpen, Christopher (1997), "The Interactive effects of communication quality and job involvement on managerial job satisfaction and work motivation", *Journal of Psychology*, Sept, Vol 131(5), 519-522.

Pareek, U. (1997), *Training Instruments for Human Resource Development*, Tata McGraw-Hill, New Delhi.

Shukla, Prabhavati (1995), *Psycho Lingua*, Jan-July, Vol 25(1-2), 23-30.

Silverthorne, Colin P. (1996), "Motivation and management styles in the public and private sectors in Taiwan and a comparison with the United States", *Journal of Applied Social Psychology*, Oct, Vol 26(20), 1827-1837.

2

A Case Study of Product Development Activities in Small and Medium Food Beverage Industry

Aarte Aggarwal*

Amit Aggarwal*

Dr. Pradip Manjrekar**

The purpose of this research is to study the cases of Product Development practices undertaken at XYZ Company. XYZ Company falls under the category of small and medium enterprise, is involved in production of cakes and buns for ten years.

INTRODUCTION

The changing needs of food consumer for new and better products are increasing rapidly. In order to succeed in the food business industry, food manufacturers have to meet the customer requirement. Innovation and the introduction of new food products developments are essential to food manufacturers in order to gain competitive advantage and be successful in the marketplace. According to Marvin (1995), the concept of food product development process begins with a concept and ends with either the entry of the product in the market or the maintenance of the product in the market place. Alison (2003), quoted that normally the activities and types of product development by Small and Medium-sized Enterprises (SMEs) are unreported. The purpose of this paper is to study the cases of Product Development Practices undertaken at XYZ Company. XYZ Company is involved in produce cakes and buns for ten years. The purpose of selecting food and beverage industries is because of this industry contributes major income for the Maharashtra's economy. The company is located at Pune.

FOOD PROCESSING INDUSTRY IN MAHARASHTRA

The food processing industry makes a major contribution to the economy of Maharashtra. It has a turnover in excess of US $1.6 billion and a labour force of more than 99,300. The food processing sector accounts for about 20% of Maharashtra's manufacturing output in 2005.

*   Faculty, ITM, Business School, Kharghar, Navi Mumbai.
** Professor, Dr. D.Y. Patil Institute of Management Studies, CBD Belapur, Navi Mumbai.

Processed foods are exported to 80 countries, with an annual export value of more than Rs 6 billion which amounts to two-thirds of the total export of over Rs 16.2 billion.

According to MSSIDC (2007), Small and Medium enterprises in the manufacturing are enterprises with full-time employees not exceeding 150 or with annual turnover not exceeding Rs 25 million.

Food production in Maharashtra is diversified. The major business categories are listed as follows:

(a) Production of palm oil products,

(b) Livestock products,

(c) Sea food products,

(d) Flour-based products,

(e) Fruits and vegetables,

(f) Food ingredient, and

(g) Animal feed.

THE CONCEPT OF PRODUCT DEVELOPMENT WITHIN FOOD INDUSTRY

New Product Development (NPD) has become critical to the growth and future prosperity of organizations (Helen, 2005). The rate of NPD in particular is considered a crucial factor in a company's success (Sethi, 2001). More recently, Calantone *et al*, (2003) state, that environmental turbulence (i.e., uncertainty) is also an important factor that directly affects NPD strategic planning. As competition is now global, companies must harness knowledge from sources in multiple countries to generate new products, as well as to build operational know-how and technological strength (Subramaniam, 2001). Thus, managers need to have better understanding and skill in managing the NPD process, including how to practise scanning the external information that is useful in making their NPD more effective and efficient. They should have more extensive knowledge of how to practically implement environmental scanning, the role of their own company's technology strategy, and the influence of technology turbulence in using environmental scanning in their NPD (Chittipa, 2005). This involves quickly identifying changing customer needs; developing more complex products to satisfy those needs worldwide; and providing better customer service, while also utilizing the power of technology in managing performance and reliability (Cooper, 2001).

Innovation and the introduction of new food products are effective ways for SMEs to gain advantage in the marketplace (Rudder *et al*, 2001), for example, Avermaete *et al*, (2003), discussed the need for smaller food companies to continuously introduce new products, develop new processes, make changes in organizational structure and explore new markets. There are several important challenges in developing successful new food products, not the least of which are making sure that new products fit market needs and that the technology embodied in the food product itself and in its production process is up-to-date and efficient. Thus, to fully utilize New Product Development (NPD) as a competitive tool in food industries, SMEs must make effective use of environmental scanning. SMEs should have long-term vision, supported by a systematic, formal scanning process (McGee and Sawyerr, 2003; Temtime, 2004). Product development essentially involves the control of stages, from receipt or preparation of an initial concept through to scale-up and transfer to production. According to Graf *et al.* (1991), there are five product development process, broadly defined phases:

- *Screening:* Initial evaluation of ideas, with possible consumer testing and technology screening to ensure achievement of desired quality attributes, processing, packaging, distribution and shelf-life stability. Idea generation should be linked to current consumer needs and trends and these ideas are usually translated into kitchen samples and compared with existing products. At this stage, it is also essential to understand the profit impact of doing nothing; a consideration which is often overlooked.

- *Feasibility Evaluation:* Initiating a concept brief and assessing its feasibility from a technical, manufacturing and financial viewpoint. Ideally, a development evaluation must be completed before there is any commitment to capital expenditure, budget or customer launch requirements.

- *Development:* Identifying and resolving scale-up issues, product/process/packing interactions, shelf-life (to ensure a microbiologically and chemically safe, physically stable and organoleptically satisfactory product to the end of the designated shelf-life), tolerance testing to produce an allowable range of deviations from a standard and documentation with procedures and specifications for both ingredients and product.

- *Commercialization:* With start-up, process optimization and quality approval.

- *Maintenance:* Most major food product lines require some degree of continuous R&D support throughout the product lifetime, and a mistake that many companies make is not to realize this. Equally important is the ongoing improvement process to maximize quality and/or profits.

New Product Development (NPD) should, therefore, have a proactive role with marketing, production and other departments in:

- Keeping a current list of key projects, stages reached, terms of reference, timetable targets and team members.

- Providing regular updates on major projects; to identify successes as well as potential problem areas and help to maintain project relevance as well as controlling the actual NPD systems.

RESEARCH STRATEGY

The research design employed was a case study approach. Semi-structured interview with individuals involved in the Product Development process were among the methods employed to gather the data. Interviews were also conducted with those personnel from the operations department who interface with the Product Development process.

The objective of this research is to observe the product development process in the small and medium industry.

BACKGROUND OF THE CASE

XYZ Company was established in 1997, producing variety breads and cakes such as: milk bread, corn bread, cream bread, butter bread, chocolate bread, and cheese bread. The types of cake that were produce by this company such as; butter cake, chocolate cake, cheese cake, strawberry cake, pandan cake and banana cakes. Although, XYZ Company operating with 100 full-time employees but the breads and cakes not only marketed in Maharashtra but also has penetrated overseas market.

XYZ Company is committed to produce the best quality bread products for their customers. The customer for the company includes housewife, restaurant, canteen school, hypermarkets, small sundry shops, hypermarket and others. Consequently, the major customers who purchase the bread and cakes from XYZ Company come from all over the country.

Product Development in XYZ Company

XYZ Company is involved in creating new products and developing the existing product to fulfill the needs of their customers. The first step, before product development, teamwork will be develop, the committee consist of selected employee from all department (sales department, design department, human resources department, marketing department and production department). The particular teamwork was responsible to meet and cooperate with supervisor and production manager throughout the new product development process. In this phase the communication and the information exchange are very important. There are seven phases of product development at XYZ Company. The process undertaken by the company begins with idea generation, idea screening, concept development, test marketing and commercialization XYZ Company is aggressive in its to product development and it is proactive in identifying opportunities. The idea generation is the initial stage of the product development process in this company. They will generate a large number of ideas for product introduction purpose. Most of ideas come from an assessment of what the market or customer actually needs. The brainstorming method is well implemented among teamwork, supervisor, and manager. Before that, the committee will get the information from various sources such as customer, competitors and supplier. However, customers of this company are involved in keeping-up with market trends and looking-out for new opportunities. After a product idea has been developed, it will evaluate to determine its likelihood of success. The committee will evaluates the product design idea according to the needs of the market. The unsuitable idea will be dropped out and the good idea will be evaluated. There are few criteria that will be reviewed, such as:

- Does the new idea (product) meet the customer needs?
- Is there any additional value to the new idea (product)?
- Target market
- Competition
- Costs
- Time development
- Profit

Concept development is the process of shaping and refining the idea into a complete product concept. Concept testing is then used to get the potential customers to evaluate product concept. This stage involves developing a concept and defining a product. After that, testing of the product will be carved out. Normally, the customers were given samples of new products. After that they will be asked to respond to various questions about new products, such as the taste, texture, colour, flavour and price. Any feedback gained would be assessed. The detailed marketing strategy will be developed such as target market, planning of production, positioning, sales, market share, price, and distribution.

In marketing test stage, company will test a new product and its marketing strategy in an actual situation.

The information gathered will be used for improvement. At this level, management attempts to reduce to make a major financial mistake. During the commercialization stage, XYZ Company is ready to launch the product into full-scale production and sale. These involve monitoring the product over several weeks, monitoring progression of production process and finally, monitoring the reaction the consumer to the product. XYZ Company continuously monitors a product and makes improvement when necessary.

Case Study Conclusion

The decision to evaluate XYZ Company was taken due to the difficulty of ascertaining the report of product development among SMEs. The overview of the XYZ Company product development gives us an example on the NPD approach of small and medium food and beverage enterprise to meet the demand of both the retailers and consumers. Innovation and the introduction of new food product developments are essential to food companies in order to gain competitive advantage and become successful in the marketplace.

References

Avermaete, T., Viaene, J., Morgan, E.J., Crawford, N. 2003, "Determinants of innovation in small food firms", *European Journal of Innovation Management*, Vol. 6, No.1, pp. 8-17.

Calantone, R., Garcia, R., Droge, C., 2003, "The effects of environmental turbulence on new product development strategy planning", *Journal of New Production and Innovation Management*, Vol. 20, pp. 90-103.

Chittipa, N., Mark, S., Nicholas J. D., 2005, "Environmental scanning in Thai food SMEs, The impact of technology strategy and technology turbulence", *British Food Journal*, Vol. 107, No. 5, pp. 285-305.

Cooper, R.G. 2001, "Winning at New Products", *Perseus Books*, Scranton, PA.

Graf, E., Saguy, I.S., 1991, "Food Product Development from Concept to the Marketplace", Reinhold, New York, NY.

Helen R.P.G., Kulwant A.P. 2005, "Measuring international NPD projects: an evaluation process", *Journal of Business & Industrial Marketing*, Vol. 20, No. 2, pp. 79-87.

McGee, J.E., Sawyer, O.O. 2003, "Uncertainty and information search activities: a study of owner-managers of small high-technology manufacturing firms", *Journal of Small Business Management*, Vol. 41, No.4, pp. 385-401.

Rudder, A., Ainsworth, P., Holgate, D. 2001, "New food product development: Strategies for success?", *British Food Journal*, Vol. 103, No.9, pp. 657-71.

Sethi, R., Smith, D.C., Park, C.W., 2001, "Cross-functional product development systems integration and the innovativeness of new consumer products", *Journal of Marketing Research*, Vol. 38, February, pp. 73-85.

Subramaniam, M., Venkatraman, N., 2001, "Determinants of Transnational New Product Development Capability", *Strategic Management Journal*, Vol. 22, pp. 359-78.

e-Governance for Urban Poor Development through Women Entrepreneurs

Krishna Rohit*
Dr. Pradip Manjrekar**

INTRODUCTION

Women power is the heart of the urban poor system both for family maintenance and job for earning a livelihood. However, they are generally neglected by the indifferent attitude of society and social organizations. They are found to have a good potential if given encouragement and support to bring out their entrepreneurial talents and operating from home, add/create wealth to themselves and the nation through a cottage and similar industries. Experiments in countries like in India with 'Lijjat Papad' and 'Grameen Bank' of Bangladesh, have shown tremendous results and can be emulated here. The proposal plans to forward a working plan for development of the women 'entrepreneurial talent' and building up a potential '(wo)manpower' base into a creative and productive outfit on a team/cooperative oriented basis.

LITERATURE REVIEW

In "Digital Kiosk in South Africa", the efforts to facilitate digital use at the urban poor pace was attempted and the experiences noted. This was initiated by efforts in India of a similar nature.

In "Exploring e-Commerce Benefits for Businesses in Developing Countries", (*Information Society*, 2007, Vol. 23, 2) Molla, Alemmayehu, Heeks and Richards, notes that e-Commerce benefits are limited to improvements in inter and intra-organizational communications.

Problem Statement

There are opportunities for development of the urban poor ghettos which have been neglected because the efforts needed are high, not cost effective and complex logistics in management. Experiments of multimedia applications seem to be the solution and e-Learning, Internet

---

* Business Development Manager, L&T Infotech Ltd., Navi Mumbai.
** Professor, Dr. D. Y. Patil Institute of Management Studies, Navi Mumbai.

usage in the right direction the best option, but more is desired than done. The research looks at pinpointing options available and the optimal way of solving the problem so that an integrated urban poor development model can be created in a cost effective manner for duplication elsewhere.

Problems and Constraints of the Study

Due to time and funds constraint the field research was made through a team of students, reviewing two retail chains, one well developed and another yet to develop, ignoring without any logical reason the opportunity that is there but not perceived by them, as confirmed by our literature study.

Further, due to the confidentiality of the information, no data or financial figures could be published that would have thrown some light on the real benefits, and also key information have been suppressed, but the study has its own relevance that corporate and researchers would benefit from, overlooking these constraints.

Vision Statement

To have an all round development of the urban poor place through the women power such that no urban poor person need to come beyond an acceptable range for his functioning productively and for enabling optimization of the local resources.

Objectives of this Study

- To develop a working plan for e-Development of the urban poor place with the entrepreneurial talent of women and canalize the same into an economy profitable activity with the necessary support.

- To build a sound urban poor economy.

- To shift the manpower to the urban poor places (with increased labour opportunities).

- To promote products from the urban poor sector to the cities with value addition in the process, through optimization of information and knowledge needs for development of the resources.

- To promote education through a structured (customized) e-Learning mode that would facilitate the gap between the interests of the urban poor women and the availability. This would bridge the gap between the gender and also due to the demographic profiles with the special opportunity for self-enhancement/development made possible.

Theoretical Framework

Schematically, the framework shall be as follows:

(a) Face to Face + e-Learning → Cost and Time Training animated tools effective training.

(b) Multi-user rich media + Central location → Urban poor women entrepreneur.

Applications with Information Officer (any time service).

The framework is to optimize these and integrate them into one project operating on a scheduled time basis for both outcomes (a) and (b) above.

Research Methodology

A brief study was made at the secondary level of the literature review as indicated above. This was followed by a discussion with people involved with urban poor development projects. A review was made of possible areas of *e-Development* office to improve business through better networked and self learning or information tools. The study, therefore, plans to integrate the technical, *e-Business* and *e-Marketing* issues optimally as they govern the success of the *e-Development* office. The additional benefit would be the administrative and statutory compliances made simple that may get the rural places better organized. The future plans of the development of these areas respectively need to be after discussions with potential entrepreneurs of the acceptability and adaptability of the model.

Recommendations

We recommend a centralized *e-Development* office as per the model below:

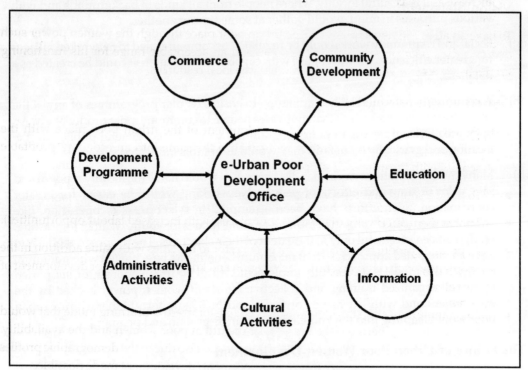

Figure 1: e-Urban Poor Development Model

We have to create a model, the highlights of the *e-Office* proposed are:

(a) Availability of all commercial details and transaction possible. A few potential units can link directly to company and get the best rates; similarly, procurement could be made on an e-Mode from the best source.

(b)   All administrative activities handled many miles away can be undertaken now at nearer points, i.e., the Post Office where this e-Development model is located. Land records, birth and death certificates, etc., can be updated for effective coordination with the central development office of the state. Medical records too can perhaps be handled.

(c)   Information on important policies and advice on emergencies/calamities, government policies, etc., can all be imparted through the *e-Mode* so that diffusion of information (regulated and right own please) is faster and more accurate. Ethical and cultural issues have to be protected here.

(d)   Education (adult learning) and on an *e-Learning* mode can be taken up so as to motivate these who feel deprived of their opportunity to advance to the extent possible. This could be had at the convenience of the urban folks and not at the convenience of the teachers, as is happening today, defeating the very objectives of educational efforts.

(e)   Developmental programmes could be guided to the urban folks in a networked manner and direct studies of outcomes could be obtained rather than through a Marketing Research agency, which is costly and not very effective.

(f)   Cultural programmes could be had to empower the use of the facility and awareness increase as it is a central locality, where people from all kinds of backgrounds and with various purposes in mind, would gather at some time or another.

(g)   Social and community works could be regulated or communicated to networked villages for greater efficiency. Volunteer base with capabilities and interest could be created as a database.

(h)   A community hall could be had adjoining to ensure regular programmes of any of the above functions taking place that motivates people to commune more productively. An open area in front for urban poor programmes would attract general public into the location and gradually by default they would adopt this innovated system.

(i)   Many more applications can be handled here, that would make the locality modern and save a lot of time and efforts of people. Networking would be easier for greater coordination. Such efforts have been attempted in select areas of operation, like administration (SETU® project in India), *e-Learning* modes for youth, weather forecasting, etc. It has been successful only to the extent of their objectives. The proposed model is to have an integrated approach so that maximum benefits can be achieved with minimum energy. If this model is successfully implemented in all the urban poor sector, supported by a well organized training and collective efforts of women power backed by the government and with extensive corporate and NGO support, Maharashtra's urban poor would leapfrog into the knowledge area in its growth and prosperity.

The Future of Urban Poor Women Development

The future of urban poor development lies in the hands of the authorities and social development bodies. There are no standard formulae and it has to be fitted in on a case-to-case basis. Hence, an accountable system implemented in a planned and committed manner is crucial for urban poor development. The model we have created would be easy to replicate. A holistic approach would be ensuring a long-term perspective of the development. The future of urban poor economy, if planned well, is bright as utilization of resources (for the urban poor) and much lesser for the branded products of the better off.

CONCLUSION

Urban poor development can be speeded up using women power and *e-Governance*. Perfected as a model in one centre, the same can be extended in all other centres homogeneously. With adequate training to the urban poor women force in IT and operations of this *e-Office* where a small team of trained operators would guide them into proper functioning, the development would be phenomenal; prosperity would be the hallmark of effective use of this *e-Office*.

References

Gupta P.K., *Strategic Entrepreneurship*, Everest Publishing House, 2000.

Desai Vasant, *Dynamics of Entrepreneurial Development and Management*, Himalaya Publishing House, 2001.

Women's Self-Help Groups and Credit for the poor: A Case Study from Andhra Pradesh – by Smriti Rao, *Financial Liberalisation and Rural Credit in India* – Edited by V. K. Ramachandran and Madhura Swaminathan.

State Bank of India (SBI) Bulletin – various issues.

Economic Survey – various reports.

Entrepreneurship – *Harvard Business Journal* (HBJ).

®SETU – Government of Maharashtra's initiative to integrated citizen facilitation centers through Information Technology.

4

Pharmacy Students' Entrepreneurial Inclination

Aarti T. More (Mhatre)*
Dr. R. K. Srivastava**

The purpose of this research paper is to identify students who are inclined towards becoming future entrepreneurs in the pharmacy profession. Identifying potential entrepreneurs before they prove themselves, or take on the challenge, was the focus of the study. The study included responses from 150 students of D. Pharm, B. Pharm and M. Pharm students of three institutes in Nasik city. The primary data were gathered through well designed questionnaire regarding their inclination towards entrepreneurial tendencies with independent pharmacy practice and ownership. The study confirms the hypothesis that students prefer working in research and development after completing B. Pharm and M.Pharm course (H-1). The study also confirms the hypothesis that students prefer establishing own enterprise—a retail outlet after completion of D.Pharm course. (H-2).

Keywords: *Entrepreneurial Orientation, Retail Pharmacies, Pharmacy Student, Survey*

INTRODUCTION

In terms of career choices, an individual has three options: To work for someone else, be self-employed in a profession, or be an entrepreneur (P. C. Jain, 1998).

A major agenda of the pharmacy profession is to herald in the era of pharmaceutical care, in part, by assisting individual pharmacists in their efforts to develop and promote new and innovative pharmacy services. New books, professional association meetings, research funding, pharmacy continuing education and pharmacy course work provide opportunities for educating and motivating pharmacists and pharmacy students in hopes they will develop, manage and market new services as part of the pharmaceutical care movement. Some of these instructional and motivational efforts come from entrepreneurs which have proven themselves capable and are willing to pass along what they have learned. Identifying potential

---

* Lecturer, MET, Institute of Management, Bhujbal Knowledge City, Adgoan, Nasik.
  PhD. Student, D.Y. Patil Institute of Management Studies, Navi Mumbai.
** Head Research Cell, SIMSR, Mumbai.

entrepreneurs before they prove themselves, or take on the challenge, is the focus of this study. Such identification may be one way to hasten the fulfillment of this professional agenda. Academic interest in how to better develop an entrepreneurial spirit among pharmacy students is the need of the hour. Indeed, time spent on teaching and nurturing student's entrepreneurial inclinations and providing needed resources could be a valuable means by which the academy, in particular, can contribute to advancing the professional status of pharmacists, the financial stability and growth of pharmacies, and the quality of pharmacists—provided patient care (Carol, 2004).

Identifying students who are inclined to be future entrepreneurs in the profession could be a helpful way to identify and target these students regarding entrepreneurial pursuits, encouraging and supporting them with real resources before and after graduation.

PROBLEMS AND ISSUES

Will today's pharmacy education serve the students by equipping them for entrepreneurial applications?

This simple dichotomous question can be asked to support the desire to move the profession forward.

Entrepreneurial activity is supported by knowledge of marketing, management and finance. But in today's pharmacy curriculum these subjects are neglected or given least priority in India.

Personal encouragement and needed skills can be given to nurture the students who are inclined towards entrepreneurship.

Hypotheses

(H-1): Students prefer working in research and development after completing B. Pharm & M. Pharm course.

(H-2): Students prefer establishing own enterprise – a retail outlet after completion of D. Pharm course.

Primary Objective

To identify students who are inclined towards becoming future entrepreneurs within their chosen pharmacy work environments.

Secondary Objective

- To know wether today's pharmacy education can support the development of entrepreneurial skills for the students.

- To understand students' inclinations to various job setting after completing the course work.

RESEARCH METHODOLOGY

Research Design, Population, Sampling

This research was carried out in Nasik city. 150 students of D. Pharm, B. Pharm and M. Pharm course of three institutes were selected. 60 students were from D. Pharm, 60 were from B. Pharm and 30 were from M. Pharm. Student's choices of job setting upon completion of course work and their career aspirations were collected. Students were given the option to indicate their first, second and third choices of job setting after completion of course work. Data was also gathered regarding whether students were satisfied with curriculum of the university if they were inclined towards entrepreneurship. A descriptive, cross-sectional design was used. All the students from respective institutes enrolled in Pune University during 2006-07 academic year were eligible (N=150). Students from final year of each course were invited to participate in the voluntary survey by completing self-administered questionnaire. The interview and data collection were done in classroom of respective institutes, stratified random sampling of students who were in attendance and who consented to participate.

Survey Methods

Personal interview involving face-to-face basis was utilized.

Questionnaire technique was used as a tool to gather information. Questionnaire focused on preference for job after completion of course work.

Results and Discussion

Association of D. Pharm, B. Pharm and M.Pharm students and their choice of job after course completion, like, to be an entrepreneur (establishing own enterprise), to work in pharmaceutical research and development, to work in manufacturing unit, to work as hospital pharmacists, to join academia/teaching, were analyzed using *chi-square* statistical technique.

At 95% confidence level the calculated value of *chi-square* is 78.630 and the table value of it is 15. 507 for 8 degrees of freedom.

It shows that the difference is highly significant; three variables are not independent and are highly associated. Therefore, hypotheses (H-1, H-2) are accepted.

Sample size: No. of students 150

Table 1

D.Pharm	B.Pharm	M.Pharm
60	60	30

Table 1.a: Association between D. Pharm, B. Pharm and M. Pharm students and their choice of job setting after course completion

Course/inclination	A(f)	%	B(f)	%	C(f)	%	D(f)	%	E(f)	%
D.Pharm	30	50	9	15	4	6.66%	13	21.66%	4	6.66%
B.Pharm	5	8.33	30	50	20	33.33%	1	1.66%	4	6.66%
M.Pharm	6	9	13	43	9	30%	0	0%	8	26.66%

X2 = 78.630. Students prefer pharmacy entrepreneurship as first choice of job setting after completion of B. Pharm and M. Pharm course on chi-square test.

A = Entrepreneurship (establishing own enterprise)

B = Research and development

C = Manufacturing unit

D = Hospital Pharmacist

E = Academia/Teaching

F = Frequency

Graph 1

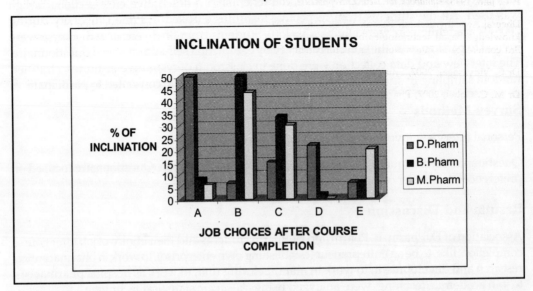

Limitations and Scope

Sample size is restricted to Nasik city, which can restrict the results from being generalized to other populations. More studies including larger student groups should be conducted to reach generalized conclusions. Although career aspirations were sought from students, some may have answered in terms of that for which they will settle, rather than that for which they truly aspire.

Identifying the students may provide faculty members, advisors and student themselves, with the opportunity for discovery or affirmation, as well as more informed dialogue regarding the future career plans. Ascertaining pharmacy student's entrepreneurial orientation sheds light, just a glimpse, on the future of profession of Pharmacy as it strives for Entrepreneurship.

CONCLUSION

The study shows that there is more entrepreneurial inclination of D. Pharm students as compared to B. Pharm and M. Pharm students who are more inclined towards working in research and development, or in a manufacturing unit. Thus, students prefer to or in a entrepreneurship as first choice of job setting after completion of D. Pharm course work. It was observed that students according to their courses have different perceptions of job setting after completion of course work. A spirit of entrepreneurialism can be nurtured by convincingly communicating to the students. Both the professional and financial rewards will be resulted from pharmacy entrepreneurship. Inclusion of business management subjects in a substantial proportion in the curriculum can certainly help these students for developing their entrepreneurial skills.

References

Carol J. Hermansen-Kobulnicky, PhD, & Corwyn L.Moss, PharmD (2004), Pharmacy student entrepreneurial orientation: A measure to identify potential pharmacists entrepreneurs, *American Journal of Pharmaceutical Education*, 2004, 68 (5) Article, 113.

P. C. Jain, 1998, *Handbook for New Entrepreneurs*, edited by Entrepreneurship Development Institute of India.

Dheeraj Awasthy, Rakesh Basant, Vivek Gupta, IIM, Ahmedabad, (2003), Commercialization of traditional knowledge based technologies by small entrepreneurs: An exploration of strategic and policy options, 3rd conference of International Entrepreneurship Forum.

Dr G. Vidyasagar, 2007, Entrepreneurship Development in Pharmacy – Need of the hour.

Dr M. C. Gohel, 2007, Pharmabiz.com

5

Micro-Finance in India: Issues and Prospects with Respect to Rural Poor Entrepreneurship

Anil Mahajan*
Dr. Pradip Manjrekar**

The 1990s saw a nationwide attempt pioneered by Non-Governmental Organizations (NGOs) to create links between commercial banks, NGOs, and informal groups (Self-Help Groups or SHGs) scaling up access to finance for India's rural poor entrepreneurs to meet their diverse financial needs through flexible products at competitive prices.

INTRODUCTION

This paper is divided into three sections. Section-I is devoted to the discussion of the micro-finance in the light of experience of Andhra Pradesh where self help programme is concentrated most. Section-II provides a broad review of policy initiatives undertaken by RBI, NABARD and government along with discussion of general trends specially in Maharashtra. Section-III summarises the findings of the paper and offers our concluding remarks.

SECTION I

Micro-credit and Andhra Pradesh Experience

The researchers have taken up Andhra Pradesh, which showed maximum enthusiasm having about 60 per cent of self help groups nationwide. This apparent success is hailed as a model for other states to follow. That apart, there are many studies worldwide about the potential and limitation of this instrument for poverty alleviation and empowerment of women. The merit of micro finance is seen in its potential to provide cheap credit whose lack of collateral excludes them from formal finance making them to rely on informal sector. With this channel opened, they are freed from clutches of moneylender. Cheap credit would act as capital generating income thereby brings about both poverty alleviation and empowerment. Increased availability of credit is likely to result in increase in economic decision-making role in household as well as community life. This will also lead to increase in participation in larger political processes.

* Sr. Lecturer, IES College of Management Studies & Research, Bandra, Mumbai.
** Professor & Head, Dr. D. Y. Patil Institute of Management Studies, Navi Mumbai.

With this background, we may turn to the self-help group programme. Each group consists of about 10-20 homogeneous members where they are expected to save some minimum amount like Re 1 a day. For availing of loan the group should be in existence for some time prescribed and fulfill certain conditions like regular meeting, book keeping etc., leader is responsible for functioning, which is supposed to be related so it consists of two stages. In the first part, women save and multiply by lending among themselves. In the second stage, external infusion of credit takes place. Banks can lend either directly to groups or to micro finance institutions for on-lending. This fund is circulated among themselves. Banks increase the size as the group proves its creditworthiness. The maximum loan that can be sanctioned in a minimum saving to loan ratio is of 1:4. The larger the corpus and longer the existence greater is the loan. Self-help group women are in full control of funds. The rate and the lending decision are taken in their weekly/monthly meetings. The books of accounts and minutes are to be maintained by themselves. The Bank does not have staff to supervise functioning of all groups. This is done with the help of NGOs. About 2,800 NGOs are helping SHGs. This is also supposed to help decentralization and democratization of the process. However, these NGOs are not accountable to the people. Further, they are not permanent bodies. Life is determined by donor's agenda. So, their increasing involvement has its own problems.

Despite such large number of Self-Help Groups, bank loans to the groups accounted for only 0.6 per cent of total credit disbursed in the state in 2002. Andhra Pradesh accounts for 51 per cent of total bank credit to SHGs in the country as a whole. The average size of loan per beneficiary group member disbursed through SHG was only Rs 1,316 in 2002. The SHG Bank linkage was dependent on NGOs. Only 2% of bank loans in 2002 going to groups were not formed or administered by NGOs.

Smriti Rao in a very comprehensive study of two villages in the state found that these groups were there for those who have (to have is to be rich). Most dalit women with annual subscription of Rs. 24 were often distinguished from other groups. The former were referred to as two-rupee groups and others as 30-rupee groups. Thus the membership was related to economic status. Over the period the dropout was very high. There was caste dimension. They were largely mono caste — the tribal and Dalit women had no members from other castes. This is the main factor whereby the members were not judged by only the risk factor. School teachers played important role in group formation.

For procedural dealings with bank account maintain etc., support of men was crucial in case of groups working without NGO support. Men from upper middle caste like the Reddys were supportive enabling that group to get DWCRA loan. But for Dalits and tribals the process of sustainability differed from higher caste. The role of village panchayat or gram sevika was very limited. Thus the social and economic inequalities were found to be reflected if not accentuated in these SHGs.

There are cases of benefits like contract for certain government schemes being appropriated by leaders of the group. The solution advocated is monitoring externally of group activities. But there were cases when NGOs withdrew after initial phases. In such situations, groups can be fragile and viable to disintegrate, requiring NGOs' intervention again without institutional provision of long-term administrative assistance.

The pattern of use of funds is another indicator worth exploring. In most of the cases the corpus is really very small. Most of them were reported using these for consumption purposes such as marriage or health or household assets, household repairs, etc. The findings that typical micro-finance members find it difficult to launch business activities is consistent with much of the literature and our experience of field visits and discussion with concerned members on micro-finance.

These groups have total freedom with regard to interest rate for on lending, terms of repayment with no restrictions on end use. This increases flexibility and reduces monitoring costs of banks. But it also remains essentially short-term and expensive credit for consumption purpose. The minimum rate observed is 2.5 per cent per month. Further, these loans were meant for a very short-term of three to four months. Finally, for repayment the families had to borrow from elsewhere. Thus, the structure is very similar to that of informal sector. Yet apart from micro credit there is no policy initiative by the state to provide cheap, minimum and long-term credit to the poor.

As regards empowerment, a great deal of debate is on. This assumes women as independent entities. But in majority women represent households getting support from family for repayment, etc. There was no condition that assets to be bought in women's name. So, it was found that these self help groups reinforced existing unequal independence between the genders. Pressure from peers in the group caused drop out of members, if not suicides. Thus, there existed possibility for getting such women apart from other women, instead of bringing together.

The sum effect has been women from lower castes and classes remained outside the network. So despite large groups in Andhra Pradesh bank loans to these groups formed a mere 0.6 % of total bank credit disbursed in year 2002. Individuals received small loans well below Rs 5,000 at very high interest rates of 2.5 to 3 % per month. All these factors limit the potential that self help group have to empower women. These limitations stem from the design of the programme itself. The state delegating administrative NGOs who are neither permanent nor accountable are no substitutes for states' responsibility to its citizens.

The poor are willing and capable to pay the cost. According to NABARD, the rates of interest charged by SHGs should be market-related. The RBI monetary and credit policy stated that while small loans directly given by banks will continue to be subject to the interest ceiling as prescribed by the RBI from time-to-time, interest rates applicable to loans given by banks to micro credit organisations or by these organizations to the members/beneficiaries will be left to their discretion. This leads to the question: What have been the actual rates of interest on micro credit in India? The availability evidence shows that the practice has resulted in significantly high cost of borrowers. Official studies from NABARD also present a similar structure—the interest rates charged to members continues to be high. This is happening in spite of reduced transaction costs of lending of banks. This is because of transfer of many responsibilities like loan provisioning, monitoring to SHG promoting institutions. So, in actual practice, the costs are not reduced the responsibilities are not reduced but only transferred. In other words, this is one kind of outsourcing resorted by banks. NGOs are doing the work of monitoring the projects.

SECTION II

Micro-credit and Policy Initiatives

The micro credit programme formally heralded in 1992 with a modest pilot project of linking around 500 SHGs, has made rapid strides in India. The SHG-Bank Linkage Programme was formally launched in the year 1992 as a flagship programme by NABARD and aptly supported by the Reserve Bank through its policy support. The programme envisages organisation of the rural poor into SHGs for building their capacities to manage their own finances and then negotiate bank credit on commercial terms. The poor are encouraged to voluntarily come together to save small amounts regularly and extend micro loans among themselves. Once the group attains required maturity of handling larger resources, the bank credit follows.

Over the years, the SHG-Bank linkage programme has emerged as the major micro-finance programme in the country. In all, 554 banks (47 commercial banks, 177 RRBs and 330 co-operative banks) are now actively involved in the operation of this programme. The 5,39,365 new SHGs credit-linked during 2004-05 represent an increase of 49 per cent over the previous year. As on March 31, 2005, the total of 16.18 lakh SHGs credit linked by banks covered an estimated 242 lakh poor families, with an average loan disbursement per family of Rs 3,044. A highlight of the programme was that about 90% of the groups linked with banks were exclusively women groups.

India has adopted a multi-agency approach for the development of its micro-finance programme. All the major credit institutions, *viz.,* commercial banks, co-operative banks, RRBs along with Non-Governmental Organisations (NGOs) have been associated with the micro-finance programme. The role of the delivering agents and their interface has led to alternative models of micro-finance.

AGENCY MODEL AND MICROFINANCE

Three distinct linkage models of micro-credit are currently being followed in India. Under Model-I, banks themselves take up the work of forming and nurturing the groups, opening their saving accounts and providing them bank loans. Up to March 2005, 15% of the total number of SHGs financed were in this category. Under Model-II, SHGs are formed by NGOs and formal agencies but are directly financed by banks. This model continues to have a lion's share, with 80 percent of SHGs financed up to March 2005, falling under this category. Under Model-III, SHGs are financed by banks using NGOs and other agencies as financial intermediaries. In areas where formal banking system faces constraints, the NGOs are encouraged to approach suitable bank for bulk loan assistance. The share of cumulative number of SHGs linked under this model up to end-March 2005 continued to be relatively small.

Agency Model adopted in countries such as Brazil and South Africa has attracted wider attention in recent years. Under this model, banks are permitted to appoint wide range of entities as correspondent-agents, which are in close proximity to the people such as post offices, supermarkets, small stores, petrol pumps and drug *stores.* Such agents use kiosks or Automated Teller Machines to accept payment, open accounts, take small deposits, provide micro-credits, sell saving bonds and insurance. ACCION International, a micro-finance institution has developed "Service Company Model" to expand micro-finance operations. A Micro-finance Service Company is a non-financial company that provides loan origination and credit administration services to a bank by way of sponsoring, evaluating, approving, tracking and collecting loans for a certain fee. The deployment of such external entities and civil society organisations by banks help in reducing the transaction costs and enlarging the outreach to hitherto unbanked population. These successful experiments in other parts of the world underscore the need for exploring the feasibility of similar possibilities in the Indian context.

Recognising their importance, both the Reserve Bank and NABARD have been spearheading the promotion and linkage of SHGs to the banking system through initiating proactive policies and systems. NABARD has been extending refinance support to the banking system and promotional grant support to NGOs and developing capacity building outreach of various partners. The microfinance initiative of NABARD, *i.e.,* SHG-Bank linkage programme has passed through various phases over the last one and half decades, *viz.,* (i) pilot testing during 1992 to 1995, (ii) mainstreaming during 1996 to 1998, and (iii) expansion from 1998 onwards. The programme has now assumed the form of a micro-finance movement in many parts of the country and has started making inroads in the resource poor regions of the country as well. The target of covering one third of the rural poor through linkage of 1 million SHGs to be achieved by 2007 was realised much ahead by end-March 2004.

NGOs have clearly emerged as facilitator and promoter of SHG concept amongst the rural poor in the country. The SHG-Bank Linkage Programme has been continuously supported by a large number of NGOs and similar partner agencies. It was, otherwise, a difficult task to organise rural poor into smaller homogeneous groups called Self-Help Groups (SHGs), build their capacities to manage their own finances and then negotiate bank credit on commercial terms. The poor are encouraged and supported to voluntarily come together to save small amount of savings, called thrift regularly and extend micro loans among themselves to meet their emergent needs. Once the group attains required maturity of handling larger resources, the NGOs support the SHGs in getting bank loans. During all these stages of transformation, NGOs and other Self-Help Promoting Institutions (SHPIs) have been supporting and hand-holding the SHGs/members of the SHGs. About 85% of the SHGs were formed through NGO interventions.

Table 1: Model-wise Linkage Position in Percentage

Model Type	Description	As on March 31, 2004		As on March 31, 2005	
		No. of SHGs	Bank Loans Rs crores	No. of SHGs	Bank Loans Rs crores
I.	SHGs promoted, guided and financed by banks.	20	14	21	15
II.	SHGs promoted by NGOs government agencies and financed by banks.	72	81	72	80
III.	SHGs promoted by NGOs and financed by banks using NGOs formal agencies as financial intermediaries.	8	5	7	5
	Total	1079.09	3904	1618.48	6898
		100	100	100	100

Table 2: Progress of SHG-Bank Linkage Programme

(Amount in Rs. crore)

Year	Total SHGs financed by banks (Numbers in'000)		Bank Loans		Refinance	
	During the year	Cumulative	During the year	Cumulative	During the year	Cumulative
1999-00	81.78	114.78	136	193	98	150
2000-01	149.05	263.83	288	481	251	401
2001-02	197.65	461.48	546	1,026	396	797

Contd...

2001-02	197.65	461.48	546	1,026	396	797
2002-03	255.88	717.36	1,022	2,049	622	1,419
2003-04	361.73	1,079.09	1,856	3,904	705	2,124
2004-05	539.39	1,618.48	2,994	6,899	968	3,092
2005-06#	211.39	1,829.84	1,421	8,319		

 # Up to December 31, 2005

Historically, there has been a concentration of SHGs in the southern states. On account of the head start of the programme and also due to some major initiatives taken by the state governments, the programme has gained the form of a movement in the southern states. However, the programme expanded rapidly in other states also during last two years. During 2004-05, SHGs which were creditlinked with banks in non-southern states shows an increase of 82%. The share of cumulative SHGs credit linked with banks in the southern states remained at about 60% of the total SHG credit linkages in the country at end-March 2005.

MICRO-CREDIT AND NABARD

To spread the outreach of micro-credit in other states, NABARD has taken up intensification of SHG Bank Linkage Programme in 13 identified priority states which account for 70% of the rural poor population, *viz.,* Uttar Pradesh, Maharashtra, Orissa, West Bengal, Madhya Pradesh, Gujarat, Rajasthan, Chattisgarh, Jharkhand, Bihar, Uttaranchal, Assam and Himachal Pradesh. NABARD has adopted a multi-pronged strategy to spread the outreach of micro-finance in the country.

Of over 16 lakh SHGs credit linked with banks, over 4 lakh SHGs are now over three years old. The core needs of savings and credit for consumption and production of these SHGs are being met by the banking system. These SHGs have not only availed loans, but have also availed loans more than once. It is being emphasised that a member of the older SHGs would now be in a position to graduate into micro-enterprises by taking up income generating activities. It is a difficult task to find viable micro-enterprises for millions of poor households in rural areas. Though micro-enterprises are not a panacea for the complex problem of chronic unemployment and poverty, yet their promotion is a viable and effective strategy for achieving significant gains in incomes and assets of poor and marginalized people. However, in the absence of any specific hand-holding strategy to provide financial and non-financial services in an integrated manner, graduation of SHG members from micro-finance to micro-enterprises has not been smooth due to several obstacles. NABARD is, therefore, undertaking a pilot project in select districts, particularly for members of matured SHGs for promotion to the stage of micro-enterprises. NGOs have been selected in each district for implementing the pilot projects.

MICRO-FINANCE AND THE GOVERNMENT

It was announced in the Union Budget for 2005-06 that the Government of India intends to promote Micro-Finance Institutions (MFIs) in a big way. For this purpose, the Micro-Finance Development Fund (MFDF) was redesignated as Micro-Finance Development and Equity Fund (MFDEF) and the corpus of the fund was increased from Rs. 100 crore to Rs. 200 crore. MFDEF is expected to play a vital role in capitalising the MFIs and thereby improving their access to commercial loans.

The Central Government is considering the need to identify and classify the MFIs and rate such institutions to empower them to intermediate between the lending banks and the clients.

To facilitate the process of rating of MFls, NABARD has decided to extend financial assistance to commercial banks and RRBs by way of grants to enable them to avail the services of credit rating agencies for rating of MFls.

MICRO-FINANCE AND THE RESERVE BANK

In view of the new paradigm shift in micro-finance, the Reserve Bank decided to revisit the issue of micro-finance in a comprehensive manner. Accordingly, several initiatives were taken in the recent period. First, consultations were arranged with several representatives of micro-finance institutions in select centres to obtain their views. Second, based on such consultations, a Technical Paper on Policy relating to Development, Regulation and Supervision of Micro-finance Services was prepared and was discussed with the representatives of MFls on July 18, 2005. The recommendations of the Paper are being considered in consultation with the Government. Third, an Internal Group of the Reserve Bank on Rural Credit and Micro-Finance (Chairman: H.R. Khan) was set up to examine the issues relating to micro-finance.

Following the announcement made in the Union Budget, 2005-06, an Internal Group (Chairman: H.R. Khan) was set up in the Reserve Bank, *inter-alia,* to examine the issue of allowing banks to adopt the agency model by using the infrastructure of Civil Society Organisations (CSOs), rural kiosks, and village knowledge centers to provide credit support to rural and farm sectors and examine the feasibility and modalities for appointment of "banking correspondents" to function as intermediaries between lending banks and beneficiaries. After examining these issues, the Group felt that linkages could be established under two broad models. One, the "Business Facilitator Model", wherein banks may use wide array of CSOs and others for supporting them by undertaking non-financial services. Under the second model, *i.e.,* "Business Correspondent Model", institutional agents/other entities could be used to support the banks for extending financial services.

PROGRESS IN IMPLEMENTATION OF SHG BANK LINKAGE PROGRAMME IN MAHARASHTRA

SHG Bank Linkage Programme launched in 1991-92 as an experiment in providing hassle free institutional credit to rural poor has achieved phenomenal success over last 13 years and is now acclaimed as largest micro-credit programme in the world. The programme received a further boost during 2004-05 in the country and state of Maharashtra is no exception to this. The overview presented below covers various aspects of implementation of the programme in the state in 2004-05. Credit Linkage of New SHGs bank linkage programme witnessed significant growth during the year 2004-05 in the state of Maharashtra. During the year, new SHGs were credit linked showing growth of 302%. During the same period, bank loan of Rs 8,811.64 lakh was disbursed to new SHGs showed 299% growth.

SHG Bank linkage programme is heading towards sustainable movement as seen from the fact that SHGs are increasingly accessing bank credit frequently. Banks in the state provided repeat finance to 5,777 SHGs during 2004-05 as against 3,820 SHGs during previous year. But its share in total finance declined in 2004-05.

The cumulative position of credit linkage reached to 71,146 SHGs as on 31 March, 2005 in the state of Maharashtra. Considering average size of SHG membership 15, the number of poor families having access to bank credit through mode reached to 10.67 lakh. The share of commercial banks in credit linkage increased significantly from 36% in 2003-04 to 52% in 2004-05. Agency-wise share of credit linkage during the last two years is as below:

Among the commercial banks, the State Bank of India credit-linked the highest number of SHGs. It financed 12,786 SHGs followed by Bank of India – 1,818 SHGs and Bank of Maharashtra – 1,217 SHGs. These major banks together credit linked SHGs which come to 93% SHGs credit linked by Commercial Banks. In case of Regional Rural Banks, Marathwada Gramin Bank headed the list with credit linkage of 1,763 SHGs followed by Chandrapur Gadchiroli Gramin bank – 1,542 and Bhandara Gramin Bank 1,133. Although cooperative banks are comparatively late entrants in SHG Bank Linkage Programme, their involvement in the programme is increasing every year. Chandrapur District central cooperative bank took big leap by financing 3,669 SHGs during the year and the share of bank among the cooperatives was 41%. The Kolhapur DCCB and Gadchiroli DCCB with credit linkage of 1,497 and 569 SHGs secured second and third position respectively. Around 68 % of bank branches in rural and semi-urban areas of the state are involved in financing of SHGs. In case of Regional Rural Banks almost all branches are involved in SHG credit linkage.

Chandrapur district had always been in the forefront in implementation of the programme. During the year the district has further consolidated the leading position with credit linkage of 5,747 SHGs (18 % of total inkapes in the state). Promotion and nurturing SHGs by NGOs as well as by banks and continuous capacity building of SHGs. NGOs and bank staff since inception of the programme and excellent coordination between all partners resulted in the district becoming a leader in micro finance movement in the state. However, with conscious efforts from NABARD, the movement is picking up in the other districts of the state. Emphasis was given during the year to sensitize the bankers in other districts of the state on credit linkage of SHG. As on March 31, 2005, as many as 26 districts are having more than 500 SHGs credit linked. The following four districts in the state were leading in credit linkage during 2004-05.

The state, government took the initiative by forming around 60,000 SHGs in five districts of Pune Revenue Division.

SECTION III

CONCLUSION

The year 2005 was declared as an International year of Micro-credit. The World Bank, ADB and other funding organisations like OXFAM are the biggest donors to MFls. The origin is traced to Mohammad Yunus who launched Bangladesh Grameen Bank. After 20 years, the observation of the minister is given here to give an idea of state of affairs. In India this SHG Bank linkage has been institutionalized within states. Anti-poverty programmes through Swarna Jayanti Gram Swarojgar Yojana (SGSY), a self promotion scheme, which claims to provide loan-cum-subsidy to the rural poor, officially certified as Below Poverty Line (BPL). SGSY was launched after the scrapping of the IRDP (Integrated Rural Development Programme) in 1999-00. These SHGs under MFls could determine their own interest. Cooperative credit institutions after nationalization of major domestic banks and RRBs were the major players in rural credit market. Since the 1990s, increasing attention is being given to recovery and profitability. So the formal institutions withdraw from this terrain, the alternative presented was micro-finance services.

But the experience over the past one-and-a-half decade shows that despite several policy initiatives, it has not succeeded in motivating banks. Micro finance disbursement constituted 0.06% in Andhra Pradesh and 0.4 per cent of total and priority sector loan disbursement. For India, micro-credit disbursement accounted for only 0.4% of total loan disbursement in year 2004-05. So in spite of high returns, the banks find it riskier proposition. Moreover, the role of the moneylender over the period increased specially in Andhra Pradesh, which is held as a success case. For repayment, the poor are pushed into the clutches of the moneylender. So it has become a way of mobilizing savings rather than providing credit. This is accompanied by corporates becoming interested in SHGs as consumers of their products. Under SGSY model, SHGs complain of imposition of some activity on them e.g., toy making, embroidery, candle making without any market support. In the absence of strong domestic local market, small enterprises find difficult to survive. All claims of employment generation through rearing cattle, making papad, pickles, etc., have become a joke when people are getting displaced. Micro-finance was propagated as a safety valve to contain dissatisfaction. This decade witnessed finance capital in the globalisation process making deep inroads into rural India— directly and brazenly. With low interest prevailing in international market, the rural market in India provided the good margin to the players. Institutional bottlenecks along with the low purchasing power resulting in absence of the local market make their sustainability appear a doubtful proposition.

Given the fungible character of finance capital the end use is not ensured. The consequence is creating additional or new/parallel source of funds will not have intended affect. The role of other agents viz, traders, moneylenders who have other linkages with land, labour, agri produce and input market ensures their repayment. Mere supply of funds without forging these links will not ensure the repayment. The issue should be discussed in the framework of credit market and not simply credit delivery.

To conclude, in a country like India, given its size and diversities we have to critically evaluate the past experience of rural credit institutions especially Cooperative Societies RRBs and development programme like IRDP, EGS. The idea of micro-credit as an integral component of village cooperative credit societies and not parallel source may be explored. This credit plan will have to be integrated with development plan of the village, which will be administered by people's representatives. Solutions should emerge through local initiatives within democratic decentralized framework. At present, the stimulus to the programme is entirely external.

Bangladesh's internationally known Non-Governmental Organizations have proved that the poor are bankable, but some are now being accused of making money on the poor and charging high interest rates on loans. Finance minister Shah Kibria blasted NGOs for taking between 20 and 25% interest from small borrower. "If this trend continues, NGOs will turn into rent-seeking financial institutions", he told a workshop. Without identifying the NGOs, he said, they were taking microcredit from the Pally Karma Shahayo Foundation, the national apex foundation funding NGOs, at just 3 to 5% interest. "This cannot be accepted" he warned. "It becomes an exploitation when an NGO is borrowing at lower rates of interest and lending the same money to poor clients at four times higher rates", he observed, while underlining the need for regulatory mechanisms to streamline the micro-finance programmes of the NGOs. Micro-credit and saving schemes organized by NGOs like Grameen Bank, Brac and many others have benefited nearly five million families countrywide, raising their capacity to earn and climb out of the poverty trap. The gradual empowerment of rural women is seen by many as the remarkable success of the NGOs. At the same time, the NGOs are regularly accused of fostering a "Pajero culture" (four-wheel drive jeeps that are now counted among the status symbols of NGOs), lack of transparency and discriminating against low-level employees in the wage structure. Some of the big NGOs, like Brac and Grameen Bank, have become veritable corporations: Owners of banks, shopping complexes, telephone systems, cold storages, transport services, among other things. They are also big employers of educated young people.

References

Report on Trend and Progress of Banking in India – various reports.

RBI Annual Report – various reports.

RBI Bulletin – various issues.

Economic Survey – various reports.

NABARD – Reports.

Women's Self-Help Groups and Credit for the Poor: A Case Study from Andhra Pradesh – by Smriti Rao, *Financial Liberalisation and Rural Credit in India* – Edited by V. K. Ramachandran and Madhura Swaminathan.

Why Self-Help Groups and Why Not the Small Village Co-operatives for Rural Development; A Critical Perspective Vision – Ashwin Ramesh, *Cooperative Perspective*, Vol 35, No 3, Oct-Dec., 2000.

6

A Case Study on Om Creations

Gavin Vaz*

Prasad Shete*

INTRODUCTION

The S. P. J. Sadhana School for the Mentally Challenged is an NGO that has been pushing the frontiers for the development of mentally challenged for the past 33 years. The school, for many years, has been striving to bring out the potential of their students in public to show their very rewarding efforts. The school employs a total of 34 persons. The trainers at the school are totally dedicated to their jobs. There is no comparison to what they do. They deal with the children on a one-to-one basis to concentrate more on maximizing the efficiency of individual creativity and talent to make them ready for the professional world.

The prime motive of the study is to understand the behaviour and working pattern of the people working at Om Creations and also to clear the dilemma that people have about the capability of these students. It also focuses the training and the academic aspects which Sadhana School provides. This project also emphasizes on the entrepreneurship abilities in making such a business model realistic and profitable.

OBJECTIVE

To study the current business model of Om Creations, a cake and chocolate factory where the mentally challenged employees work.

Vision

To be productive members of society globally.

Mission

To convert the students' disabilities into abilities.

About S. P. J. Sadhana School

In 1986-87, five year innovative training programmes were created at Sadhana School; these programmes were so developed or created so as to create a perfect individual in these kids.

* MBA Student, Kohinoor IMI School of Hospitality Management, Khandala, Maharashtra.

The programmes deal with all possible variations of life. Just as a mother would teach her child from the time it is a baby, these dedicated professionals train their children. The school realized that these kids are very special and need few interesting ways of teaching which led them to introduce more innovative and creative teaching methods than normal institutes. This was done so as to create an adult who would be ready for the tough competitive world outside. Since the training is dedicated solely on training the children for work the major emphasis is placed on correct behaviour at work, their communication skills and majorly the employment criteria today. The curriculum is also enriched with Yoga, Indian Music, Laughing Therapy, Instrumental Enrichment and Brain Gym. All these make for a holistic approach maximizing the potential of each student.

The Hospitality and Catering Course prepares the students for industry with chopping, serving, baking and cooking skills. We teach Indian, Chinese, Thai, Mexican, Italian cuisines. Students also learn to make pickles and squashes. A café on the premises caters to in-house training which has led to self-employment. The school is also linked with Om Creations which is a trust dealing with catering on a large scale with the all employees employed from Sadhana School itself, who work with the aid of a few helpers.

THE CATERING AND HOSPITALITY COURSE

The Catering and Hospitality course at the S. P. J. Sadhana School is a five-year training programme for young adults. The main aim of this course is to train students so as to get employed in the food industry. Sadhana School has been successful in training the severely cognitively multiplied handicapped as chefs for five star hotels. Some of the various hotels that the students have been employed in are:

1.   Taj Group

2.   Orchid

3.   Taj President

Students are trained also with the various new trends and changes brought about in the hospitality industry. This awareness is of utmost importance. Normally, when a student starts working in this course it is the duty of the trainers to identify particular skills like cutting, frying, packaging, etc. After a certain skill has been identified in an individual the trainers concentrate on that particular skill itself till the student has totally mastered it. These students are such that a monotonous activity is much easier for them and unlike a normal individual they don't know the meaning of boredom. After this skill has been perfected by the student, they are trained to aim at their particular goals in life and what they would be doing in the future. The students like any other hospitality student are sent for internship programmes in various hotels; this helps them to learn how to work in a normal environment amongst other people who are strangers to them.

The course also aims at training the students with social and communicative skills. These skills help them to interact better on a professional level when they actually work with a particular hospitality organization. Most of these students show a lot of shyness and backwardness. These are a few things which are enforced on changing before they join the industry. Some of the subjects taught to them in this course are as follows:

•   Cookery

•   Bakery and Patisserie

- Café-Counter service
- Service
- Nutrition and Hygiene
- Hospitality
- Social Communication – Skills with clients
- Self Care Skills
- Behaviour in the work place
- Domestic Skills/Survival skills
- Methods of counting measuring and weighing
- Basic principles of food production
- Foundation ingredients, nutrition and hygiene
- Food and beverage service (basic)
- Hospitality and social skills.

Course Objective

The main objective of having a course like this is to train students in the field of food production in order to make competent enough at least for the basic level. It also helps in developing social etiquette and discipline in the students. The students are also taught various cuisines. The major aim is to identify a skill in the student and then to maximize the efficiency of that particular skill.

The students love to explore their skill where creativity is concerned in cookery and you will be amazed by how much they value their own ability to do something so productive. These students have never experienced the feel of productiveness. Hence this course brings out the true potential in a particular individual and helps to portray it better to themselves so as to encourage them.

The Students

The students are the only reason why this school is even functioning in the first place. The students are extra special; they need a lot of love and affection for any task they have to undertake. A little recognition makes a lot of difference to the way they work. The students working in the cookery department were in the beginning taught how to memorize recipies. But it was only later that it was realized that memorizing of ingredients was a better option. The students are able to do cutting and chopping as well. Like any other hospitality college they are shown a sample of what has to be cut and the result to be obtained. Then they further do it themselves with a little guidance from their trainers. They are also exposed to all the major equipments which are used in a hospitality kitchen on a day-to-day basis. They work on a daily basis except the weekends. They have two trainers taking care of the cookery department. One is Ms. Ranjana who takes care of cooking, cutting, frying, etc. Whereas the other is Ms. Saloni who takes care of the bakery part of things. Some of the students are more capable than others; hence they are given an opportunity to even give exams for H.S.C, S.S.C, etc. The school also has counsellors who are especially for students to help them to think. Most of the students fees go according to parent's salaries. 80% of their fees are subsidised. The course on the whole is a very gradual process so as to teach them properly and they are able to grasp. The students are also able to modify recipes if necessary with guidance of course.

The Issue

Most of us today have no clue about these students. We have never seen these students in actual day-to-day activities. We always think that they are not capable, but we are wrong, these students are more capable than some of us normal adults. They are happy with what they do and get. Whereas we are the one's always looking for better prospective in life, sometimes too lazy to do our own jobs. This is not the case with these special adults. The major issue is that no one knows them. Hence, it is difficult for them to get into the industry. It would be very grateful if people would at least give them a chance to see what they can actually do.

Certain Facts

A few facts about these students are that even though they may have special needs, it is astonishing to know what dedicated workers they are. They love what they do and will do it without a complaint. The student is normally trained to do one thing only. For example, if he has the skill to bake, he will do the task of baking only. This is mainly because if he has to do something with a little variation it becomes difficult for him to grasp it and might be very time-consuming to the organization. Their needs and wants are limited. As long as they are happy with what they do, you don't have anything to worry about. Another important fact is that they don't realize things. For example, when we light gas we make sure we take necessary precautions so as not to get hurt in any way. These kids don't realize this; they might do things unknowingly. However, they are very well trained in whatever they do. So, once they reach the industry they are as good as any other professional.

Om Creations

Om Creations is a trust which takes care of various catering orders. They are basically like a bakery and patisserie shop that have a variety of goods on sale by the order. They also take on bulk orders for special occasions like Diwali, Christmas, etc.

- *State-of-the-art industrial kitchen:* All the savouries, cakes and snacks prepared at the food section at Om Creations are wholesome and hygienic, while being extremely tasty. The central kitchen is equipped with industrial grade equipment and staffed by our team of special workers. Each of our workers comes to Om Creations after five years of thorough training at SPJ Sadhana School. They are passionate about their work and are proud of being able to stand on their own feet, despite being disadvantaged.

- *High standards of hygiene and organized workflow:* The kitchen is kept very clean and there is a regimen of cleanliness and hygiene that is comparable to the best industrial kitchens. Even the work flow is well planned and orderly. The atmosphere is completely friendly the ability of our adults to work as a team is both a revelation and heart warming. It puts to rest many myths about the 'abilities' and 'capabilities' of mentally challenged people.

- *Om Creations is holding a valid Licence*

  Food Licence No.   -   160643

  Validity Till   -   31.12.2007 (Renewable Every Year)

- *Their standard fare includes:* Handmade Chocolates, Assorted chocolates—with cashew crunch, plain, almond rock, mint and orange. Sugar free chocolate and much more.

Each student who has been employed here gets a stipend. There are totally 11 disabled adults, 1 teacher/project coordinator and 3 helpers among the staff at Om Creations. The staffs are divided into three divisions. Cutting, working on fire, packaging. They work from 9 a.m. till 5 p.m. It normally takes them months together to actually master a particular skill before they are left to work alone. Parents are the major base for sale of products at Om Creations. There are also two more among the staff. One takes care of accounts and the other looks all office administration. These adults sometimes find it difficult to work on certain days and therefore have to be excused.

The office administrator takes care of funding donations, thank you letters, basic administration, renovations and overall operations. He also deals with a marketing consultant who gives his guidelines and strategies to the trust free of cost. Certain other jobs include insurance, licenses, project proposals, etc.

The accountant handles sales accounting, order placements, daily sales report and other day-to-day accounts.

Scope for Marketing Strategies

It has been noticed that it is a possibility for further research to take place in the field of marketing as far as Om Creations is concerned.

CONCLUSION

After an in-depth research of the Sadhana School and their chocolate factory which is Om Creations, I would have to say it has been a fabulous journey never thought of. In the beginning my mindset about these students was that they are challenged. How would they be able to work like normal people? But to my surprise it was astonishing to see that they have better skills and talent than some of us. They are very hardworking, need some recognition from time-to-time and are excellent team players once they get used to the people around them.

A Few Recommendations

1. It was noticed that a lot of advertisement that is needed, is not being done, which can bring out Om Creations in the real market. I suggest they should start advertising commercially rather than by just word-of-mouth.

2. If possible try to get someone to sponsor the restructuring of Om Creations so as to make it a more professional organization that can be compared with the same sector in the market.

7

Rural Tourism in Maharashtra: Entrepreneurial Opportunities

Prof. J. John Peter*
Prof. A. Ramakumar*

INTRODUCTION

"When was the last time you chased chickens? Roamed in the fields with pure wind on your face? Found yourself jiggling up and down to the thrills of a bullock cart ride?"

This quote from Rabindranath Tagore's poem "Must have awaken the child in you", to experience the unforgettable whiff of the countryside…. plant baby seeds…enjoy the delights of organic food and experience many spontaneous joys of nature.

The same is the theme for 'Rural Tourism'. Rural India has a rich tradition of art and culture and can thus provide a unique experience to tourists. Rural India has much to offer to the world. Rich in traditions of arts, crafts and culture, rural India can emerge as important tourist spots. Those in the developed world who have a craze for knowledge about the traditional ways of life, arts and crafts will be attracted to visit rural India if the concept of rural tourism is marketed well.

India is a multi-destination country with a variety of tourist attractions and facilities. India's rich religious and cultural past has created distinctive architectural styles, temple towns and famous monuments. With the Himalayas as backdrop, India's mountain hideaways offer some of the best places in the world to literally chill out and rejuvenate the body and soul. The stunning beaches that line India's vast coastline; offers unique experience, apart from the inevitable tan. A year ago, India was listed as the 4th chosen destination in the world. India received an estimated 3.5 million foreign tourists and 366 million domestic tourists in the year 2005, a rise of almost 30 per cent from 2003. The domestic tourism is expected to grow by 20 per cent over the next five years. It is the third largest foreign exchange earner after gems, jewellery and ready-made garments.

Tourism create more jobs than any other sector for every rupee invested. For every Rs. 10 lakh of investment in manufacturing, there is employment generation for 12.6 people; in tourism it is four times higher at 47.5, even higher than in agriculture, which is 44.7. In India direct employment from tourism contributes 4.59% of the total employment while indirect employment

* Faculty, Sinhgad Institute of Management, STE Society, Vadgaon Budruk, Pune.

bumps that figure up to 8.27% or around 40 million. The forecast by the World Travel and Tourism Council pegs industry growth in India at 9.7%, which translates into the creation of nearly seven million jobs over the next 10 years. It has a major role in promoting large-scale employment opportunities, keeping this in view, it has been granted the status of industry.

The above figures may sound big from India's point of view, but when we compare with France (75.1 million foreign tourist arrivals in 2004-2005), Spain (53.6 million), U.S.A. (46.1 million), our figure 3.5 million seems negligible. Small countries like Malaysia (11.7 million) and Thailand (11.7 million) are far ahead in tourism with their limited resources. In view of the fierce competition in tourist generating markets from several countries, it becomes necessary for India to strengthen its promotional and marketing efforts continuously to maintain and improve its existing market share. Steps are, therefore, being taken to develop and implement strategic marketing programmes. Efforts are continuing to focus on cultural heritage as well as pilgrim tourism, extensive use of technology measures to improve tourist information, laying stress on NRI and ethnic segments, special campaigns for promoting India in summer and monsoon months, promotion of yoga and Ayurveda for mental and physical health and traditional value and cultural based rural tourism.

Rural tourism is emerging as one of the best options available with its proven results in west, to promote incredible India both for domestic and foreign tourists. In absence of any promotional activity for rural tourism, thousands of foreign tourists visit rural areas in Rajasthan, Gujarat and south India every year. This is the proof of viability of the concept of rural tourism. The market for rural tourism is around Rs. 4, 300 crore per annum. Rural tourism has the potential of attracting both foreign and domestic tourists.

The stresses of urban lifestyles have led to a 'counter-urbanization' syndrome. This has led to growing interest in the rural areas. There are other factors, which are shifting the trend towards rural tourism like increasing levels of awareness, growing interest in heritage and culture and improved accessibility, and environmental consciousness. In the developed countries, this has resulted in a new style of tourism of visiting villages to experience and live a relaxed and healthy lifestyle.

CONCEPT OF RURAL TOURISM

As per Gannon, rural tourism covers, "A range of activities provided by farmers and rural people to attract tourists to their area in order to generate extra income for their business".

In the Indian context, any form of tourism that showcases the rural life either real or recreated, and that which involves rural folk (as artists and guides, etc.) at such locations, thereby benefiting the local community economically and socially, as well as enabling interactions between the tourists and locals for a more enriching tourism experience would classify as rural tourism.

That means rural tourism takes place in the countryside and creates value from rural opportunities. Typical characteristics of rural tourism are:

• Sparsely populated locations.

• Predominant natural environment.

• Focus on outdoor activities.

- Small establishments with mainly part time involvement in tourism by the local community.

- Locally owned enterprises.

- Meshing with seasonal and local events.

- Fewer guests.

- Based on preservation of culture, heritage and traditions.

The important elements of rural tourism are:

- Tourists rent out cottages in country side or sometimes become paying guests of villagers by residing with them.

- Village tourism activities like farm-camping, horse riding will be provided to tourists in villages.

- Traditionally furnished accommodation and food.

In nutshell, rural tourism promotes non-urban lifestyle.

Rural tourism has great potential in attracting tourists of various interests, as it is a mix of various tourism concepts. It provides everything in single package and works in non-urban setting with rural essence for the benefit of local community while preserving rural assets, values and heritage. Rural tourism inculcate following concepts of tourism:

(i)   Heritage and Culture (Ethnic Tourism)

(ii)   Learning and Education from natural environment about rural lifestyle, art and culture (Eco-tourism)

(iii)   Scenic value (Nature Tourism)

(iv)   Religious value (Pilgrim Tourism)

(v)   Adventure/Sports based activities (Adventure Tourism)

(vi)   Rural/Agrarian lifestyle (Farm Tourism)

ECONOMIC IMPORTANCE

Rural tourism is gaining importance in Indian tourism with its economic and social benefits. It is estimated that Rs. 4, 300 crore additional revenue can be generated through rural tourism. It is going to play a vital role in bridging the gap between rural and urban India by balancing urbanization and counter urbanization syndromes.

GOVERNMENT INITIATIVES IN PROMOTING RURAL TOURISM

The government, of late, has realised what the rural India can offer to the world. The Tenth Plan has notified Tourism as one of the major sources for generating employment and promoting sustainable livelihoods. The Union ministry of tourism in collaboration with UNDP has launched the Endogenous Tourism Project linked to the existing rural tourism scheme of the government. The UNDP has committed $ 2.5 million for the project. UNDP will help in areas of capacity building, involvement of NGOs, local communities and artisans forge strong community-private and public sector partnerships. The government has decided to develop necessary infrastructure for facilitating rural tourism. So far, the government has identified 31 villages across the country as tourist spots and providing Rs. 50 lakh as financial assistance for each project. Besides, an additional amount of Rs 20 lakh would be provided for developing logistic facilities and starting community participation centers through self-help groups. The implementation of his scheme would be done through a convergence committee to be set-up under the district collector. Out of these projects, Raghurajpur (Orissa), Jageshwar (Uttaranchal), Kokkare Bellur (Karnataka) have already been sanctioned for implementation. There are many other spots of potential tourist interest where adequate infrastructure needs to be developed. The concept of rural tourism has been developed within the product/infrastructure development of destinations and circuits. In the Annual Plan 2006-2007, an amount of Rs. 439 crore has been allocated for the purpose against Rs. 369 crore allocated in 2005-06.

Some states have by their own initiatives have begun promoting rural tourism. For instance, the forest department of the Uttaranchal government has set-up 'Centre for Ecotourism and Sustainable Livelihoods'. This centre aims at capacity building of local communities and promotion of rural tourism.

RURAL TOURISM IN MAHARASHTRA

Maharashtra, the land whose sheer size and diversity, the Sahyadri mountain range that stretches out into the mists as far as the eye can see, innumerous forts that stand proud and strong and scores of temples, sculpted into and out of basalt rock will stun the tourists. Diverse and colourful cultures, woven in one gigantic quilt, festivals that galvanize the sleepy into fervent motion, miles of silver white beaches and green forest, certainly potential enough to attract both domestic and foreign tourists. *'Atithi Devo Bhava'* is more practiced in rural Maharashtra than anywhere else.

Significance of Rural Tourism

- Tourism growth can be harnessed as a strategy for rural development. The development of a strong platform around the concept of rural tourism is definitely useful for a state like Maharashtra where majority of population resides in villages. Neighbouring states like Gujarat, Madhya Pradesh, and Andhra Pradesh are already started putting their high efforts in exploring the rural tourism potential.

- The trend of 'urbanization' has led to falling income levels, lesser job opportunities in the rural areas leading to an urbanization syndrome in the rural areas. Rural tourism is one of the few activities, which can provide a solution to this problem.

- In many parts of Maharashtra the rural economy is in the doldrums due to the increase in input costs and decrease in income. Many debt-ridden farmers are committing suicide. Efforts to promote rural tourism as a subsidiary occupation can arrest this trend with balanced regional development. This can be a subsidiary profession for farming community with least investment.

- The lucrative rural tourism proposals from Maharashtra can attract more investment from big industrial houses including valuable Foreign Direct Investment and ultimately increase in GDP of the country by creating value from rural opportunities and not by simply substituting value in new concepts.

Current Status

Rural tourism in Maharashtra is in its infancy stage. Maharashtra started moving in this direction, though rather late and slow. The Central government identified 'Sulibhanjan-Khultabad' in Aurangabad district in Maharashtra under UNDP–supported, Ministry of Tourism's Endogenous Tourism Project. By taking inspiration from a farmer in Alibaug, who adopted agri-tourism three years ago and began earning Rs.12 lakh every year through his venture, Agri Tourism Development Corporation (ATDC), Pune has started its pilot project in Malegaon near Baramati and has managed to increase the annual income of farmers by almost 25%. The trail has now encouraged ATDC to replicate the model on a nationwide scale 25 centers have been identified across Maharashtra. NGOs like Agriculture Development Trust taking keen interest in the development of rural tourism with their initiative called 'Maharashtra Krishi Vistar Yojana' to help farmers in diversifying their operations. The government's recent announcement on eco-tourism clearly pronounces the increasing importance of rural tourism.

STRATEGIC INSIGHTS

In India, we find different tourism destinations in different stages of what is termed as the product life cycle. For example, a region like Goa, a city like Shimla or a leisure spot like the Badkal Lake have reached a maturity level. They no more require promotion and have similarly exhausted their carrying capacity (infrastructural, environmental or social impacts). Their problem on the contrary is of retaining their image, checking the decline and doing away with the negative impacts of tourism. In marketing jargon, what they require is internal marketing, product improvement, checking the decline, proper maintenance, etc. On the contrary, look at the regions like Konkan, Vidarbha and Marathwada in Maharashtra which are struggling hard to promote their attractions in rural areas and develop their tourism products.

Marketing becomes a major problem for the promotion of rural tourism in Maharashtra. This is because the local bodies are either not aware about the developmental role of tourism or are constrained by their own politics or lack of funds. While marketing a rural tourism destination (region, village or leisure spots) there is need of study and development in following:

- Attractions – Finding the potential rural tourism destinations.

- Infrastructure (accommodation, cuisine, hygiene, clean water (basic amenities, etc.).

- Accessibility (roads, means of transportation) – should not be too far from railhead or airport: 2-21/2 hr.

- Carrying capacity of the destination.

- Environmental issues (Pollution, Eco-fragility, etc.)

- Safety, law and order situation (for both the local population as well as tourists), etc.

There is a need of research from government and related organizations to find out the suitable locations, ascertain market size, tourist profile, perceptions and expectations, to demarcate roles and responsibilities among public and private sector, complete package to tourists, to design macro-plan for state and micro-plan for locations, provision and management of infrastructure, accommodation and food facilities and more importantly about the role of NGOs/local government and community.

Another important aspect is the integration of Rural Tourism projects with Heritage, Pilgrim, Medical and Adventure tourism.

ENTREPRENEURIAL OPPORTUNITIES

The overall goal of the rural tourism is to create a community managed rural tourism model through strengthening livelihoods of the local communities and the preservation and development of local heritage of the villages.

Due to the initiatives taken by the Ministry of Tourism to promote rural tourism, a number of avenues for entrepreneurship of local population have opened. The direct and indirect sources of income are enumerated below:

- The employment of local youths as tour guides has given gainful employment to a large number of unemployed youth in the village.

- The concept of home stays with toilets has supplemented the income of the host population.

- A large number of tea stalls, small restaurants, pan shops etc., have started functioning due to the increase in inflow of tourists, which has again improved the socio-economic conditions of the local people.

- As local resources (labour and material) can be used to construct the hardware structure under this scheme in the villages, a number of people have got employed.

- The revival of tourism products like folk arts by formation of activity groups has also helped the local population. These folk arts provides a link with the past and bring alive ancient traditional art forms and culture. They also helped in perpetuating legacy for the future. The support to rejuvenate the folk arts has lead to the revival of the folk arts and also providing livelihoods to the practitioners of the arts.

- A vital aspect of the Rural Tourism Scheme was to check the migration of the artisans from the village. To tackle the problem of migration, artisans in different categories like stone carvers, pot makers, wood carvers, painters, weavers, etc., have been given trainings and exposure visits. Their product has been effectively promoted via different means and they have been taught about product diversification and demand of market, which has ultimately enhanced their income and stopped the migration.

- The travel agents and tour operators are playing an important role in promotion of the destinations. Most of these places were till recently unknown to many domestic and foreign tourists. However, most tour operators who conduct package tours (taking the people for sightseeing to different places and arrange for their accommodation and food too) have started taking the visitors to these sites now.

- Though it is still at a nascent stage, with volume of tourists slowly increasing to the sites, however the efforts are in place to promote these sites. During interaction with private tour operators, it has been reported that the situation is slowly changing and visitors are now desirous to see these destinations.

CONCLUSION

There is ample scope for the rural entrepreneurs to venture into rural tourism projects by way of creating and developing projects, by taking part in hospitality and travel services. There is a need of proper training; financing and marketing support are needed for further growth.

The involvement of the government, local community and financial institutions can ensure the success of rural entrepreneurs in this area.

References

Tourism Marketing – Jha S.M.

Foundation for Tourism Development – Negi, Jagmohan

Tourism Marketing – M. V. Kulkarni

Marketing Research – Aaker Kumar Day

Marketing Research – Tull Hawkins

Marketing Strategy – Walker Boyd Mullins

Strategic Marketing – Bowerson Cooper

Strategic Marketing Management – ICFAI

Indian Journal of Marketing

Journal of Marketing

www.ficci.com

www.india.agnesscott.edu

Report prepared by AF Ferguson & Co.

India Today

Indian Express

Reports of Parliamentary committees on Tourism

Reports of Ministry of Tourism, Govt. of India

8

Entrepreneurship: Special Reference "Human Resource Management"

Helen Mary Selvaraj*
V. Veena Prasad*
Dr. Pradip Manjrekar**

As environment become more complex and dynamic, firms must become more entrepreneurial in order to identify new opportunities for sustained superior performance. Corporate Entrepreneurship (CE) involves organizational learning, driven by collaboration, creativity and individual commitment. Therefore, it is widely held that Human Resource Management practices are an important driver of success. However, there is a pressing need for empirical research that addresses the contributions that HRM makes to a firm's ability to accept risk, be innovative and be proactive. This paper reviews empirical research linking Human Resource Management (HRM) practices with CE. It is found that although there is consensus as to the importance of HRM to CE, the empirical evidence is mixed and tends to lack a clear theoretical explanation. This review identifies two central themes that need to be addressed as we seek a theoretical explanation for this important relationship: Individual risk acceptance and the encouragement of discretionary entrepreneurial contributions. It is suggested that these two issues are interdependent. Potential theoretical avenues and future research directions are discussed.

In this paper, entrepreneurial activities in human resource management are examined by first analyzing changes occurring in the field of human resource management during the past few decades. Entrepreneurial and intrapreneurial activities in human resource management are then described. Finally, the resulting changes for the field of human resource management are discussed.

INTRODUCTION

In a world where ideas drive economies, it is no wonder that innovation and entrepreneurship are often seen as inseparable bedfellows. The governments around the world are beginning to

*   Faculty, S.I.W.S. College, Wadala (West), Mumbai.
** Professor, Dr. D.Y. Patil Institute of Management Studies, CBD Belapur, Navi Mumbai.

realize that in order to sustain progress and improve a country's economy, the people have to be encouraged and trained to think out-of-the-box and be constantly developing innovative products and services. The once feasible ways of doing business are no longer guarantees for future economic success.

In response to this inevitable change, some governments are rethinking the way the young are educated by infusing creative thinking and innovation in their nation's educational curriculum. In the same vein, they are putting much emphasis on the need to train future entrepreneurs through infusing entrepreneurship components within the educational system, especially at the tertiary level. Some countries have taken this initiative to a higher level by introducing entrepreneurship education at elementary schools and encouraging them to be future entrepreneurs when they are of age. In a series of survey funded by Kauffman Center for Entrepreneurial Leadership, it was found that nearly seven out of ten youths (aged 14-19) were interested in becoming entrepreneurs. Being an entrepreneur is now the choice of the new generation as compared to the preferred career choices of yesteryears such as being a doctor, lawyer or a fighter pilot. In a recent visit to the bustling city of Shanghai in China, an informal survey was carried out among Chinese youths by the author. The results of the survey showed that being an entrepreneur, especially in the field of computer and e-commerce, is perceived as a 'cool' career and is an aspiration for many Chinese youths. Prior to the 'opening up' of modern China, being an entrepreneur was perceived as the outcome of one's inability to hold a good government job and those who dared to venture, were often scorned at by their peers. Times have changed indeed. With this change in mindset and the relative knowledge that entrepreneurs bring forth increased job creations, the awareness and academic studies of entrepreneurship have also heightened. In many tertiary institutes, many courses of entrepreneurship and innovation are being developed and offered to cater to the increasing demand. The term "entrepreneurship" has also evolved with numerous variations. The proliferation of jargons such as netpreneur, biotechpreneur, technopreneur and multipreneur are coined to keep-up with the ever-changing times and business conditions that surround us.

In view of these changes, it is important that the definition of entrepreneurship be refined or redefined to enable its application in this 21st century. To put it succinctly, "Good science has to begin with good definitions", without the proper definition, it will be laborious for policymakers to develop successful programmes to inculcate entrepreneurial qualities in their people and organizations within their country.

OBJECTIVES

- To develop an appreciation and understanding of entrepreneurship and its role in human resource management.

- To understand, foster and maintain creativity and innovation in individuals and organisations.

- To identify and understand the role of HRM function in support of entrepreneurship and creativity in organisations.

- To explore change management models and tools in consideration of meeting entrepreneurial challenges of managing new venture.

ENTREPRENEURSHIP

Entrepreneurship has three dimensions: innovation, risk-taking and proactive behaviour. Innovation requires an emphasis on developing new and unique products, services and processes. Risk-taking involves a willingness to pursue opportunities having a chance of costly failure. Proactive behaviour is concerned with implementation and doing whatever is necessary to bring a concept to fruition.

For an increasing number of firms, the issue is not whether they should embrace entrepreneurship, but how they can encourage innovation, risk-taking and proactive behavior. An entrepreneurial orientation requires employees to think and act in new ways, taking individual responsibility for change while also cooperating with teams. Employees must be more opportunistic, creative and achievement-oriented, yet tolerant of ambiguity and willing to take risks.

ENTREPRENEURSHIP THROUGH THE YEARS

It was discovered that the term 'entrepreneurship' could be found from the French word *'entreprende'* in the twelfth century though the meaning may not be that applicable today. This meaning of the word then was to do something without any link to economic profits, which is the antithesis of what entrepreneurship is all about today. It was only in the early 1700s, when French economist, Richard Cantillon, described an entrepreneur as *one who bears risks by buying at certain prices and selling at uncertain prices*. This is probably closer to the term as applied today.

In his 1776 thought-provoking book, *The Wealth of Nations*, Adam Smith explained clearly that it was not the benevolence of the baker but self-interest that motivated him to provide bread. From Smith's standpoint, entrepreneurs were the *economic agents who transformed demand into supply for profits*.

In 1848, the famous economist John Stuart Mill described entrepreneurship as the founding of a private enterprise. This encompassed the *risk takers, the decision-makers, and the individuals who desire wealth by managing limited resources to create new business ventures*.

INNOVATION

One of the definitions that the author feels best exemplifies entrepreneurship was coined by Joseph Schumpeter (1934). He stated that the entrepreneur is one who applies "innovation" within the context of the business to satisfy unfulfilled market demand (Liebenstein, 1995). In elaboration, he saw an entrepreneur as an innovator who implements change within markets through the carrying out of new combinations. The carrying out of new combinations can take several forms:

- The introduction of a new good or standard of quality;

- The introduction of a novel method of production;

- The opening of a new market;

- The acquisition of a new source of new materials supply; and

- The carrying out of the new organization in any industry.

Though the term 'innovation' has different meanings to different people, several writers tended to see "innovation" in the form of entrepreneurship as one not of incremental change but quantum change in the new business start-ups and the goods/services that they provide.

Drucker (1985), perceived entrepreneurship as the creation of a new organization, regardless of its ability to sustain itself, let alone make a profit. The notion of an individual who starts a new business venture would be sufficient for him/her to be labeled as an entrepreneur. It is this characteristic that distinguishes entrepreneurship from the routine management tasks of allocating resources in an already established business organization. Though the definition tends to be somewhat simplistic in nature, it firmly attaches the nature of entrepreneurial action with risk-taking and the bearing of uncertainty by the individual (Swoboda, 1983).

Innovation can be perceived simply as the transformation of creative ideas into useful applications by combining resources in new or unusual ways to provide value to society for or improved products, technology, or services.

An individual could be termed as an entrepreneur if he or she sells a product or service using new systems and/or mediums of marketing, distribution or production methods as a basis for a new business venture.

Innovation: Special Reference Innovation in Human Resource Management Practices

Human resource management practices are especially critical for encouraging entrepreneurial behaviours. The question becomes one of determining which particular practices-recruitment, selection, training, job design, evaluations or rewards-are most conducive to fostering the entrepreneurial spirit.

Managers from firms in seven industries participated in a survey to determine which HR practices promote and facilitate entrepreneurship. Two questionnaires were designed for the survey. The first was mailed to the senior HR manager of a firm, the second to the marketing manager at the same firm. The HR manager was asked to characterize the company's HR practices, while the marketing manager was asked to characterize its entrepreneurial orientation. This article summarizes the results of those surveys and identifies practices that successful firms use to promote entrepreneurship.

PRACTICES THAT MAKE A DIFFERENCE

(a) Difference between Entrepreneurial and Non-Entrepreneurial Firms in HRM Practices

The greatest differences between entrepreneurial and non-entrepreneurial firms are found in performance appraisal practices, compensation practices and training practices. In the area of performance appraisals, firms with a more entrepreneurial orientation tend to encourage higher levels of employee involvement in the appraisal process. They are also more concerned with evaluating results, rather than the methods used to achieve them (ends versus means). And although individual performance remains a primary focus, group performance is more likely to be part of the appraisal process in highly entrepreneurial firms.

Entrepreneurial firms tend to include innovation in their employee evaluations and encourage risk-taking behaviors. Building a greater tolerance for failure into the appraisal process and evaluating performance over a longer period of time complements the entrepreneurial emphasis. In compensation practices, firms with a more entrepreneurial orientation tend to base pay rates on market comparisons more so than on internal equity concerns. These firms frequently provide a lower base pay, but have significantly greater opportunities in the form of performance-based pay incentives, including a greater variety of pay incentives in higher dollar amounts. Entrepreneurial firms also tend to base pay on a balance of short and long-term accomplishments by both the individual and his or her work group. Finally, entrepreneurial firms appear to spend more time and effort on orienting new employees and helping them adapt to the organization's culture. These firms also emphasize more participative, group-oriented training programmes requiring a systematic, planned approach. Training in these firms is more likely to be approached as an ongoing activity linked to an employee's career.

When hiring managers, entrepreneurial firms rely more on external sources for candidates, and are more likely to communicate job openings to a wider audience. Firms with an entrepreneurial orientation also provide a greater variety of career path options than firms with a more traditional orientation.

Once employed, managers in entrepreneurial firms find their jobs less structured and more complex than those of managers in traditional firms. Managerial positions in an entrepreneurial firm involve a greater variety of duties and responsibilities, as well as more discretionary authority and freedom in carrying out assignments.

On the basis of the survey's findings, it appears *HR systems can be designed to promote and reinforce entrepreneurial behaviours in employees*. Entrepreneurial organizations in the survey differed from their less entrepreneurial counterparts in specific areas of HR policy design.

The changing nature of human resource management fostered the development of entrepreneurial activities in human resource management. Some of these changes were forced on human resource management through activities such as downsizing, which affected human resource staff as well as other employees. Other changes were the consequence of human resource management's need to demonstrate its ability to add value to a firm. Entrepreneurial activity was demonstrated through an entrepreneurial philosophy, treating other departments within the firm as customers when they utilized the services of human resource departments, and the development of new firms who provided human resource services. Like all entrepreneurial endeavors, human resource entrepreneurs have varied in their success.

The successful entrepreneurs have been able to identify better and more cost-effective ways to provide human resource services. They have also demonstrated the ability of human resource management to add value to a firm.

The field of human resource management typically has not been associated with entrepreneurial activities. In fact, some observers might argue that "entrepreneurial human resource management" is an oxymoron. However, analysis of changes in human resource management reveal that entrepreneurial activities indeed have occurred. Some of these activities resulted from a changing business environment. Other changes were consequences of changes in the field human resource management.

(b) Entrepreneurial Activities in Human Resource Management

Since human resource management needs to be a value-added function, the cost and benefits of the human resource function have been analyzed in order to maximize the value of any resources directed toward this function. This analysis requires consideration of specific human resource functions (that is, job analysis, human resource planning, recruitment, selection, compensation system development, benefits administration, performance appraisal, career planning, training, etc.). Each function is analyzed to determine whether or not services related to this function should continue. If the specific services are considered worth providing, the next decision requires identifying the most cost-effective way to provide these services. Should the firm provide these services or should these services be provided by someone outside the firm?

The process of analyzing the cost-effectiveness of specific human resource functions has led to specific changes and entrepreneurial activities related to human resource management. The most obvious outcomes of these changes are outsourcing all or some of the human resource activities, an entrepreneurial philosophy of the human resource professionals providing services to other parts of the firm, and the development of human resource firms who provide the services to firms who have outsourced some or all of their human resource function.

(c) Outsourcing all or some of the Human Resource Activities

When an organization decides whether or not to outsource a specific function, the usual criteria for making this decision concerns the place of the function in the overall business strategy. If the function is considered "non-core", it is a likely target for outsourcing. When a firm outsources strategically and emphasizes its core competencies, it can leverage its skills and resources in order to make it more competitive.

By doing this the firm can concentrate its resources on a set of core competencies in which it can achieve preeminence and provide unique value to its customers (Quinn, Doorley, & Paquette, 1990). A carefully planned outsourcing of specific human resource activities can help a firm gain or retain its competitive advantage (Jeffay, Bohannon, & Laspisa, 1997).

When downsizing became a method for cost cutting and/or increasing shareholder value, most firms looked to the human resource department to reduce the number of employees. When this was accomplished, human resource departments then were asked to reduce the headcount in their own department. They moved from being the implementers of downsizing to the target of downsizing (Greer, Youngblood, & Gray, 1999). Many human resource departments saw their size decrease dramatically (Csoka, 1995).

Therefore, firms who see human resources as a non-core function often will decide to outsource all or some of the human resource function. This outsourcing is made to outside vendors who can perform the specific human resource function(s) better, faster, and more cost-effectively (Davidson, 1998).

In general, firms should first outsource the less critical areas of human resources—for example, payroll. They can outsource other activities after they have gained experience from outsourcing these less critical functions (Quinn & Hilmer, 1994). Carrig (1997), offered a specific classification of human resource activities that identifies a recommended order for outsourcing human resource activities. Carrig's classification includes three categories: transactional, traditional, and transformational. The transactional activities are the easiest to outsource. These activities include (in order from least difficult to most difficult to outsource) benefits administration, record keeping, employee services, communication, and performance management. Traditional activities are moderately difficult to outsource. These activities include (in order from least difficult to most difficult to outsource) training, recruiting, employee and labour relations, compensation, and management development. Transformational activities are the most difficult to outsource. These activities include (in order from least difficult to most difficult to outsource) business partner, strategic planning, organization development, and knowledge management.

Outsourcing of human resources started as a way to control human resource costs. Its popularity is gaining, but it is not a new concept (Haynes, 1999). Now outsourcing of human resources is seen as a strategic tool that heightens efficiency and allows firms to focus on their core business. Also, the popularity of mergers and acquisitions makes firms concerned about controlling fixed costs such as the wages for the human resource department (Gault, 1998).

The use of outsourcing can change the nature of human resources. Carrig's (1997) analysis of human resource practices lead to the conclusion that the human resource department of the future will have its greatest value if it extends outsourcing to a strategic partnership. In this way outsourcing is more than shifting the responsibility of specific tasks to a contractor.

CASE STUDY

An example of the partnership model for outsourcing is provided by the relationship between Corning and CCFL (College Center of the Finger Lakes), a nonprofit education and training organization founded as a consortium of colleges and chartered by the New York Board of Regents. Corning gradually shifted responsibility for much of its training from Corning's training department to CCFL. Corning still monitors the quality of the training provided by CCFL, and Corning does not outsource training related to the firm's core competencies. The initial partnership started by having CCFL administer sixty skill courses while Corning retained responsibility for education and training processes. This partnership progressed to a point where CCFL and Corning formed a joint organization in which CCFL managed skills courses, administered core competency courses, and developed training curricula; Corning installed systems and provided consulting. In the final stages of this partnership CCFL was responsible for delivering all training courses while the Corning training department provided strategic leadership, was responsible for the training content of employee orientation and leadership courses, focused on competency centered learning, and conducted research (DeRose & McLaughlin, 1995).

Corning's training department was characterized as entrepreneurial before the partnership with CCFL (DeRose & McLaughlin, 1995). It continued to be entrepreneurial with its partnership with CCFL, which was mutually beneficial. Corning was able to outsource most of its training to CCFL and control training costs. CCFL was able to expand its market, develop its entrepreneurial skills, and learn from a topnotch corporate training department (DeRose & McLaughlin, 1995).

An Entrepreneurial Philosophy of the Human Resource Professionals providing Services to Other Parts of the Firm

When firms identified separate business units, human resource departments often were not identified initially as a business unit. They generated costs, not income. Therefore, they could not produce profits. However, when human resource management departments are expected to deliver economic value, a firm's various constituencies are willing to pay for these services (Beatty & Schneir, 1997).

As human resource departments developed and, in some cases, redefined their role in the firm, they proved that they could also generate income and, therefore, profits. This change often was accomplished by defining other departments in the firm as internal customers. The human resource department provided services needed by other departments, for example, training and recruitment. Therefore, internal customers could pay the human resource department for these services in the same way that they could hire an outside vendor to provide these services.

If a truly competitive model is used, departments or business units within a firm can be allowed to choose who will provide needed human resource services—the firm's human resource department or one of various outside vendors. Under such a model, the human resource department is forced to adopt an entrepreneurial philosophy and look for better and more cost-effective ways to provide human resource services. If other business units are potential internal customers for the human resource department, the human resource department must create services that satisfy these internal customers and demonstrate value (Csoka, 1994).

Examples of this model are provided by Hewlett-Packard and Levi Strauss. Hewlett-Packard has a personnel manager in most of its divisions. These personnel managers purchase services through the regional or national organization. Levi Strauss developed a human resource consulting unit that does research on best practices and provides consulting services (Csoka, 1994).

Development of Human Resource Firms who provide the Services to Firms who have Outsourced some or all of their Human Resource Function

When firms outsource one or more human resource activities, these activities still must be performed successfully. In some cases these activities are performed by consulting firms who have existed for many years and developed expertise in one or more human resource areas (for example, Hay Associates). In other cases, increased outsourcing has resulted in new opportunities for entrepreneurial firms who provide the needed human resource services. In fact, some of the new entrepreneurs are the human resource staff who formerly worked for one of the firms who has decided to outsource some of its human resource activities.

DISCUSSION

The field of human resource management initially may seem like an unlikely place for entrepreneurial activities. However, it is a place where various entrepreneurial activities have occurred.

These entrepreneurial activities have resulted in new and better ways to provide human resource services. Some of these entrepreneurial activities have occurred through classic ways by the development of new firms started by entrepreneurs with expertise in human resource management. Other entrepreneurial activities have occurred through new activities and/or partnerships between existing firms or through intrapreneurial activities by human resource departments.

CONCLUSION

Development of these entrepreneurial activities has reinforced the development of human resource management as a function that adds value to a firm. Like all changing activities, any changes in human resource activities or method delivery must be monitored carefully to guarantee its success. The advantages and disadvantages of encouraging and utilizing the services of specific human resource entrepreneurs must be carefully assessed before deciding to value these entrepreneurs more than human resource professionals who operate in more traditional human resource departments.

In general, the most successful human resource entrepreneurs are found in firms known for quality human resource management. *This finding is especially apparent when human resource management is one of the firm's core competencies.*

References

James C. Hayton, Promoting corporate entrepreneurship through human resource management practices: A Review of empirical research, February, 2005. College of Business, Utah State University, United States.

Mitchell, Margaret E., Entrepreneurial Activities in Human Resource Management, American International College, *Journal of Business*, March 22, 2000 *Entrepreneurship* (*Usage*), Human Resource Management (Methods), United States.

www.allbusiness.com

www.sciencedirect.com

www.findarticles.com

9

Achieving Excellence in Corporate Entrepreneurship: Can Management Education be the Ladder?

Prof. S. S. Dhond*
Dr. Pradip Manjrekar**

Corporates around the world, in their quest to rejuvenate their organizations are frazzled to reorganize the basic theories of management education and put them in practice, to match with the present prerequisite of the knowledge based economy. In this present tryst, corporate entrepreneurship seems to be the new terminology in the world of business. It provides an apparent belief that it is possible to restart the engines of growth not just by uptight attainment, but through internal self replenishment. Corporate professionals put efforts to expand their dynasty either by preaching the philosophy of Small is Beautiful or Bigger is Better. The real difficulty arises when the harmonization needs to be done of both the philosophies simultaneously. The reason for that may be because of the fundamental differences in the scale of thinking, the duration of time, and the amount of resources needed to exploit bigger versus smaller opportunities. The need for sustainable market development in this era of knowledge-based business requires the talent to innovate, create new ideas and develop new market trends and open-up new areas of business in the old and established cycle of service business. The mission of management education seems to be half truth when it comes to fulfill the need for corporate entrepreneurs. In this context, the present paper explores the various facets of management education in India and deal with the needs of enhanced industry-institute endeavours as one of the major catalyst for the inception of corporate entrepreneurship in the mindset of future managers.

INTRODUCTION

Entrepreneurship is considered to be a vital component in the process of economic growth and development for various reasons. It is a mechanism by which society converts technological information into products and services (Shane & Venkatarmana, 2000). This type of entrepreneurially driven innovation in products or services and processes is a crucial engine that drives the change process in a capitalist society (Schumpeter, 1934).

---

* Director, Vasantdada Patil Institute of Management & Research, Chunabhatti, Mumbai.
** Professor, Dr. D. Y. Patil Institute of Management, Navi Mumbai.

Entrepreneurship discovers and mitigates not only technological, but also temporal and spatial inefficiencies in an economy (Shane and Venkatarmana, 2000). It is clear that entrepreneurship is an essential component of the business.

Entrepreneurship has long been seen as a synonym for establishing new small firms as a suitable vehicle for entrepreneurial endeavour. Over the year, a parallel strand in literature was developed stressing the importance of entrepreneurship for and within existing corporations. A widely accepted label for this branch in entrepreneurship theory aiming at bewildering existing companies with an entrepreneurial spirit is corporate entrepreneurship. Factors that have stimulated the emergence of corporate entrepreneurship as a field of research and practice are related to perceived weaknesses of the traditional methods of corporate management (e.g., highly regulated, strict hierarchy, short-term focus, premeditation with cost minimization and cutting slack, narrowly defined jobs etc.). These traditional management methods can lead companies onto a bureaucratic or administrative pathway, often ignoring the need for change and smoldering innovative initiatives. This type of management is expected to be self-reinforcing since disappointed entrepreneurial-minded employees and executives tend to leave a company managed by strict bureaucratic rules and regulations.

Corporate entrepreneurship is thought of as rejuvenating and revitalizing existing companies. It is brought into practice as a tool for business development, revenue growth, profitability enhancement and pioneering the development of new products, services and processes (Lumpkin and Dess, 1996; Miles and Covin, 2002; Zehra, 1991; Zahra and Covin, 1995; Zahra *et al.*, 1999).

Realizing the need of corporate entrepreneurship in the knowledge based economy and equally justified need of role of management education, the present paper attempts to discuss the need, benefit of corporate entrepreneurship, factors responsible for corporate entrepreneurship. It also attempts to study the role of management education in achieving excellence in corporate entrepreneurship. The organization of the paper is as follows: section two deals with growth and type of corporate entrepreneurship; section three and section four discuss the need and benefit of corporate entrepreneurship; section five deals with factors responsible for success of corporate entrepreneurship; section six justifies the role of management education in the present context; section seven gives a conclusion of the study.

GROWTH AND TYPES OF CORPORATE ENTREPRENEURSHIP

Recently, there has been a growing interest in the use of corporate entrepreneurship as a means for corporations to enhance the innovative abilities of their employees and at the same time, increase corporate success through the creation of new corporate ventures. However, the creation of corporate activity is difficult since it involves radically changing internal organizational behaviour patterns. A number of studies have been conducted to understand the factors that stimulate corporate entrepreneurship. They examined the effect of a firm's strategy, organization and external environment. It appears that the environment plays a profound role in influencing corporate entrepreneurship whereas there is consensus that the external environment is an important antecedent of corporate entrepreneurship.

For despite the growing interest in corporate entrepreneurship, there appears to be nothing near a consensus on what it is. Some scholars emphasizing its analogue to new business creation by individual entrepreneurs, view corporate entrepreneurship as a concept that is limited to new venture creation within existing organizations (Burgelman, 1983). Others argue that the concept of corporate entrepreneurship should encompass the struggle of large firms to renew them by carrying out new combinations of resources that alter the relationship between them and their environments (Burgelman, 1983). According to Zahra (1991), corporate entrepreneurship refers to the process of creating new business within established firms to improve organizational profitability and enhance a firm's competitive position or the strategic renewal of existing business.

Thus, corporate entrepreneurship is conceived of as the effort to extend an organisation's competitive advantage through internally generated innovations that significantly alter the balance of competition within an industry or create entirely new industries. Corporate entrepreneurship is a process of organizational renewal (Sathe, 1989) that has two distinct but related dimensions: Innovation and venturing, and strategic stress creating new business through market developments by undertaking product, process, technological and administrative innovations. The second dimension of corporate entrepreneurship embodies renewal activities that enhance a firm's ability to compete and take risks (Miller, 1983). Renewal has many facets, including the redefinition of the business concept, reorganization, and the introduction of system-wide changes for innovation.

Corporate entrepreneurship activities can be internally or externally oriented. Internal activities are typified as the development within a large organisation of internal markets and relatively small and independent units designed to create internal test-markets or expand improved or innovative staff services, technologies, or production methods within the organisation. These activities may cover product, process, and administrative innovations at various levels of the firm (Zahra, 1991). Schollhammer (1982), has proposed that internal entrepreneurship expresses itself in a variety of modes on strategies—administrative (management of research and development), opportunistic (search and exploitation), imitative (internalization of an external development, technical or organizational), acquisitive (acquisitions and mergers, divestments) and incubative (formation of semi-autonomous units within existing organizations).

External entrepreneurship can be defined as the first phenomenon that consists of the process of combining resources dispersed in the environment by individual entrepreneurs with his or her own unique resources to create a new resource combination independent of all others. External efforts entail mergers, joint ventures, corporate venture; venture nurturing, venture spin-off and others.

Whether internal or external in focus, corporate entrepreneurship can be formal or informal. Informal efforts occur autonomously, with or without the blessing of the official organisation. Such informal activities can result from individual creativity or pursuit of self-interest, and some of these efforts eventually receive the firm's formal recognition and, thus, become an integral part of the business concept. According to Zahra (1991), a comprehensive of corporate entrepreneurship must incorporate both formal and informal aspects of corporate venturing, as follows: "corporate entrepreneurship refers to formal and informal activities aimed at creating new business in established companies through product and process innovations and market developments". These activities may take place at the corporate, division (business), functional, or project levels, with the unifying objective of improving a firm's competitive position and financial performance (Morris *et al.*, 1988).

In light of these manifestations, it is evident that corporate entrepreneurship is not confined to a particular business size or a particular stage in an organisation's life cycle, such as the start-up phase. In a competitive environment, entrepreneurship is an essential element in the long-range success of every business organisation, small or large, new or long established.

The strategy literature identifies three types of corporate entrepreneurship. One is the creation of new business within an existing organisation – corporate venturing or intrapreneurship as it is called (Bugelman, 1983). Another is the more persistent activity associated with the transformation or renewal of existing organisations (Stopford & Fuller, 1994). The third is where the enterprise changes the rules of competition for its industry in the manner suggested by Schumpeter (Stevenson and Gumpert, 1985).

Changes in the pattern of resource deployment new combinations of resources in Schumpeter's terms – transform the firm into something significantly different from what it was before – something 'new'. This transformation of the firm from the old to the new reflects entrepreneurial behaviour. Corporate venturing, or new business development within an existing firm, is only one of the possible ways to achieve strategic renewal. Strategic renewal involves the creation of new wealth through new combinations of resources. This includes actions such as refocusing a business competitively, making major changes in marketing or distribution, redirecting product development, and reshaping operations (Guth and Ginsberg, 1990).

Various terms have been used in literature to describe *Corporate Entrepreneurship* including *Intrapreneurship, Internal Corporate Entrepreneurship, Corporate Ventures, Venture Management, New Ventures and Internal Corporate Venturing*. In the context of this paper, we use the definition: "CE is the process whereby an individual or a group of individuals, in association with an existing organization, create a new organization or instigate renewal or innovation within that organization". This definition briefly captures the paradoxes inherent in the concept of CE namely, the coexistence of "new" and "existing", and the close association of the "individual" and the "organization" which usually are located on different planes. This naturally leads to a number of questions: How can innovation and individual initiative flourish in the midst of a highly structured environment? Should corporations rely on individuals to foster innovation? How can individuals and organizations associate?

WHY CORPORATE ENTREPRENEURSHIP?

Building a new venture within the walls of an established corporation is an uncommon initiative. So perhaps, it is not surprising that any corporation presented with "lower hanging fruit" that is, growth opportunities that are less difficult to capture – would naturally seek to avoid the risk and complexity of entrepreneurship. So, when would a corporation risk a significant portion of its earnings on a risky new venture? We cite a few motives behind establishing corporate ventures.

From the literature, it is evident that the need to pursue corporate entrepreneurship has arisen from a variety of pressing problems including:

- Threats to businesses from potentially disruptive technologies or changes in external environment.

- Growth and Diversification of businesses due to nature markets.

- To retain talent and to satisfy the ambitions of key employees.

- Required changes, innovations, and improvements in the marketplace to avoid stagnation and decline.

- Perceived weakness in the traditional methods of corporate management.

- Turnover of innovative-minded employees who are disenchanted with bureaucratic organisations.

However, the pursuit of corporate entrepreneurship as a strategy to counter these problems creates a newer and potentially more complex set of challenges on both a practical and theoretical level.

BENEFITS OF CORPORATE ENTREPRENEURSHIP

It is observed that in most of the developed and developing countries, about 80% of all new ventures fail within the five years (Kanter, 1990). In this context, the question arises that can these firms stand to gain by pursuing risky CE ventures? The answer to this is associated with the benefit of practicing CE and this section looks at some of the possible answers to the above question.

Scope for Pre-testing: CE initiatives, by virtue of being small, get thoroughly sieved before big investments are made. Corporates can decide whether to exercise or extinguish the initiatives at an early stage, thereby improving the pay-off from its various strategic choices.

Cost Effectiveness: Almost all CE initiatives require very less upfront investment and use far less resources than a regular development project. Also, by pursuing multiple ventures the firm can diversify its risk.

Flexibility and Manageability: Managing a small team of people would be far easier than managing organizational entities. Also, resource endowments made to the CE initiatives are highly flexible – investments can be made progressively.

Synergy between Internal and External Ventures: For today's corporations, traditional internal expansions, efficiency improvements and "Synergistic" acquisitions are no longer sufficient sources of growth. The new challenge is to search for emerging "white space" opportunities that would meet the unmet needs of customers in emerging markets". The value created for the firm is maximum when there is perfect synergy between the internal and external ventures of the firm.

FACTORS RESPONSIBLE FOR ACHIEVING EXCELLENCE IN CORPORATE ENTREPRENEURSHIP

In this section, we examine some of the internal and external factors that facilitate a successful CE culture in an organization.

- *Dynamism and Competitiveness of the Environment of the Corporation:* Dynamic and competitive environments shorten the life of competitive advantages and force corporations to engage into constant innovation. It is undeniable that with the twin forces of globalization and digital revolution, the potential for radical change in any industry is greater now than ever before.

- *The Values and Traits of the Top Management Team:* Cultural orientations such as authorizing the expression of unorthodox ideas and perceiving change positively are correlated with the adoption of an entrepreneurial posture. These values can be seen in abundance in HCL Technologies founder Shiv Nadar who provided the early support to Rajendra Pawar and Vijay Thadani to set up NIIT, which became a pioneer in the field of IT education in India.

- *The Culture and Structure of the Corporation:* A corporation structured as a learning organization is more likely to be conducive to CE than any other structure. The learning organization is based on equality, open information, little hierarchy, and a culture that encourages adaptability and participations, enabling ideas to bubble up from anywhere that can help an organization seize opportunities and handle crises.

- *The Level of Performance of Organization:* There are diverse perspectives possible on this. For some organizations, poor corporate performance could lead to conservatism. Others perceive crises as an excellent innovation opportunity. For instance, New York Times Company, when faced with an onslaught from dotcoms offering free content to readers, responded by seeding and funding a new media business unit to counter the threat.

- *Right Selection Mechanisms:* These selection mechanisms should ensure strategic alignment of CE initiatives while preserving their operational autonomy. This could take the form of explicit programme goals, norms and procedures, standardized project evaluation criteria and methods or formal approval instances. Such processes reduce the risks inherent to CE by insuring that the various selected initiatives fall within an acceptable scope, that they are reasonably resources conserving and that they do not generate excessive conflict.

- *Right Retention Mechanisms:* Corporate entrepreneurs are key resources whose exit can damage the corporation's human and social capital. Research has established corporate entrepreneurs in large organizations considered the non-pecuniary motives more important. Therefore, managers should monitor the motivations and expectations of each corporate entrepreneur and appropriately tailor the rewards and incentives.

- *Right Structure for the Corporate Venture:* The choice of structure for a new venture depends on a number of factors, the most fundamental being how close the activities are to the core of the business. Other factors include the level and urgency of the venturing activity, the nature and number of ventures to be established, and the corporate culture and experience. Based on the balance between the desire to learn new competencies and the need to leverage existing competencies, one can identify four possible structures.

ROLE OF MANAGEMENT EDUCATION

A firm may establish a corporate venture for a number of reasons – to improve its competitiveness by exploiting existing processes, to explore more attractive product markets or to grow new business based on new technologies, products or markets. However, studies show that most corporations struggle to manage the inherent contradictions of CE, which include issues like strategic misalignment and competitive erosion. Are these strategic risks acceptable? The answers to these questions are conditional. They depend on the corporate manager's risk perception and controllability which are in turn influenced by various internal and external factors. Adopting the right structure for the corporate venture, monitoring its performance and controlling the strategic risks are keys to the success of the venture.

Even though, the concept of Corporate Entrepreneurship has been in vogue in management literature for decades now, in India, the idea has gained acceptance in recent times with its adoption by corporate like HLL and HCL. The IT services sector in India seems to be the sector that is most likely to its open culture and idea-intensive nature. This industry, which has a high attrition rate, also stands to gain from the increased retention of high caliber employees. This is evident from the successful ventures being followed at HCL and Wipro. Other sectors which are also seeing matured markets and increased competition will gain by adopting CE practices within their organizations.

Realizing the increasing role of management knowledge and education in the corporate world, this section will discuss below, management education can be used to make the factors effective, which are responsible for achieving excellence in corporate entrepreneurship. It will also examine whether management education is successful in doing that assignment.

Demand for management and management education is growing rapidly for the success of CE initiatives in specific and performance of organization in general. Management is seen as a major force for change, growth, and prosperity. The diversifying and competitive industrial and market scenario across the nation is demanding for risk taking behaviour by the management or to say the managers. Management education in India has come a long way from the traditional approach to management subjects to broad specified subject orientation. But the unparalleled growth in business and its activities demands more of risk taking and challenge–oriented managers. The competitive edge in any sector/type of business is a threat for the process owners to think and rethink for issues related to sustainable development in the particular field. They would look more at the young mangers to overcome the challenges of the growing and demanding business scenario.

The growth in management education and management institutes obviously shows a good sign of prosperity for the business challengers, but the care needs to be taken whether in the urge of increasing the number of management institutes in quantity and volume, the really demanding owners of these management institutes give up the need to strive hard for the quality they look for. The gap between theory and practice of management education somehow leads towards high cost of training and development for the companies to make them aware of the realities and competitive behaviour of the market. Making them understand the fact that functional expertise (Theory to Practice) covers only one-eighth for the managers overall development up the ladder in the organization, takes away a lot of time and energy of the organization. The young managers need to have a holistic approach when working in the organisation. Awareness of the outside world and business and competition should be a parallel and constant thought in the back of their mind.

Again, having a subject on Corporate Entrepreneurship in Management Education may not be a complete solution for the future managers to be compatible with the growing needs of the corporate world. But the ground level fact is to make them aware of their strengths and weakness during there tenure of management level education and also aware of the growing and demanding business scenario. The need of time is a revamp in the structure of management education away from the exam-oriented and grade-oriented approach, which at times hinders the students from looking at the corporate scenario with a holistic approach. Sensitivity and creativity of the future managers need to nurture to stand with confidence and handle the business situations with high innovations at workplace. The future managers as per there interest need to be nurtured for developing skills leading towards an insight into identifying opportunities, creating and opening new ventures in established systems.

Strategic management education with increased Industry-Institute interface is the urgent need of time. The cultivation of young corporate entrepreneurs with high functional abilities, innovative mind and leadership qualities would seamlessly serve the purpose of the growing and competitive business environment. The traditional manager outlook of being a servant bearing no risk involved in the enterprise in the present business scenario is asked to be risk taker and bear the uncertainty involved in the enterprise. The managers are now asked to be change agents who are given full support for conceptualizing new goods and services to meet the changing needs of the customer. Understanding the demand of Corporate entrepreneurs by the corporate sector the management education need to undergo a thorough rejuvenation of its present course structures and develop strategies to identify potential future managers through improved and effective psychological behaviour testing and then providing careful guidance and motivation. A mere course work shall not serve the purpose of the high demand in the real life situations. The various variables for testing of the students can be their entrepreneurial capacity, their capacity to take risks, motivation level, problem resolving, positive self image and their interest in setting up and trying something new or unconventional. And in the process the industry-institute interface needs to be the parallel drive for the making of highly motivated corporate entrepreneurs. Companies need to come forward by providing opportunities for the young future managers with simulated business scenario for developing new ventures or markets in the present established systems. One of the major advantages of doing this would be the saving of high cost involved in training and developing the young managers as per the requirement of the companies. The industries need to support the management institutes in harnessing talents and helping them educate, train and provide exposure at early stages for the potential corporate entrepreneurs. It is incumbent on the part of the planners and policy formulators to take note of the emerging needs of the industries and develop strategies to identify and inculcate corporate entrepreneurship skills in potential future managers.

CONCLUSION

The present paper has made a modest attempt to identify the merits of CE and factors responsible for the success of CE to achieve excellence in the organisation's performance. It also tries to justify the role of management education for the success of CE. It can be concluded that a systematic theoretical knowledge and equally balanced practical exposure should be provided by the management institute to the students, so that they can implement their knowledge and experiences effectively for achieving excellence in CE. Apart form this, there is need of a conducive and dynamic environment in the organisation and enhanced industry-institute endeavours as one of the major catalysts for the inception of corporate entrepreneurship in the mindset of future managers.

References

Burgelman, (1983), Corporate Entrepreneurship and Strategic Management: Insights from a Process Study", *Management Science*, 29(12).

Guth, W. D. and Ginsberg, A. (1990), Guest Editor's Introduction on Corporate Entrepreneurship, *Strategic Management Journal*, 11, 5-15.

Kumar, S. A. (2004), "Entrepreneurship Development", New Age International (P) Ltd.

Kuratko *et al.*, (1990), "Developing an Entrepreneurial Instrument for an Effective Corporate Entrepreneurial Environment", *Strategic Management Journal*, 11, 49-58.

Lumpkin, G. T., & Dess, G.G. (1996), "Clarifying the Entrepreneurial Orientation Construct and Impact of Industry Technological Opportunities", *Academy of Journal, Academy of Management Review*, 21(1): 135-173.

Miller, D (1983), "The Correlates of Entrepreneurship in Three Types of Firm", *Management Science*, 29(7), 770-791.

Morris *et al.*, (1988), "Individualism and Modern Corporation: Implications for Innovation and Entrepreneurship", *Journal of Management* 19 (3), 595-613.

Sathe, V (1989), *Managing an Entrepreneurial*.

"Dilemma: Nurturing Entrepreneurship and Control in Large Corporation", *Frontier in Entrepreneur Research*, 636-656.

Schollhammer, H. (1982), "Internal Corporate Entrepreneurship", *Encyclopedia of Entrepreneurship*, Prentice Hall.

Shane, S. and Venkatarmana, S. (2000), "The Promise of Entrepreneurship as a Field of Research", *The Academy of Management Review*, 25(1), 217-226.

Stopford, J. M. & C. W. Fuller (1994), "Creating Corporate Entrepreneurship", *Strategic Management Journal*, 15(7), 521-536.

Zahra *et al.*, (1999), "Entrepreneurship and the Acquisition of Dynamic Organisational Capabilities", *Entrepreneurship Theory and Practice*, 23(3), 5-10.

Zahra, S.A. (1991), "Predictors and Financial Outcome of Corporate Entrepreneurship", *Journal of Business Venturing*, 6, 259-165.

Zahra, S.A. and C. Covin, (1995), "Contextual Influence on the Corporate Entrepreneurship – Performance Relationship: A Longitudinal Analysis", *Journal of Business Venturing*, 10, 43-58.

10

Are Entrepreneurs Control Freaks?

Col E. J. Sanchis*

A new idea is like a newborn baby: delicate and without a past. An entrepreneurship idea about making the automotive industry's delivery of cars with spare wheels superfluous is a novel idea.

HOW DOES A COMPANY GET STARTED?

It is important that roles and responsibilities of the individual employees have been determined so that decisions are made at the right places in the company. It is also important to map the key risks that are permanent parameters for customer requirements and/or own production and services to the customer. It may be technical, but also sales, financial and delivery terms, which may be key areas.

The mapping of these parameters forms the actual basis of which conditions are necessary to make decisions on after thorough analysis. The result of the analysis also provides important indications how the company should take measures which counteract factors, which are either known or unknown.

Do you have it in you?

If you think you want to be your own boss and run your own business, but are not sure you have the right qualifications to be an entrepreneur then you need to know what stuff entrepreneurs are made up of. What are the characteristics of an entrepreneur? How does an entrepreneur think?

Until recently, entrepreneurs were not widely studied. There was a general lack of knowledge and information about what made them tick. The recent interest in revitalizing America's dormant productivity has changed all that. India has gone global. Most business universities now offer courses in entrepreneurship. As a result, business professionals have learnt a lot about what it takes to become a successful entrepreneur. Although no one has found the perfect entrepreneurial profile, there are many characteristics that show up repeatedly. In this paper, I will endeavour to cover several important characteristics of entrepreneurs for you to consider and dispel the entrepreneurial myths. And also decide whether an entrepreneur is a "control freak".

---

*   Faculty, St Francis Institute of Management and Research (SFIMAR), Borivili, Mumbai.

ENTREPRENEURIAL CHARACTERISTICS

A series of interviews were conducted with distinguished entrepreneurs. They were asked what characteristics they felt were essential to succeed as an entrepreneur. A few are listed below:

Sound Health

A characteristic mentioned by every entrepreneur interviewed. Entrepreneurs are physically resilient and in good health. They can work for extended periods of time, and while they are in the process of building their business, they refuse to get sick.

Supermen

In small businesses, where there is no depth of management, the leader must be there. You may not be able to afford a support staff to cover all business functions, and therefore you will need to work long hours. At the end of the eight-hour day, when everyone else leaves for home, the entrepreneur will often continue to work into the evening, developing new business ideas.

Self-Control

Entrepreneurs do not function well in structured organizations and do not like someone having authority over them. Most believe they can do the job better than anyone else and will strive for maximum responsibility and accountability. They enjoy creating business strategies and thrive on the process of achieving their goals. Once they achieve a goal, they quickly replace it with a greater goal. They *strive to exert whatever influence they can over future events.*

In large, structured organizations, entrepreneurs are easy to recognize by the statements they make: "If they wanted that job done right, they should have given it to me". A dominant characteristic of entrepreneurs is their *belief that they are smarter than their peers and superiors.* They have a compelling need to do their own thing in their own way. They need the freedom to choose and to act according to their own perception of what actions will result in success.

Self-Confidence

Entrepreneurs are *self-confident when they are in control of what they're doing* and working alone. They tackle problems immediately with confidence and are persistent in their pursuit of their objectives. Most are at their best in the face of adversity, since they thrive on their own self-confidence.

Sense of Urgency

Entrepreneurs have a *never-ending sense of urgency* to develop their ideas. Inactivity makes them impatient, tense, and uneasy. They thrive on activity and are not likely to be found sitting on their haunches. When they are in the entrepreneurial mode, they are like cats on a hot tinned roof.

Entrepreneurs *prefer individual sports*, such as golf, skiing, or tennis, over team sports. They prefer games in which their own brawn and brain directly influence the outcome and pace of the game. They have drive and high energy levels, they are achievement-oriented, and they are tireless in the pursuit of their goals.

Comprehensive Awareness

Successful entrepreneurs can comprehend complex situations that may include planning, making strategic decisions, and *working on multiple business ideas simultaneously*. They are *farsighted* and aware of important details, and they will *continuously review all possibilities* to achieve their business objectives. At the same time, they devote their energy for completing the tasks immediately before them.

Realism

Entrepreneurs accept things as they are and deal with them accordingly. They may or may not be idealistic, but they are seldom unrealistic. They will change their direction when they see that change will improve their prospects for achieving their goals. They *want to know the status of a given situation at all times*. News interests them if it is timely, and factual, and provides them with information they need. They *will verify any information they receive before they use it* in making a decision. Entrepreneurs say what they mean and assume that everyone else does too.

Conceptual Ability

Entrepreneurs possess the ability to identify relationships quickly in the midst of complex situations. They are natural leaders and are usually the first to identify a problem to be overcome and begin working on their solution faster than other people. They are not troubled by ambiguity and uncertainty because they are used to solving problems. If it is pointed out to them that their solution to a problem will not work for some valid reason, they will quickly identify an alternative problem-solving approach.

Status Requirements

Entrepreneurs find satisfaction in symbols of success that are external to themselves. *They like the business they have built to be praised*, but they are often embarrassed by praise directed at them personally. Their egos do not prevent them from seeking facts, data, and guidance. When they need help, they will not hesitate to admit it especially in areas that are outside of their expertise. During tough business periods, entrepreneurs will concentrate their resources and energies on essential business operations. They *want to be where the action is* and will not stay in the office for extended periods of time.

Symbols of achievement such as position have little relevance to them. Successful entrepreneurs find their satisfaction of status needs in the performance of their business, not in the appearance they present to their peers and to the public.

Interpersonal Relationships

Entrepreneurs are *more concerned with people's accomplishments than with their feelings*. They generally avoid becoming personally involved and *will not hesitate to sever relationships that could hinder the progress of their business*. During the business-building period, when resources are scarce, they seldom devote time to dealing with satisfying people's feelings beyond what is essential to achieving their goals. Their lack of sensitivity to people's feelings can cause turmoil and turnover in their organization.

Entrepreneurs *are impatient and drive themselves and everyone around them*. They don't have the tolerance or empathy necessary for team building unless it's their team, and they *will delegate very few key decisions*.

As the business grows and assumes an organizational structure, entrepreneurs go through a classic management crisis. For many of them, *their need for control makes it difficult for them to delegate authority in the way that a structured organization demands*. Their strong direct approach induces them to seek information directly from its source, bypassing the structured chains of authority and responsibility.

Their moderate interpersonal skills, which were adequate during the start-up phases, will cause them problems as they try to adjust to the structured or corporate organization. Entrepreneurs with good interpersonal skills will be able to adjust and survive as their organization grows and becomes more structured. The rest won't make it.

Emotional Stability

Entrepreneurs have a considerable amount of self-control and can handle business pressures. They *are comfortable in stress situations* and are challenged rather than discouraged by setbacks or failures. Entrepreneurs *are uncomfortable when things are going well*. They'll frequently find some new activity on which to vent their pent-up energy. They are not content to leave well enough alone. Entrepreneurs *tend to handle people problems with action plans without empathy*.

PERSONALITY CHARACTERISTICS OF SUCCESSFUL ENTREPRENEURS

Most important for success as an entrepreneur:

- Perseverance
- Desire and willingness to take the initiative
- Competitiveness
- Self-reliance
- A strong need to achieve
- Self-confidence
- Good physical health

Important for success as an entrepreneur:

- A willingness to take risks
- A high level of energy
- An ability to get along with employees
- Versatility
- A desire to create
- Innovation

Least importance for success as an entrepreneur:

- Ability to lead effectively
- A willingness to tolerate uncertainty

- A strong desire for money
- Patience
- Being well organized
- A need for power
- A need to closely associate with others.

ARE ENTREPRENEURS BORN OR MADE? (NATURE OR NURTURE?)

Two-thirds of entrepreneurs claim they were inspired by innate desire, not education or training. According to a new survey (2006), "The verdict: born". At least, that's according to the survey by Northeastern University's School of Technological Entrepreneurship.

Nearly, two-thirds of entrepreneurs claim they were inspired to start their own companies by their innate desire and determination, rather than by their education or work experience.

Only 1 per cent of more than 200 U.S. entrepreneurs surveyed cited higher education as a significant motivator toward starting their own venture, while 61 per cent cited their "innate drive". Other motivators cited were work experience (21 per cent) and success of entrepreneurial peers within their industry (16 per cent).

"The survey results indicate a major issue in academia today: Institutions of higher education are not adequately preparing students for careers in entrepreneurship", said Paul Zavracky, Dean of School of Technological Entrepreneurship.

While entrepreneurship skills can be taught, the survey results suggest that the desire to be an entrepreneur usually is not. Rather, as 42% of survey respondents said they launched their first venture in childhood, it seems as though the enterprising spirit is discovered within the individual, not developed by the individual's experience.

Thirty-three per cent of respondents launched their first venture between the ages of 18 and 30; 13 per cent between 30 and 40; and only 12 per cent started their first business after the age of 40.

The survey also suggests that the majority of entrepreneurs were confident about the success of their first venture. Thirty-two per cent said they had no fear that their venture would not succeed, while 42% had some fear but characterized themselves as confident. Only 14% said they experienced significant fear that their first venture would fail, while 12 per cent said fear of failure delayed their leap into entrepreneurship.

Psychological studies prove that the genetic contribution to personality is around 75% and 25% is due to environmental influence. This implies entrepreneurs are born. Books on entrepreneurship propound that entrepreneurship like other disciplines can be taught and mastered. This suggests entrepreneurs can be made. Whether the born/made ratio is 75/25 or 40/60, the environment is an important parameter with which something can be done.

Where Entrepreneurs come from?

Considering their roots and the surrounding influence, they can be grouped as under:

Family Background – entrepreneurial heritage.

Education and Age – aspirants do not give too much of importance to education. Majority are young.

Work Experience – 90% entrepreneurs start their business in the same area as their work experience.

Control Freak

In psychology-related slang, *control freak* is a derogatory term for a person who attempts to dictate how everything around him or her is done. It can also refer to someone with a limited number of things that they want done a specific way; Professor of clinical psychology, Les Parrott, wrote that "Control freaks are people who care more than you do about something and won't stop at being pushy to get their way". In some cases, the control freak might honestly believe that their constant intervention is beneficial or even necessary; this can be caused by feelings of superiority, believing that others are incapable of handling things properly, or the fear that things will go wrong they don't attend to every detail. In other cases, they may simply enjoy the feeling of power it gives them so much that they automatically try to gain control of everything around them.

An Acid Comment on Control Freaks

"Control freak" is one of those terms for which the meaning is starting to get distorted; its actual meaning is "One who has an obsessive need to exert control over people and situations".

A Typical Conversation

Me: Are you ready to go?

Him: Yes, let's go.

Me: It's gotten chilly in the past hour; I'll get my jacket.

Him: You don't need a jacket.

Me: Yes, I do.

Him: No, you don't, it's not that cold.

Me: I'll be cold without a jacket, so I'm getting it.

Him: You're not going to need it.

Me: Yes, I am, and I'm taking it with me.

Him: Why do you always have to be such a control freak?

Me: It's not being a control freak to make the decisions for my own life.

Him: But... yeah... but... er...

Me: A control freak is someone trying to enforce their preferences on someone ELSE'S life; that'd make you the control freak in this scenario, not me.

Him: Yeah, but... but you don't need... if you're insisting on doing something unnecessary...

Me: It has nothing to do with being a control freak. Furthermore, it's extremely arrogant for you to assume that you have the ability and authority to decide what other people need, especially in circumstances where someone else's physical perceptions, about which you know nothing, are involved.

Him: Yeah, but...

Me: Can we go now?

Him: Yeah, fine... I still say you won't need the jacket...

If this description reminds you of someone in your life, be aware that they feel powerless and resentful, and can be expected to pull passive aggressive stunts such as always being late and forgetting things to even the scales.

It's important to be on the lookout for control freakism in those around us, especially in the early days of relationships (romantic or platonic) when people are normally on their best behaviour; everybody likes to get their way, but control freaks get a charge out of making you do whatever they ask, including things that don't involve their own welfare but are purely to showcase their power... and that makes them bad relationship choices.

CHECKLIST: ARE YOU A CONTROL FREAK?

Check all that apply to you or that you agree with.

- It's difficult for you to trust people.

- You make lists for everything in your life.

- You can't stand it when you're in a car but not driving.

- As much as possible, you need to do everything yourself.

- You rarely think that you're wrong.

- You love to be the centre of attention.

- When it comes to social gatherings, you prefer to do the planning.

- You get bored when you have to listen to other people talk.

- Your vacations tend to be structured and active.

- You tend to think that you know what's best for other people.

- You don't like people touching your stuff.

- You are definitely a perfectionist – and your own worst critic.

- It's hard for you to get used to a new hair style or a new pair of jeans.

- You would not really enjoy a surprise party thrown for you.

- You can't stand to wait for people who are a few minutes late.

- You are a completely stubborn person.

- You tend to interrupt people a lot.

- You don't like taking orders.

- You don't take it lightly when people disagree with you.

- Other people's messes really bother you.

- When you're watching TV with other people, you always have to have the remote.
- You are easily irritated.
- You are insulted when people don't take your advice.

Control freaks will often:

- Try to control every aspect of your life.
- Dictate what you and your friends should do.
- Hate you doing anything without them.
- Seem threatened by any opinions that don't fall in line with what they think.
- Feel threatened by areas of your life that don't directly concern them and may criticize things they don't even know about.
- Always assume they know what's best for you regardless of your point of view and give advice whether you asked for it or not.
- Resent other people in your life who seem to exert influence over you in some way such as your boss, or good friends or even family members. They may constantly criticize or even try to keep you away from such people.
- Check up on you to see what you are up to. They may even go through your phone numbers or interrogate friends, colleagues as to your whereabouts.

We all have a basic need for a sense of control but the control freak has a need that is out of control. They may tell you their controlling possessive ways are signs of caring for you but that's part of the control.

CONCLUSION

Exerting control over our environment is a fundamental human need, but in a certain portion of the population, the 'release' mechanism simply doesn't exist. Control freaks try and control every aspect of the environment.

Control freaks not only try to dominate the environment by putting order on what they perceive as chaos, but they also try to control how other people think and behave.

Do you know anybody who always has to have the last word? Do you know anybody who asks you your opinion, and then when you give it, they tell you why you're wrong? Doesn't that just curdle your blood?

Think about the abuse this person inflicts on everybody else. Abuse seems to be the most evil outcome of controlling behaviour. But I'd say that's one of the basic fallacies of the control myth. It is awful and I would never wish that kind of abuse on anybody, but what's really more evil than the abuse is how much it harms the control freak – him or her.

Think about it: They can't get away from the critical, controlling thoughts that are always there in their own darn head! Imagine living a life that is fully controlled... it couldn't be much fun!

The 'successful' businessman or entrepreneur has control over their emotions... and their lives... and their business... and the results their employees produce. We believe that small changes in the business are okay, but anything that happens quickly or without planning is bad and should be avoided and controlled somehow.

Attention to detail and a determination to do things properly are admirable traits. But for some, these virtues curdle into obsessive behaviour that stifles all self-expression in the workplace. At one end of the spectrum, the control freak is a motivated and organised employee; at the other, an obsessional, temperamental bully who can't see the big picture and makes everyone else's life a fun-free zone. Control freaks, in other words, function to a high standard but few can bear to work with them.

11

Service Quality as Competitive Advantage: An Entrepreneurship Case from Indonesia

Nelly Nailatie Ma'arif*

The research findings indicated that in a developing country like Indonesia, with 220 million people, there are big potentialities of starting a business and becoming entrepreneur. In line with the global trend, where " bigger companies " tend to focus on their core business, "services" products and businesses are being handled by third party—whose core business is in that particular services. Since, labour is considerably cheap and many manufacturers have found that the combination of display and enthusiastic SPGs is a cost-effective tactical promotion tool. Consistency in nurturing a product and business and combine with endless effort to improve the quality of the offer are key to a successful entrepreneurship. Key to survival is offering the quality of service and maintaining it all the way, across the areas and cities and across the clients. Competitive advantage has to be built by offering a difference in the service.

BACKGROUND

Indonesia has a population estimated at close to 220 million, concentrated most heavily in Java which accounts for 59% of the total. The island of Java includes the three major cities of Jakarta, Surabaya and Bandung. Sumatra accounts for a further 21% of population with Medan as the main city. The remaining islands are widespread and include such major cities as Ujung Pandang and Banjarmasin. This huge market offers a very attractive potential for anybody who would like to set-up his own business and become an entrepreneur. This vast population also indicates a large consumption of consumer goods by the people of this country.

Consumer products will always be in high demand as long as human beings exist in this world. Consumer products are mostly sold through retail stores . Therefore, the understanding of retail trade is becoming very important.

At the other side, "SPG Services" means "human services". The role of each individual service provider is significant. One of the most important factors that influence the human services is the motivation of the person.

---

* Senior Researcher/Senior Lecturer, Widia Research Center, JWC, Universitas Bina Nusantara Jl. Jakarta, Indonesia.

Theoretical Foundation

In business circles now-a-days, every organization is competing toward others by always improving their departmental performance. Derived from Portalhr.com, one of the strategies that they used to improve their departmental performance is by synergizing the values of the employees.

Caterina C. Bulgarella, Ph.D, Guide Star Research Analyst (2005), said that satisfied employees are motivated employees; that is, they have the motivational resources to deliver adequate effort and care. Satisfied employees are empowered employees; in other words, they have the resources, training and responsibilities to understand and serve customer needs and demands. Satisfied employees have high energy and willingness to give good service: At a very minimum, they can deliver a more positive perception of the service/product provided. Satisfied employees can provide customers with interpersonal sensibility and social account (i.e., adequate explanations for undesirable outcomes).

It has been suggested that these components of inter-action have a significant impact on customer satisfaction. According to this view, because satisfied employees experience interaction, they can deliver it; that is, satisfied employees have enough emotional resources to show empathy, understanding, respect, and concern. Employees can strongly contribute to an organization's success by having a customer-centric approach in their work and in their work-related interactions (Gunawan, Vera, 2007).

Overview on Indonesia's Market

The retail trade in Indonesia is one on the verge of momentous change and, indeed, it could be said that the moment of truth is close at hand. Indonesian retailers have been protected from foreign competition for many years but there are signs that the strict rules restricting foreign entry will be relaxed or that means will be found to overcome these rules through franchising or other arrangements.

International department stores from Japan, including Sogo and Seibu, have already established a presence. Moreover, international wholesalers, notably Makro from the Netherlands and Davids from Australia, have recently entered the market.

The Retail Trade in Indonesia

For most manufacturers of Fast-Moving Consumer Goods (FMCG), the target consumers are in urban areas (approximately 70 million). Many manufacturers focus on the more cosmopolitan areas in the big cities where the growth of supermarkets has developed most strongly. AB consumers are moving into supermarkets and away from traditional shops and wet markets, especially for products that are heavily advertised and where choice is desirable. However, in Jakarta, the key choice factors for using a particular supermarket cited by consumers are "convenience" and "value for money".

To understand the nature of supermarket retailing in Indonesia, it is necessary also to understand certain features of society which impact on retailing. In general, relatively affluent families will employ a maid who has usually come into the city from the rural areas. This maid will be responsible for shopping, especially for the basic family needs and fresh produce. Typically, she will go to the traditional wet market every day, usually around 5.00 a.m., and purchase meat, vegetable and so on.

Furthermore, looking at individual brands in Jakarta, the situation can be even more dramatic with certain brands relying very heavily on supermarkets. This applies in particular to premium brands targeted at the AB consumer. In some cases, brand owners now care relatively little about what is happening outside the supermarkets. They know the trends and they know that their consumers visit supermarkets rather than the traditional trade.

Point-of-sale activity, though not currently measurable, appears to have grown dramatically in the past three years. It is rare to visit a supermarket without noting an abundance of Sales Promotion Girls (SPGs). Labour is not very expensive and *many manufacturers have found that the combination of display and enthusiastic SPGs is a cost-effective tactical tool* (Walker, 1996).

Research Objective

To get indication on how an entrepreneur start, survive and compete in a free market.

Research Method

Personal Interview

Name of the Company

P.T. Gelatik Supra

Product

Service of SPG (Sales Promotion Girl) and SPB (Sales Promotion Boy)

Respondent

1 (one) person – Mr. Hadi Suprapto the owner (100% share) and President Director of the company.

Place of Interview

Jakarta, Indonesia

Period of Interview

November 2007

Interview Proceeding

1. Questionnaires were prepared – by taking into account the theories discussed in *Entrepreneurship* by Peggy A. Lambing and Charles R. Kuehl.

2. An appointment was set-up with the respondent.

3. A personal interview was conducted, following the prepared questionnaire.

4. The question was asked one by one, from general info up to the last question.

5. The result of interview was analyzed and the findings were concluded into a paper.

P. T. GELATIK SUPRA – THE SERVICE PROVIDER

Introduction

Mid 1995 – after 12 years of service at P.T., Wicaksana, and holding various positions such as Product Manager, Sales Manager, Assistant to Managing Director, Human Resource Manager and the last position was as Corporate Manager, for some business politics reasons, Mr. Hadi Suprapto was 'advised' to leave the company. Having a separation allowance of around US $ 3,500 Hadi was trying to handle various works.

During this 'semi jobless' situation, he was asked by a friend who happened to work at Nestle Indonesia, to help doing some 'product sampling for a newly launched product – Maggi Porridge, which was targeted toward children between 3 to 12 years. Therefore, the sampling coverage was Kindergarten and Primary School. At a later stage, more and more products of Nestle Indonesia was handled by Hadi Suprapto and team, i.e., Maggi Bouillon, some chocolate products such as Kit Kat, etc.

September 1995 – Nestle Indonesia asked him to take charge of their 55 SPGs (Sales Promotion Girl). Nestle paid all the operational costs including office renting, buying computer, salary of personnel and all other operational related costs. Hadi was offered 20% fee out of total payroll for the SPGs.

In 2001, the HRD Director of Nestle Indonesia, after 26 years of service, was retired. He demanded to be given the assignment of running the SPG's operation. Nestle decided to offer the "company's ex Director "about 80% of its SPG's operation and 20% left with Gelatik Supra. This condition forced Gelatik Supra to "look for other clients". One by one, companies who have heard about "Gelatik reputation" in handling SPG operation, approached him and was welcome warmly.

Currently, P.T. Gelatik Supra has more than 15 companies as client, i.e., Indofood group, Gizindo Group, Pepsi Cola, Quaker Oath, Kraft Food, Tempo Group, Abbott, B. 29 group , and Master Food.

In 2006, a new company called 'Bina Tunas Bestari (BTB)' was set up. The nature of the service was exactly the same. The purpose of setting up this company was to accommodate competing companies which required their services. Clients of BTB include Frontier Indonesia, Johnson & Johnson, and Kimberley.

Legal Status

September 1995 – Nestle Indonesia asked him to take charge of their 55 SPGs (Sales Promotion Girl). This assignment forced Hadi to form a legal company which later on he named it PT. Supra Indonesia. (PT is Perusahaan Terbatas = A Limited Corporation)

Reason for Founder to become an Entrepreneur

Hadi Suprapto, after being 'advised' to leave PT wicaksana after 12 years of service, was approached by a friend to do some product sampling for a newly launched product, Maggi Porridge, targeted at children between 3 and 12 years of age.

By accident, he was offered assignments that "led him" to become an entrepreneur.

Reason for choosing Current Business

The initial assignment offered by Nestle Indonesia, which he nurtured carefully and dedicated his time and effort; was the main reason why he choose this "SPG Service" business.

Organization Structure

Pt. Gelatik Supra

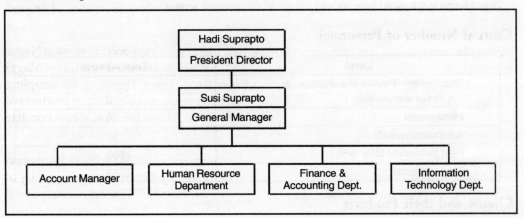

Area Coverage

Gelatik Supra divides the area of its operation into three types:

Type A: Own Office, own Representatives and SPGs.

Type B: Having Representative, but without own office. The staffs work at distributor's office.

Type C: Has no office, has no Representative, but has SPG operation.

Table 1: Area Coverage

Type of Operation	Location	Margin
A	Major big cities in Indonesia such as: • Jakarta • Medan • Bandung • Jogjakarta • Surabaya • Semarang	11 – 13 %
B	Secondary cities in Indonesia, i.e., • Manado • Makasar • Samarinda • Den Pasar • Padang • Pekanbaru • Palembang	7 – 10 %

Contd...

	15 Tertiary cities in Indonesia, i.e., 1. Purwokerto 2. Pontianak 3. Banjarmasin 4. Lampung 5. Batam 6. Mataram	
C		7 %

Note: Margin is calculated base on total payroll of the assigned service.

Current Number of Personnel

Level	Total number
Shareholders: Passive shareholders: 2 Active shareholder: 1	3
Management	6
Administrative staffs	50
Field personnel (SPG, SPB)	2500
Total personnel	2559

Clients and their Products

Currently, P.T. Gelatik Supra has more than 15 companies as client, i.e.:

1. Indofood group, with products like Indomilk, Indo Ice Crea, Fritolay, etc.

2. Gizindo Group with product i.e., Promina – Baby's food.

3. Pepsi Cola

4. Quaker Oat

5. Kraft Food with Kraft Cheese, Oreo Biscuit, Ritz Biscuit, etc.

6. Tempo Group, with products such as: Hemaviton Tonic Drink, Bodrex Flu Medicine, Marina Skin Care.

7. Abbott with products i.e., Pedia Sure Infant Milk.

8. B. 29 group with product such as B.29 cream soap.

9. Master Food – Malaysia with product such as Ali Coffee.

10. Softex and etc.

In 2006, a new company called Bina Tunas Bestari (BTB) was set up. The nature of the service was exactly the same. The purpose of setting up this company was to accommodate competing companies which required their services. Clients of BTB include:

1. Frontier Indonesia with its product Anlene Milk.

2. Johnson & Johnson with its product Clean & Clear.

3. Kimberley with its products such as Huggies, Kleenex and Kotex.

Difficulties in Starting the Business

- Finding the client to offer the service.
- Handling the office politics of the client's key employees.

Difficulties in Maintaining Business Performance

- To maintain the standard quality of offer all across clients in Indonesia.
- To control the field personnel.
- To deliver the service on time in line with client's expectation.
- To collect the information and data required by clients on time, in line with client's expectation, in term of time, schedule and type of data required.
- Keeping the service competitive – since most of the contracts with client are on annual basis.

Discussion and Conclusion

- The research findings indicated that in a developing country like Indonesia, with 220 million people, there is a large potential of starting a business and becoming entrepreneur.
- In line with the global trend, where bigger companies tend to focus on their core business, services products and business are being handled by third party – whose core business is in that particular services.
- The key to survival is offering the quality of service and maintaining it all the way, across the areas and cities and across the clients.
- Competitive advantage has to be built by offering a different in the service. For P.T. Gelatik Supra, currently they offer the:
  - ❖ On time, online information and data of the performance of the client's product across the market.
  - ❖ Standard quality of the performance of the field personnel across the markets and across clients.

Limitation and Future Research

- Interview and data were gathered based on only 1 (one) company. Therefore, in the future, a bigger number of entrepreneurs to be interviewed would be recommendable.

References

Brenda Jamieson, "Retailing – getting it right", *Nutrition & Food Science*, Number 4, 14–18 (July/August 1996).

Hisrich, Robert D., Peters, Michael P., Shepherd, Dean A., *Entrepreneurship*, 8th ed., McGraw-Hill, New York. (2005).

Hisrich, Robert D. and Peters, Michael P., *Entrepreneurship*, 5th ed., McGraw Hill, New York., USA (2005).

Lambing, Peggy A. and Kuehl, Charles R, *Entrepreneurship*, 3rd ed., Prentice Hall, New Jersey, USA (2003).

Ma'arif, Nelly N., *The Power of Marketing*, Penerbit Salemba, Jakarta, Indonesia, (2007).

Northouse, Peter G., *Leadership, Theory and Practice*, Sage Publications, London, UK (1997).

Walker, David, "Moment of truth for Indonesia's food retailers", *International Journal of Retail & Distribution Management*, Volume 24, Number 8, (1996).

Gunawan, Vera, *Relationship between Employee Attitudes, Customer Satisfaction and Departmental Performance*, A thesis to fulfill graduation requirements at School of Marketing, Binus International, Universitas Bina Nusantara, Jakarta, Indonesia (2007).

RESEARCH ON ENTREPRENEURSHIP

NOVEMBER 2007

I.   Data of Respondent

Name	
Position	
Gender	
Office	
Office Address	
Office Phone	
Direct Phone Number	
Mobile Number	
E-mail address	

II.   Research Questions

1.   Why are you interested in becoming an entrepreneur ?

2.   What is your product ?

3.   When did you start your business ?

4.   Why do you choose your current business ?

5.   What is your current revenue ?

6.   What is your net revenue ?

7.   What is the area of your operation?

8.   How many people do you have now?

9.   What is your organizational structure ?

10. What are the key success factors in becoming entrepreneur ?

11. What are the difficulties in starting business ?

12. What are your difficulties at present ?

12

A Study on Trends of Entrepreneurship Quotient in MBA Students

Leena Nandanwar*
Makarand V. Nandanwar**

Professional educational institutions and entrepreneurship go side by side. It has been observed that students of these professional educational institutions opt for starting their own ventures. Management institutes, nowadays are showing the same trend. This is a study about the trends of entrepreneurship quotient of MBA students and their inclination towards starting their own ventures. This study also tries to find out driving and restricting forces for student entrepreneurs to start their ventures.

ONSET

From the primitive age, history reveals that our ancestors were all entrepreneurs. Till the bronze era and the 'Barter System' it went through lots of improvement. Then, as businesses were began growing, people started employing other people in a business. This was the time of a paradigm shift from entrepreneurship to service class. With the passage of time people tended more towards softer options like service than having their own ventures.

But now, are we aiming to create elite obedient clerks or technicians in India? Is doing things differently is our motto or is doing different things also important?

Over the years in India, we were able to increase the number of professional institutes and the students opting for such courses are also increased manifold. These courses are intend to groom the students in various aspects of the business and make them self sufficient. The idea is also to inculcate entrepreneurship and boost innovative thinking so that they not only do things differently but also dare venture into different things.

But the figures clearly indicate the truth; from the concept of age-old family business, with education, students are more inclined towards the jobs. Take a simple case of agriculture – 67% of the students studying in these institutes not want to continue with their family owned farming.

* Faculty, Dr. D. Y. Patil Institute of Management Studies, CBD Belapur, Navi Mumbai.
** Ph.D Scholar, Dr. D. Y. Patil Institute of Management Studies, CBD Belapur, Navi Mumbai.

So, do you want to apply your ideas and efforts to be the master of your own destiny or you want others to flourish their businesses at your cost? This was the question we have asked to professional MBA students in this study.

First of all, it was very important to ascertain whether with passing time have we lost it i.e., urge to be an entrepreneur? Not in terms of abilities but in our hearts and minds? Is there any "Chromosomal Shift" in us over the years? Various studies have shown that there needs to be certain traits or characteristics which are prominent in today's entrepreneurs. These characteristics are the certainly the measures of one's capabilities or potential to become future entrepreneurs. These specific traits represent "Entrepreneurship Quotient" i.e., EQ in this study. The study also intends, on the basis of the results of interaction with the respondents, to suggest some measures to convert these abilities into actions.

Limitation of the Study

To do justice with available time, resources and objectives of the study, it has been only limited to MBA students in the Navi Mumbai area.

Wrong responses from some respondents can also be also one of the limitations.

Reliability test of the instrument used in this study was also calculated on a pilot survey of another 21 respondents and was found out to be 0.623.

Objective of the Study

The study has following objectives:

1.   To assess entrepreneurship potential in MBA students.

2.   To judge the willingness of students to be self-employed.

3.   To analyse the factors leading to low or high entrepreneur quotient among different strata of MBA students.

Plan of Action

It was consciously decided that MBA students of various colleges would be approached and served with standard questionnaire to approximately 100 students distributed randomly. An explorative study was conducted with a simple data analysis done on the basis of comparing mean and average scores of the each group. The instrument for the survey was a simple self–assessment questionnaire of eleven questions. It reflects the characteristics of an entrepreneur followed by questions about their willingness to start an entrepreneurship firm and type of venture they would start. Towards the end, the questionnaire focused its attention on personal details of the respondents. The higher total of entrepreneurial quotient shows that the student has entrepreneurship characteristics.

Data Analysis

The total of questionnaires served was 135. Only 110 responded back; around 20 questionnaires where not responded at all; only 5 questionnaires were incomplete and hence rejected.

Data analysis is done on simple comparison of average score of Entrepreneurial Quotient. The total data was stratified into following components: Age, Gender, Willingness to start entrepreneurship firm.

Observations

Following are the observations under different heads:

Entrepreneurial Quotient

1. The average entrepreneurial quotient of all MBA student is 86.23.

2. The average entrepreneurial quotient of male student is 43.27 and female student is 42.96.

3. There difference between the different parameters of Entrepreneurial quotients rang from 0.01 in leadership qualities to 0.38 in the confidence level of students.

Age

1. Average age of male student is 23.4 years.

2. Average age of female student is 22.2 years.

3. The average entrepreneurial quotient of students below 23 and less age is 42.23.

4. The average entrepreneurial quotient of male students below 23 and less age is 40.72.

5. The average entrepreneurial quotient of female students below 23 and less age is 40.73.

Gender

1. Male students has higher averages as compare to female student in entrepreneur characteristics like: goal-driven, risk-taking abilities, confidence level, decision-making and knowing their competitors.

2. Female students have higher averages as compare to male student in entrepreneur characteristics like: Leadership qualities, mentally prepared to sit for long working hours, communication skills, organised person and good team worker.

Willingness to work

1. Only 32.73% of total students are determined to start their own entrepreneurship firm.

2. Students prefer staring up services industry, mostly consultancy firms, followed by starting up manufacturing firms.

3. 14.55 % of the students are sure to take up the job and decided not to start any kind of entrepreneurship firms. Reasons given for the same vary from family business to uncertain professional future, especially in female respondents.

4. Around 52.73 % of students are not sure about starting an entrepreneurship firm. Reasons stated are: Procedural technicalities (male: 47.6% and female: 43.8%), inadequate finance (male: 28.6% and female: 25.0%), risk involved (male: 19.05% and female: 18.8%) and others (male: 4.6% and female: 12.5%).

CONCLUSION

1. EQ in MBA student was found to be very high in both genders.

2. There is no remarkable difference in entrepreneurial quotient because of empowerment of female students through education system.

3. The average age of passing out MBA is less in female students as compare to the male students.

4. Most of the students in spite of having high entrepreneurial quotient are low in confidence level.

5. EQ translating into ventures is 32.7%.

6. The main fears are finance and lack of procedural technicalities.

Recommendations

After studying the primary data, and drawing above listed conclusions, we recommend that as we assess the IQ of the student for admission in MBA course, similarly every college should identify the potential entrepreneur by assessing their entrepreneurial quotient. This entrepreneurial quotient will help us to identify future entrepreneurs. These students can be groomed during their programme, which can contribute significantly to our economy.

MBA *curriculum needs more practical orientation*, so that the budding entrepreneurs are more practical in their ventures. The main focus should be given to the practical training for preparing viable project proposals.

The *institute should act as a facilitator* between the students and financial agencies through frequent interaction with banks, financial institutions, etc.

An *"Advisory forum" and "Entrepreneur help desk" can be established* which can help students to take their decisions about their firm even after they pass out from the institutes. This Advisory forum and Entrepreneur help desk can also provide different primary data about different sectors. The above mentioned data can be collected as summer projects of first year students.

13

Learning Orientation Exporters: An Exploratory Study of Laboratory Equipments in Mumbai Region

Dr. Pradip Manjrekar*
Milind Deshpande**

This exploratory study revealed that exporters of lab equipments from Mumbai region exhibit a relatively high learning orientation. The culture of staying in touch with the market and constantly evaluating opportunities, assumptions about decision, and the quest to stay competitive are the hallmark of successful company. The Internet has been useful in keeping in touch and learning about the market. The quest to learn and develop export expertise is further enhanced through interaction with organizations that promote export development.

INTRODUCTION

Exporting presents fewer challenges for experienced exporters due to the fact that they have already acquired the knowledge needed to effectively deal with routine procedures and market conditions and to anticipate many of the problems they are likely to encounter. To new exporters, particularly from developing nations, lack of knowledge can hinder their efforts to get into international markets. They must learn new skills and develop their export marketing expertise. This paper reports a preliminary study on Indian firms' learning orientation, their perceptions toward the usefulness of the Internet and export assistance programme as sources of knowledge building.

LITERATURE REVIEW

Market knowledge is the foundation for any strategic action. The resource-based theory of competition suggests human knowledge and expertise to be a primary source for competitive advantage (Barney, 1991). Wang & Olsen (2002), found that knowledge of the foreign market and knowledge of exporting procedures have positive effects on export profitability, lending support to the resource-based theory of competitive advantage.

---

* Professor & Head, Research & Extension Centre, Dr. D. Y. Patil Institute of Management Studies, Navi Mumbai.

** Director, Agile Lifescience Technologies India Pvt. Ltd., Thane.
   Ph.D. Scholar, Dr. D. Y. Patil Institute of Management Studies, Navi Mumbai.

The resource-based view of firm recognized the transferability of a firm's resource and capabilities as a critical determinant of their capacity to confer sustainable competitive advantage. Kogut and Zander (1992), viewed knowledge as the basis for creating competencies. For a firm's marketing effort to be successful, marketing strategy needs to be based on these competencies. Proficiency of marketing activities and handling of complex patterns of coordination between people and other resources is expected to translate to export performance of the exporter. Knight and Liesch (2002), emphasized that information and knowledge are the key resources for facilitating increasing internationalization. According to Dodgson (1993), organization learning is the process through which managers acquire new knowledge, insights, associations and routines that lead to incremental adjustments and innovations in products, processes and actions. In addition to export assistance programmes initiated by many government, the advent of internet has added another dimension to the learning process which should made learning about foreign markets much easier (Nguyen & Barrett, 2006).

Objective

The purpose of this study was to find out:

1.   The learning orientation of Indian exporters.

2.   Usefulness of internet as a learning mechanism.

3.   Usefulness of export assistance programme in enhancing foreign market learning.

Method

This is an exploratory study. The setting of the study is in Mumbai, India and the eight firms are exporting lab equipment products involved in exporting. The personal interview is guided by a survey instrument. The information is provided by top management of the company. The respondents are exporting lab equipment products. Although, the export covers quite a wide region, the number of countries exported to is confined to between 2 to 5 only. The firm size as measured by the number of employee shows that 6 firms employ less than 50 persons and falls into the category of small firms, while 2 firms represent the medium-sized firms as they employ between 50 - 200 persons. There is no large-sized firm. The experience of these firms in export market is rather moderate as majority of them have exporting between 6 to 10 years. The background information about these companies is presented in Table 1.

Table 1: Characteristics of Responding Companies (n=8)

		Frequency	Per cent
Types of Lab Products	Hot Air Ovens	2	25.0
	Lab Glassware	1	12.5
	Fume Hoods	1	12.5
	Refrigerators	1	12.5
	Incubators	2	25.0
	Plastic ware	1	12.5
Type of Region for Export	South East Asia	1	12.5
	Middle East	3	37.5
	Africa	2	25.0
	North America	1	12.5
	EC	1	12.5

Contd...

Position	Managing Director/Proprietor	4	50.0
	International Sales Manager	1	12.5
	General Manager	1	12.5
	Export Manager	2	25.0
Firm Size	Small firm «=50 persons)	6	75.0
(Number of employee)	Medium firm (51-200 persons)	2	25.0
International Experience	1-5	2	25.0
(Number of years)	6-10	5	62.5
	11-15	1	12.5
(Number of countries)	0-1	0	0.0
	2-3	2	25.0
	4-5	5	62.5
	More than 5 countries	1	12.5

Learning Orientation

In developing measures to indicate the knowledge management, we synthesized perspectives from the literature with those obtained in our fieldwork. Learning orientation was measured utilizing the scale developed by Sinkula *et al*, (1997) for 7 items. The frequency of responses and the pattern of mean values presented in (Table 2) indicated that the learning orientation of Indian firms is relatively high. The continuous assessment of the marketplace as indicated by the responses to statement number 1 shows that the responding firms are keeping taps on the development and changes are taking place. The learning orientation is relatively high.

Table 2 : Frequency of Distribution

	Learning Orientation	Mean	Scale				
			1	2	3	4	5
1.	Personnel in our firm realize that the every way they perceive the marketplace must be continually questioned.	4.35	-	-	2	4	2
2.	There is total agreement on our organizational vision across all levels, functions, and divisions.	3.95	-	-	1	5	2
3.	We are not afraid to reflect critically on the shared assumptions we have made about be markets.	3.80	1	2	2	1	2
4.	We always collectively question our own biases about the way we interpret market information.	3.60	-	-	6	1	1
5.	Employees view themselves as partners in charting the direction of our firm.	3.50	-	-	6	1	1
6.	Manager basically agrees that our firm's ability to learn is the key to our competitive advantage.	3.40	-	3	2	2	1
7.	There is a commonality of purpose in our firm.	3.15	-	2	3	3	-

A five-point scale was used: 1 = strongly disagree, and 5= strongly agree.

Perceived Usefulness of the Internet

Perceived usefulness of the Internet was a construct measured adapted Nguyen & Barrett (2006), or 6 items reflecting the level of the firm believes in usefulness of the Internet for obtaining information on foreign markets. All of the other items were measured by a five-point rating scale, anchored by (1 = strongly disagree, and 5 = strongly agree). The frequency and ranking of mean values of responses to the six items are presented in Table 3. The overall pattern suggests that the Internet is very useful in staying touch with all parties involved in the transaction of international business dealings. Such open communication enabled speedy acquisition of information and decision-making process.

Table 3: Usefulness of the Internet (n = 20)

	Usefulness of the Internet	MEAN	1	2	3	4	5
1.	By using the Internet, our firm would contact supplies, customers and distributor in international market more easily.	4.60	-	-	1	1	6
2.	By using the Internet, our firm would find it more effective in making export decision.	4.55	-	-	2	5	1
3.	By using the Internet, our firm would obtain information about international markets more quickly.	4.45	-	-	-	7	1
4.	Overall, our firm would consider that the Internet is useful for conducting export activities.	4.40	-	-	-	5	3
5.	By using the Internet, our firm would obtain information about international markets more easily.	4.35	-	-	1	4	3
6.	By using the Internet, our firm would obtain information about international markets more cheaply.	4.30	-	-	1	5	2

A five-point scale was used: 1= Strongly disagree, 5= Strongly agree.

Learning from Export Assistance Programmes

The extent of usage is used as a proxy measure of usefulness of export assistance programmes offered by the Thai government. The usage of export assistance was measured by a five-point rating scale anchored by (1 = never used, and 5 = always used). The frequency of responses and the ranking of mean values are presented in Table 4. The pattern of mean values suggests that only Information Service Centre is frequently used by the responding firms. Other types of services are found to be moderately used by the responding firms. Table 5 shows the usefulness of assistance provided by non-government bodies. The pattern of mean values indicates that the usage of services hovers between moderate and frequent levels.

Table 4: Usage of Export Assistance in Govt. Support (n=20)

	Usage of Export Assistance (Government)	Mean	1	2	3	4	5
1.	Information Service Center	3.85	1	-	4	2	1
2.	Export Information System	3.55	-	2	4	2	-
3.	Distribution Network	3.50	-	-	2	4	2
4.	Seminar and Training Centre	3.45	-	-	1	5	2
5.	Product Development Centre	3.45	-	5	3	-	-
6.	Product Design Centre	3.35	1	6	1	-	-
7.	Trade Fair	3.25	-	-	-	3	5
8.	India Trade Office	2.95	1	1	1	3	2
9.	Exporter to New Market 2002-2007	2.95	1	1	3	2	1
10.	Indian Exhibition	2.75	4	2	1	1	-

A five-point scale was used: 1= Never used and 5= Always used.

Table 5: Usage of Export Assistance in Non-Govt. Support (n=20)

	Usage of Export Assistance (Non-Government)	Mean	Scale				
			1	2	3	4	5
1.	Commercial Bank	3.90	-	-	1	2	5
2.	Logistic & Transportation Company	3.55	-	1	2	5	-
3.	Distributors/Trading Company	3.55	-	-	2	3	3
4.	Member of Commerce Association	3.45	2	-	2	2	2
5.	Insurance Company	2.55	-	1	1	1	5

A five-point scale was used: 1= Never used and 5= Always used.

DISCUSSION

Experiential knowledge is vital in export ventures. The development of knowledge requires firm to allocate resources to generate both tangible and intangible assets. Such assets will contribute to firm's competitive advantage and is necessary for firms eager to expand their business abroad. The findings of this exploratory study suggest that Indian lab equipment exporters are adopting a relatively high learning orientation culture. This augurs well if such posture will generate exchange and deliberation of ideas in positioning the company's operation in servicing the needs of foreign buyers. The advent of technology which has introduced Internet as the communication and information exchange tools appears to have been embraced by the Indian lab equipment exporters. Staying in touch with the market through regular visits and face-to-face interaction are keys to successful exporter-importer relationships. However, Internet has benefited them in reducing the cost of interaction and information search and ensuring speedy decisions. Export assistance programmes can be a useful source of knowledge development. The findings' show that exporters from developing nations are using these sources to enhance their entry into foreign markets.

References

Barney, J. (1991), "Firm resources and sustained competitive advantage", *Journal of Management*, 17(1),99-120.

Dodgson, M. (1993), "Organizational learning: A review of some literature". *Organization Studies*, 4(3), 375-94.

Knight, G. A. & Liesch, P. W. (2002), "Information internalization in internationalizing the firm", *Journal of Business Research*. 55(2002),981-995.

Kogut, B. & Zander, U. (1992), "Knowledge of the firm, combinative capabilities and the replication of technology". *Organizational Science*. 3, 383-397.

Nguyen, T. D., & Barrett, N. J. (2006), "The adoption of the internet by export firms in transitional markets". *Asia Pacific Journal of Marketing and Logistics*, 18(1), 29-42.

Sinkula, M. J., Baker E. W. & Noordewier, T. (1997), "A framework for market-based organizational learning: Linking values, knowledge and behavior", *Journal of the Academy of Marketing Science*, 25(4), 305-318.

Wang, G., & Olsen, J. E. (2002), "Knowledge, performance, and exporter satisfaction: An exploratory study", *Global Marketing*, 15(3/4), 39-63.

14

Mapping of Entrepreneurial Profile:
The Case of North East Mumbai Cyber Cafes

Mangesh Patil*
Dr. Pradip Manjrekar**

Globalisation hitherto has been realized to be a double-edged sword. It has proved a boon to some industries, but curse to the others. Industries, which developed a competitive edge and went on sharpening the same, enjoyed the richest harvest and vice-versa. This paper provides bird's eye view of the internet services catered through cyber cafes and shows how they turned their radar in the right direction and enjoyed the fruits of liberalisation and globalization. It is based on primary information collected directly with the help of a structured questionnaire, by researchers, from a sample of 100 cyber cafes selected randomly in the North East Mumbai. It finds that cyber cafes provide an easy and economic access to information for the users and an easy avenue of self-employment for the operator-cum-promoters of the cyber café. Though it is a new line of business activity, it is quite simple to start with average level of skills and investment.

INTRODUCTION

Information has become one of the critical inputs for conducting business transactions in the global economy. As a measure of providing access to information, the Internet has revolutionized the way of doing business. Today, businesses are categorized as 'winners' or 'losers' on the basis of presence on the Internet. The Internet provides a new and often extremely efficient means of communicating with producers, distributors and consumers. In a way, that overcomes geographic limitations as well as greatly increases width and depth of market reach of firms.

By having an easy access to the pool of existing knowledge, current information and analytical skills for future forecasting through the Internet, one can, just by sitting on a Personal Computer (PC) in any corner of the globe, explore, collect, analyze and interpret the required information. Actually, work goes on through cyber cafes available at any corner of the towns and cities.

*   Lecturer, Dr. D. Y. Patil Institute of Management Studies, Navi Mumbai.
**   Professor, Dr. D. Y. Patil Institute of Management Studies, Navi Mumbai.

These cafés give people the freedom to work on their own terms: When they want, how they want and from wherever they happen to be. Enabling them to get more done in less time and facilitating a more collaborative environment. The cyber cafe meet both the competitive demands of companies and the diverse needs of the people.

Business devices and enhancements that integrate voice, messaging email and access to other Internet services.

Application mobility that brings support for industry-leading business applications to IT devices to increase employee's interactions with colleagues, partners and customers, while providing them access to key company information.

Consequently, there has been considerable increase in the number of Internet users. Even today, only few Indians can afford PCs. So, millions go online in 'Internet Cafes' and enjoy their low-cost anonymity. About 60% of India's Internet users access the web through a cyber café accounting for four million subscribers and 18 million users. Cyber café business contributes in making the working environment more demanding on individuals as well as companies along new dimensions, such as time and speed, customer location, and his/her ever changing needs.

BACKGROUND

The enthusiasm for radically new, yet unproven and only vaguely understood, Internet business methods has led to 'irrational exuberance (excitement)'. It has been observed in the recent past that venture capital poured into dotcoms and millions of new websites were introduced. With a wealth of cash on hand, firms focused on technological sophistication, building brands, and gaining market share (which was often measured in terms of "eyeballs" viewing the site), with little emphasis on revenue generation or profitability. Basic laws of economics appeared to have been suspended (Reichert, 2001) by those who "thought they had chopped off the invisible hand" (Benko, 2000). Hence, the irrational enthusiasm for the Internet ended abruptly in early 2000 with what has been called the 'Tech Wreck'. Investors suddenly realized that dotcoms were overcapitalized and that some might never actually show profits. Stocks plummeted overnight, leading to the demise of many dotcoms. Venture capital dried up, and the pendulum appeared to have swung to the opposite extreme of an irrational aversion to anything "dot.com". Empirical studies have also indicated that the majority of websites are currently used as publishing media for public relations and not for commerce (Dutta and Segev, 1999; Griffith and Krampf, 1998).

There is, therefore, a need for shifting emphasis in operational approach. In this regard, (Oliver, 1990) explained that dotcoms should focus on building market share rather than profits and (Allee, 2000) argued that traditional return-on-investment criteria are not adequate for evaluating dotcoms. According to Mouat (2000), Internet network operators are challenged by declining margins in their traditional businesses. Declining revenue per user represents a phenomenon that will force network operators to implement new services continuously to remain competitive and turn around the trend of the decreasing marginal revenue. Value added services will become an important new source of revenue and will accelerate the rapid growth of mobile commerce. Forecasts estimate that by 2010, mobile services will be generating about half of operator's revenue per user. The operator's role as portal providers and content aggregators – often through alliances with content and service providers – will allow them to offer customers a new, more personalized and comprehensive range of information and services, while enabling them to differentiate themselves from the competition.

Employment Potential

Information Technology (IT) has opened large avenues of employment for educated youth in the country. It is estimated that one segment of IT industry i.e., computers both-hardware and software which employs computer engineers and system analysts are having over a million jobs at present. Besides this, the IT sector provided 2.2 million jobs to computer professionals and other related personnel engaged in IT sector. NASSCOM-McKINSEY report (1999) has estimated that by next year (2008), IT enabled services will provide 11 million jobs and generate a revenue of US $ 3.5 billion expanding employment opportunities. But a disturbing aspect is that the present IT education is very costly and IT jobs are the preserve of the better-off in education. Therefore, if the government desires to develop entrepreneurship in this field it should make provisions in the form of subsidies or charge differential fees.

Research Methodology

This study is based on primary information. In this regard, this study has taken a sample of 100 cyber cafes selected randomly from the ten nodes (Assembly Constituencies) of North East Mumbai. For making the study more representative, not more than 10 cyber cafes from each node were taken. The cyber cafes from the selected nodes have been chosen randomly. Following is the sample size :

Sample Size

Node	Sample Size
Mulund	10
Bhandup	10
Vikhroli	10
Ghatkopar	10
Kanjur Marg	10
Vidya Vihar	10
Kurla	10
Tilak Nagar	10
Chembur	10
Mankhurd	10
Total	**100**

Findings

For the sake of simplicity, the findings of the study have been summarized under the following sub-heads: Profile of entrepreneurs, factors influencing decision-making, socio-economic aspects, problems and prospects, sustenance, suggestions and an integrated approach for developing cyber cafes categories.

Profile of Entrepreneurs

We tried to map the enterprise and the profile of our entrepreneurs who were the subjects of this research. The following are the characteristics:

- Cyber café business is of new origin. Two-third of the cafes have come up during 1999-2002.

- As of today, it is basically an urban-oriented business.

- About 80 per cent of the cafes are proprietary concerns.

- More than 50 per cent are located in rented premises.

- Migration of promoters from other districts/states as well as from rural to urban areas for establishing cyber cafes is quite limited. Most of them belong to same town/city where their cafes are located.

- Cyber cafes are dominated by first generation young entrepreneurs. About 90% are below the age 35 years.

- It is a new avenue of self-employment for the educated unemployed youths and thus, supports the general perception that education, entrepreneurship and economic development go hand in hand.

- Caste or social category are not a barrier for establishing cyber cafes, but cyber café owners form OBC and SC categories are quite few.

- The ownership of cyber café business is dominated by the category of general castes. About 90% of promoters belong to this category.

- It is dominated by Hindus. About 86% of the promoters are Hindus. It may be due to overwhelming majority of Hindus in the states under study.

- The entry in cyber café business is also not restricted to any particular caste, creed or family occupation. Promoters from all walks of life are coming in.

- Promoters coming from service class families are dominating the scene. Fathers of more than 50% promoters belong to the service class.

- No special skill are required for establishing cyber café. Any educated person with average socio-economic and educational background can establish and operate a cyber café.

- It is a simple and easy avenue for self employment. About 90% promoters had no exposure to any training or experience before starting their cafes.

- However, promoters who attended any training before starting their café found the training inputs highly useful for operating the café.

Factors influencing Decision-making

Entrepreneurship causes conversion of ideas into creating new venture. This requires decision-making at various steps. These decisions are of many types, in many phases and have different elements and degrees of risks. Notwithstanding, the actual entrepreneurial decisions have resulted in millions of new business throughout the world. The entrepreneurial decisions indicate that around 1.5 million new ventures have been formed each year during the recent years. The factors that influenced the sample entrepreneurs in their decision-making are given below.

There are multiple factors pulling and pushing for self employment and owning as well as operating a cyber café:

- Promoters have chosen cyber café business mainly because it requires small investment; risks are limited and are easy to set-up.

- With increasing computerization of business world where most of the persons do not own PCs, the promoters foresee a rising demand for cyber café services.

- Own urge is the most important factor for setting up a cyber café, followed by the advice from family members and friends.

- Performance of the existing cafes, easy availability of bank credit and future demand also have played important role for attracting new entrants.

- Promotional role of the government officials as well as training and financial institutions has remained limited.

- Most of the promoters are satisfied in their self employment. About 60 per cent parents want to suggest their children to go for self employment. Of them, 65 per cent want their children to set-up cyber cafes.

- The major reason for suggesting their children go for self employment is the shrinking job market, followed by freedom to take decision in one's own business and positive relation between input of hard work and earnings.

- About 40% of the owners/promoters do not support the idea of self employment for their children due to high risks, uncertainty associated with self-employment and falling rate of income.

Socio-Economic Aspects

Entrepreneurship has been associated with many challenges on the one hand and on the other hand, it provides plenty of opportunities. Those who get cowed down with the problems either do not move beyond the idea, if moved beyond the idea, fail to create a new venture and if a venture is created, the same does not survive and grow, instead it gets folded up. Those who are bold and creative look opportunities in the problems and are always in the look out for the new prospects of the business. The entrepreneurs that were surveyed showed various socio-economic characteristics given below:

- Cyber café is a new line of business for 95% of the promoters.

- It is an expanding business but at a decelerating rate.

- It is highly urban-oriented.

- Migration of rural youths for setting cyber cafes is quite limited.

- Most of the cyber café business promoters belong to low or middle income groups.

- The most typical size of cyber cafes is 8 to 10 PCs.

- The initial investment is less than rupees two lakhs in 50 per cent of the cafes, 2 to 4 lakhs rupees in another 30 per cent and more than 6 lakh rupees in only 8 per cent of the cafes.

- Investing ones own capital plays an important role for establishing cyber café business.

- The most important sources of financial assistance are the members of family and their relatives. However, 47 per cent promoters take loans from bank/FI too.

- About one-fourth cafes are operated by one person only and others by two or more persons. The average employment generation per café is three persons.

- Of the total employed persons, about 47% are promoters and 53% are workers.

- Among the workers about 51% are skilled and the rest unskilled.

- The technically skilled manpower is quite limited as promoters themselves are efficient enough to operate.

Problems and Prospects

- Establishing and operating cyber cafes is not problem-free. About 80% promoters have stated one or the other problem.

- The most important problem is getting telephone connection.

- For most of the promoters, future of cyber café is bright.

- Pessimists with dark future prospects are very few.

- Decreasing revenue/income due to cut throat competition and home-connections are anticipated as the major threats.

- Success of cyber cafes depends on many factors. Almost all promoters agree that hard work has no substitute.

- Three-fourth of them feel that perceiving right opportunities and taking risks are necessary for success.

- The banks are not very helpful to cyber café entrepreneurs.

Need for an Integrated Approach

The entrepreneurial qualities are not inherited by a person rather acquired in the process of socialization in a particular socio-economic culture. The whole process of entrepreneurship development in cyber business can be seen as a process having three distinct but integrated components, namely stimulatory, support and sustaining activities.

However, in practice, there is no watertight compartmentalization of different activities. Each of the activities classified under different component are highly interactive, supplementary and crucial through which entrepreneurial activities flourish and grow. So, most of the activities can be and should be undertaken simultaneously.

Limitations of Data

- This study is based on primary information collected from ten nodes of north eastern Mumbai. Selection of nodes was purposive. Thus the nodes are only partially representative of North East Mumbai.

- Sample data, though collected directly by the researchers, presents only broad/ approximate figures and not the information taken from written statements – balance sheet and profit and loss accounts – of the units. None of the sample units shared adequately their written statements. Thus, the study presents broad trends only.

References

Cadeaux, J. (1997), "Counter-revolutionary forces in the information revolution. Entrepreneurial action, information intensity and market transformation", *European Journal of Marketing*, 31(11/12):768-785.

Dahan, E. and Srinivasan, V. (2000), "The predictive power of Internet based product concept testing using visual depiction and animation", *Journal of Product Innovation Management*, 17(2):99-109.

Daly, J. (2000), "Sage active", *Business* 2.0, August 22: 134.

Datt, Ruddar., (1994), "Economic Policy- A Review", *Indian Journal of Labour Economics*.

DeCovny, S. (1998), "Electronic commerce comes of age", *Journal of Business Strategy*, 19(6): 38-44.

Evans, P. (2000), "Strategy: The end of the endgame?", *Journal of Business Strategy*, 21(6): 12-21.

Galvin, CB., (1997), "Telecom Trends: Opening up a World of Possibilities", *Telematics India*, July 1997.

Gurjar, B.R and Mohan, Manju., (1998), "Entrepreneurial Opportunities in Infotech Industry", *Entrepreneurship and Small Business*, Rawat Publications, New Delhi.

Khurana, M.M., (2002), "Technological Development in the Field of Customer Electronics", *Entrepreneurship and Small Business*, Rawat Publications, New Delhi.

Kolodko, Grzegorz W., (2003), "Globalisation and Transformation: Illusions and Reality", *Journal of Emerging Market Finance*, Vol 2, No.2.

Kumar, Krishna., (2003), "Electronic Industry in China: A Perspective", *Electronic Information and Planning*.

Louis, T. (2000), "What I learned at boo. com." *Business* 2.0, August 8:238.

Means, G. and Faulkner, M. (2000), "Strategic innovation in the new economy", *Journal of Business Strategy*, 21 (3):25-29.

Murthy, L. Srinivasan, (2002), "Electronic Industry, The Emerging Trends", *Indian Entrepreneurship - Theory and Practice*, Abhishek Publications, Chandigarh.

Narduzzi, E. (2001), "Is m-business the same game as the e-business?" Paper presented at M-conference: Seizing the Mobile Advantage, Rotterdam: January 19-20, 2001.

NASSCOM (2003), "Indian IT Software and Service Directory."

Nayar, Deepak, (1996), "Globalisation: The Past and Present", *The Economic Journal*, Vol.49, No.3.

Nolan, C. (2000), "Crash-test dummies", *Business* 2.0, July 11:179.

O'Keefe, R, 0' Connor, G., and Kung, H.-J. (1998), "Early adopters of the web as a retail medium: small company winners and losers", *European Journal of Marketing*, 32(7/8):629-641.

Quelch, J. and Klein, L. (1996), "The Internet and international marketing", *Sloan Management Review*, 37(3):60 - 75.

Rangarajan, C., (1993), "New Economic Policy and the Role of the State", *RBI Bulletin*.

Rastogi, Rajiv., (200 I), "Indian Electronics and IT Industry Production Profile" 2000.

Rathore, B.S., (2002), *Entrepreneurship and Small Business Development*, Rawat Publications, New Delhi.

Roberts, E. (1991), *Entrepreneurs in High Technology*, Oxford: Oxford University Press.

Sanghvi, Rashwin., (1991), "Liberalisation of the Indian Economy", *Dalal Street Journal*.

Sawhney, M and Sum ant, M. (2000), "Go global", *Business* 2.0, May: 178.

Seybold, P. (2000), "Niches bring riches", *Business* 2.0, June 13:135.

Sukuja, RA., (1998), "Entrepreneurial Opportunities in Repair and Maintenance of Electronic Products", *Entrepreneurship and Small Business*, Rawat Publications, New Delhi.

Tenth Five Year Plan, (2002-07), "Planning Commission, Government of India".

15

Challenges in Collective Entrepreneurship: A Case Study on a Co-operative Initiative by Single Mothers in Terengganu, Malaysia

Mohar Yusof*

This paper tries to shed some light on the entrepreneurial and economic activities of a co-operative in Terengganu, Malaysia, and discusses the barriers and challenges faced by the co-operative leadership and Single Mothers in implementing these activities. It was observed that the type of entrepreneurship practiced by the co-operative and its leadership falls under the ambit of social entrepreneurship. The collective efforts undertaken by Single Mothers in this case study have been observed as development towards the achievement of economic and social value creation.

INTRODUCTION

With the objective of providing the Single Mothers community a reasonable level of income and an alternative source of income to some, the Single Mothers Co-operative of Terengganu, Malaysia or KUWAT (its Malay abbreviation) was formed in 2006 and registered under the Cooperative Act, 1993, under the sponsorship of the Single Mothers Society of Terengganu. With an initial membership of one hundred single mothers, the Co-operative has operated a few collective entrepreneurial and business activities and is planning several other activities to be implemented in the next few years. The aim of this paper is to shed some light on the entrepreneurial and economic activities that had been undertaken and to discuss the barriers and challenges faced by the co-operative leadership and single mothers in implementing these activities.

DEMOGRAPHY OF TERENGGANU, MALAYSIA

Terengganu is one of the thirteen states in Malaysia. It is situated in the East Coast of West Malaysia. With the total state area of 12,955 km, Terengganu has a population of 1,055,943 (2005 census), of which Malaysia make up 94.8% of the population and Chinese, 2.6%, while Indians 0.2% and other ethnic groups comprise the remainder, 2.4%. In the year 2000,

---

* Faculty, UNITAR Study Centre, Tun Abdul Razak University, Malaysia Faculty of Business Administration, Malaysia.

the state's population was only 48.7% urban; the majority lived in rural areas. By the 2005 census, the proportions had changed significantly, with 51% of the population living in urban areas and 49% in the rural areas (Leete, 2007). Terengganu is divided into seven administrative districts (called *Daerah* in Malay).

Developing Social Entrepreneurship

Even though KUWAT is profit-oriented, it is also a social organization with focus and concern not only towards its co-operative members, but also towards the plight and well-being of approximately 18,000 Single Mothers in Terengganu. Thus, the consideration for profit and cost is not just economic in nature, but social as well.

The type of entrepreneurship practiced by the co-operative and its leadership can be said to fall under the ambit of social entrepreneurship. Dees (2001), described social entrepreneurs "as change agents in the social sector by:

- Adopting a mission to create and sustain social value,

- Relentlessly pursuing opportunities to serve their mission,

- Continuously innovating, adapting and learning,

- Acting boldly without being limited by resources currently in hand,

- Exhibiting a heightened sense of accountability to the constituencies served and for the outcomes created."

Thus, from Dees's perspective above, it can be argued that the success of the co-operative in creating and sustaining economic and social values (Mair and Marti, 2006) is partly dependent on the ability and competency of the co-operative management and leadership to act and to behave entrepreneurially and effectively.

Methodology

Data in the case study was collected through interviews and observations during a financial literacy programme and study trips to three sites where three different types of business activities had taken place. The two days financial literacy programme was organized by fourteen students of the Students In Free Enterprise (SIFE), Tun Abdul Razak University (UNITAR), Malaysia on March 7 and 8, 2007 (http://fba.unitar.edu.my/news/issue2_07/index.htm). SIFE is a global non-profit organization active in establishing student teams in university campuses, which are led by faculty advisors and challenged to develop community outreach projects, educate the community on market economics, success skills, entrepreneurship, financial literacy and business ethics and assist in the creation of economic opportunity (http://www.sife.org/).

Sixteen Single Mothers, mainly committee members of the co-operative and district leaders of the Single Mothers' society, participated in the training where they were taught on basic economics, finance and book-keeping. Some elements of entrepreneurship were also incorporated. Interestingly, the training was delivered by the SIFE team from UNITAR. A representative from Amanah Ikhtiar Malaysia, a private trust agency established in 1987 to provide financial assistance to poor households in rural areas (http://www.aim.gov.my), was also invited to talk on micro-financing.

The sites visited on March 6, 2007 include a rock melon farm, a chicken poultry farm and a cow herding farm. These agriculture farms were small and managed collectively by groups of Single Mothers. Semi-structured interviews were employed on the group leaders of these agricultural activities. Since the objective of the study was to identify barriers and challenges faced by these women entrepreneurs in developing their economic activities, semi-structured interviews were deemed appropriate since they allowed the interviewees to express their opinions and ideas in their own words and made it possible to understand what life is like from the perspective of these women entrepreneurs (Johl *et al*, 2006).

Challenges Identified

From the case studies, visits, interviews and discussions with Single Mothers who operated the agriculture farms, participants of the financial literacy programme and the Chairwoman of the society and co-operative, Madam Maimunah Omar, three broad problems faced by Single Mothers in Terengganu were identified namely lack of education, insufficient and inadequate livelihood sustenance, and, lack of awareness and understanding of family law.

There were several direct challenges faced by the co-operative leadership and Single Mothers who were running the small businesses under the co-operative. These include:

a.   Lack of management and business skills;

b.   Lack of human resources and manpower expertise;

c.   Individualistic behaviour of many single mothers which inhibit the collective efforts;

d.   Lack of interpersonal skills and social networking capabilities;

e.   Too shy to ask for help and to improve their understanding on business management;

f.   Many Single Mothers were not interested to participate in business creation and to be self-independent. Instead, they prefer to ask for aid than work; and

g.   Moral hazard and manipulation by vendors and suppliers of government assistance. These contractors had cheated and have taken advantage of the conservative attitude of single mothers by supplying poor quality equipments and tools for projects that were assisted financially by the government.

Discussion

The Single Mothers community in Terengganu is one of the poorest in Malaysia. These Single Mothers struggle from day-to-day to make a living for the family. Even though most of them are physically capable, healthy and intelligent, they lack interpersonal skills, social networking capabilities, and the connection with the right government agencies to make their voices heard. Unfortunately, while there is much government assistance for Single Mothers and rural development, middlemen and vendors tend to manipulate and treat them unfairly.

There are approximately 18,000 Single Mothers in the Terengganu but the Single Mothers Society, at the state level, does not have a computerized database system to manage membership and generate accurate profiling of its members. This significantly affects and influences decision-making at the state level. In addition to the society is not able to supply adequate and sufficient data to governmental agencies and bodies responsible for Single Mothers' welfare.

Due to lack of information, dissemination of assistance, training schemes and financial schemes is not evenly distributed and may not reach the hardcore poor.

From the training satisfaction survey of the financial literacy programme, in general, the participants found the training to be useful and had helped to improve their basic understanding of economics, finance, book-keeping and entrepreneurship. The Sife Unitar team also tried to boost the participants' self-confidence and teamwork by motivating them to persevere with their co-operative and entrepreneurial activities.

More training, self development and entrepreneurial development programmes are needed to prepare and motivate these Single Mothers to face the challenges in developing their newly established co-operative and in starting new ventures. They need to be trained to be better organized and to be capable of managing their value chain activities and processes efficiently and effectively. The critical question that can be asked is "who is going to do this?"

Further, they need to learn to beneficially utilize the financial assistance given or to be given to them by the state government, federal government, domestic private agencies or international agencies. Most importantly, the use of middlemen and contractors needs to be abolished and the assistance should be given directly to the society, co-operative or a trustworthy Non-Government Organization (NGO) to be distributed fairly and equitably to Single Mothers. Recently, Shetty (2007a; 2007b), proposed a model that can be considered for the development of women entrepreneurs in rural areas and the necessary linkages between the government, the women entrepreneurs and the required support systems.

CONCLUSION

In this paper, the co-operative's collective entrepreneurial and business activities are considered as a form of social entrepreneurship. Social entrepreneurship takes on multiple forms, depending on socio-economic and cultural circumstances (Mair and Marti, 2006). In this case study, the collective efforts undertaken by Single Mothers in Terengganu, Malaysia have been observed as development towards the achievement of economic and social value creation.

The co-operative may require and need further training and development to be able to achieve its economic and social objectives. The problems and challenges faced by them could be reduced or solved if there are people in the industry, government and academia who are willing to help and committed towards voluntarism. Thus, social entrepreneurship or collective entrepreneurship development in rural areas can be further improved with the assistance and support of social entrepreneurs within the industry, government and educational institutions, particularly universities, colleges and institutes of higher learning.

Acknowledgement

Our heartfelt appreciation goes out to SIFE World Headquarters and our Financial Literacy funding supporters, the HSBC Global Education Trust and the Corporate, Investment Banking and Markets (CIBM) division of HSBC for making this project possible with the USD900 grant, the Single Mothers Association of Kuala Terengganu for their kind co-operation and hospitality, and the Centre for Student Development, Tun Abdul Razak University, for their kind assistance, fourteen students who participated in the project and all those who made this project possible.

References

Dees, J.G. (2001), "The Meaning of Social Entrepreneurship, Social Entrepreneurship Resources, United States Association for Small Business and Entrepreneurship", Retrieved on November 13, 2007 at http://www.usasbe.org/knowledge/socialentres/Dees.pdf.

Johl, S.K., Bruce, A. & Binks, M. (2006), "Using mixed method approach in conducting a business research", *Proceedings of the International Borneo Business Conference 2006*, Hilton Hotel, Sarawak, Malaysia, December 5-7.

Leete, R. (2007), "Terengganu's Human Development Progress and Challenges", United Nations Development Programme, Retrieved on November 13, 2007 at http://www.undp.org.my/uploads/files/Terengganu HumanDevelopment.pdf.

Mair, J., and Marti, I. (2006), "Social entrepreneurship research: A source of explanation, prediction and delight", *Journal of World Business*, 41, 36-44.

Shetty, V. (2007a), "Rural development plan for women as entrepreneurs – A working model submitted to UNDP for discussions before implementation", *Proceedings of the Asia Pacific Marketing Conference 2007*, Holiday Inn Resort Damai Beach, Sarawak, Malaysia, November 2-3.

Shetty, V. (2007b), "E-Governance for rural development through women entrepreneurs", *Proceedings of the Asia Pacific Marketing Conference 2007*, Holiday Inn Resort Damai Beach, Sarawak, Malaysia, November 2-3.

16

Case Study: A.P. Mani & Sons – Mentoring Food Retail Entrepreneur

Jyotinder Kaur Chaddah*
Rabiya Jidda*
Neha Mathur*

The food retail industry has learned that one way to get shoppers back to cooking is to do most of the work for them, especially the time-consuming tasks of trimming and chopping. Jyotinder Kaur Chaddah, Rabiya Jidda and Neha Mathur dwell on this further. They have written a case study on A.P. Mani & Sons who has made a success out of selling pre-cut and packaged fruits and vegetables. In their endeavour, they found out that the lack of mentoring is the biggest impediment in the growth of Food Retailers in India.

INTRODUCTION

Situated on a bustling road leading to Chembur station in Central Mumbai, A. P. Mani and Sons appears to be just another food retail outlet. The only clues to what may lie inside are the mini vans that keep unloading precut and packaged packets of fruits, vegetables and groceries. A glimpse inside and it soon becomes clear that this is not your average store.

What makes it unique is that this entrepreneurial venture with an annual turnover of 12 crores has understood the needs of its consumers and in fact as its loyal customers say, created the need (among them) for their products. "Every other food retail outlet today is only trying to cut price, but we are trying to value add. I understood that there was a market for freshly grounded coconut and other spices for making chutneys, sambar and pulav, " says the entrepreneur who is credited with starting pre-cut and packaged vegetables and packaged idli and dosa mix in Mumbai. Sindhumani, a regular to this outlet says that it has been 7 years since she made the staple idli dough at home. Now, A. P. Mani has made her life easier. She only has to come to this one stop shop for the basic pre-cut veggies and stuff.

Regulars at A.P. Mani reminiscence the humble beginning of Nagesh Nadar, the promoter of A.P. Mani. They add, "This matriculate student of humble background started this venture in a temporary stall on the pavement outside Chembur station where he used to be penalised for

---

* Faculty, Guru Nanak Institute of Management Studies.

his `unofficial set up". Nadar who came to Mumbai as a teenager in the late 80s from a small village in Tamil Nadu says, "I had a futuristic vision of making a difference and doing things differently". At a tender age of 17, he had no concrete plan on one side of the coin and the harsh realities of doing business with the hounding civic authorities on the other. He was left an unclear future. He still recalls that on one occasion the BMC vans did not allow him to sell vegetables and hence his kitchen fire at home was not on. With a complete loss with withering vegetables left, he was in a catch 20-20 situation. Frustrated, he sorted out the good pieces, put them in small packets and stored them in a good samaritans shop. An idea dawned upon him, Why not make this his business? He then started reaching out to consumers with the packaged raw vegetables …thus the concept of pre-cut and packaged vegetables was born. Ever since then, he has not looked back. "The concept really caught on" says the entrepreneur who has a number of firsts to his credit.

A.P. Mani & Sons has three outlets with different flavours: each with a different format and a very different target segment visiting them. Three formats help in balancing out supply chain of his enterprise and overcome any discrepancies in inventory and forecasting. One of the three outlets is a supermarket where only precut and packaged vegetables are sold. The second one sells loose vegetables and fruits and the third one, *Sasta Bazar* is used for reverse logistics purposes where the unsold produce is retailed at 50% discount.

The precut and packaged vegetables are more expensive than their whole, fresh counterparts by 15-20%. The market for precut vegetables is exploding because people are constantly seeking ways to lighten the burden of cooking. They promise less drudgery, save time in selecting and weighting, there is more variety than just canned or frozen alternatives, and plenty of vitamins. And what differentiates this enterprise from the competitors is the entire business strategy.

"At A.P. Mani, my other directors and I, go and handpick the produce directly from the farmers, unlike competitors who allocate two people to pick up 20 bundles of coriander", he exults.

Taking a trip down memory lane, he says consumers today have changed a lot. Twenty years ago, consumers demanded that supermarkets take the plastic wrap off produce. They got their way and took advantage of the opportunity, choosing what was ready to eat and leaving behind the unripe, the overripe and the damaged. Now, shoppers have changed their minds: they want the vegetables wrapped up, only after they have been cut and chopped, washed and rinsed. Another significant change is the consumer's average billing. In the 1990s, a customer with Rs 100-150 billing was considered to be "big spender" and was given a special treatment. Today, an average billing is around Rs 1,000.

The man behind the show is credited for making an average Mumbaikar include exotic vegetables in his staple diet says, "The percentage of people shopping for exotic vegetables has gone up, further the quantity purchased and the regularity with which customers shop has shot up as well". He credits this to improved economy, his clients not averse to sampling different cuisines and the overall usage of these products in daily cooking due to his clients exposure to different cuisines.

While elaborating on another change he noticed, he continues, the use of credit card or shopping for food on credit. Today 50% of his clients shop using their credit card and at average credit card spending accounts for over a lakh of rupees of sales every day. While previously banks did not give him permission to use credit facilities for vegetable shopping, today the scenario has changed, banks are approaching him with better deals and urging him to install their machines for using credit cards.

Starting from a humble beginning to a large processing and packaging unit in Vashi, the entrepreneur explains the operational procedure whereafter the raw vegetables and fruits are procured, the processing that follows is fairly simple. After that, the vegetables are cut, washed in a chlorine solution to kill harmful bacteria and rinsed in plain water. Then, the vegetables are put into a zone that has a controlled atmosphere. The atmosphere inside this zone is regulated by reducing the amount of oxygen and increasing the carbon dioxide, which slows down the process of decay.

A.P. Mani has a high capacity for adaptation to regional differences, different market segmentation needs, and food consumption trends, because it can easily accommodate variations around its basic two-fold concept of freshness and convenience.

While commenting on price wars among food retailers, he says, "Price discounts do not attract a customer beyond a point. Instead one must offer quality products. This will ensure the customer will stick to you like glue".

Mr Mani is thoroughly satisfied that the brand he created is associated with freshness and quality for vegetables and fruits is gaining huge popularity and mass acceptance not only in his two retail departmental stores at Chembur, but in over 25 supermarkets and convenience store chains in Mumbai and Navi Mumbai (Akbarallys, D Mart Network of departmental stores, "Heiko Super-Market" at Hiranandani Gardens and various other super markets, star hotels, canteens and caterers and as well home delivery in Ghatkopar/Chembur areas. A third shop at the A. P. M. C. market in Vashi has been started recently, as it is in the major wholesale market complex of Mumbai.

He attributes his success to constant commitment to supply reliability, delivery deadlines and exceptional customer service. And this he says would have been unachievable without 100 employees who work tirelessly with him. The manpower mainly consists of Tamil Nadu and people from Uttar Pradesh.

A stickler for discipline and cleanliness, he provides his workers with accommodation, food, clothing, medicines, etc. Every employee is gifted with a Life Insurance Policy after successful completion of 3 years of service. He has purchased a couple of flats in order to accommodate the employees. "Looking at the quantity of the meals prepared for the employees, they can be mistaken for making preparations for a wedding".

His lean SCM and distribution system gives him a natural advantage over his other competitors. The *USP of his SCM is his philosophy of directly sourcing and directly supplying using his own infrastructure.* His vehicles are used to source the produce from the farmers and he supplies the packaged produce to his clients. This gives him a complete control over his supply chain. There is no outsourcing or middleman involved at any stage.

Among other plans is the agenda to get into farm to plate. He explains that this will let him earn better from the margins and he could also venture in reverse logistics in a bigger way.

Ask him where he sees himself against a barrage of big retail giants and he quips, "I will still be around long after they are gone". With plans of having 10-12 outlets in the next two years, he wants to have a chain of food retail outlet a la Spinach, Haiko by getting into a JV. He says he wants to get involved in all aspects of food retail right from sourcing, distributing and retailing. For all this to become a reality, he is looking for advice and support from a mentor. While seeking advice and feedback from his regular customers, one often finds Nadar asking them the quintessential question, "Is there any facility or organization which can guide on my future growth prospects?"

Nadar feels that the timing is perfect for getting into bigger things but as they say all big things begin with a small step, he too wants to embark on this new journey by writing a vision statement. And it is here that he faces the *biggest hindrance, his lack of education and no external mentoring support from any quarters.*

All the three promoters (P Suresh and R Rama Subramanium) have only studied till high school and have no formal grounding in management. They are completely dependent on accounts and other more qualified employees to do regular bank and transactional work.

This budding entrepreneur needs *advice on business plans, on financial planning, on markets, on issues related to management.* Besides they need access to companies. Therefore, Nadar must reach out to organizations like *TiE (The Indus Entrepreneur)* who under the *Entrepreneur Acceleration Programme* are making special efforts to provide free of charge *mentoring to food retail entrepreneurs.* Based on the plan and proposal, TiE will organize the mentoring sessions with the relevant TiE Charter members at a mutually convenient time. While mentoring sessions will be scheduled at the mutual convenience of mentor and mentee, mentoring clinics will be fixed on a particular day in every quarter. At these clinics, a large number of charter members as well as other appropriate invitees (e.g. senior professionals, entrepreneurs outside the TiE network, academicians, etc.) can spend half a day mentoring entrepreneurs in 30-45 minute sessions.

Analysis

Proprietary Position:

Currently, few competitors and maximum retailers in Mumbai are dependent on AP Mani for their supplies.

Product Description:

Fresh, washed, bite-sized, contained in a sealed, transparent, polypropylene bag.

Product Categories:

1.   Packaged raw vegetables and fruits,

2.   Pre-cut vegetables and fruits,

3.   Ready to make chutneys, dosas, idlis, papad mix, and

4.   Repackaged dals, besan, sugar, atta.

Package Size:

Institutional packs in different sizes and weights: 1kg, 500 gms packets.

Products available

1.   The packaged version of raw vegetables and fruits places it in the rapidly growing group of high-quality, premium-priced, convenience-based products which fit with the emerging Indian family and lifestyle.

2.   Variety of ingredients used for sambar, chutney in the right proportion eliminates need to buy larger quantities of these ingredients, mix portions of these and store the unused portions.

3.   Sustained freshness for longer time if bag is maintained at proper temperature.

4. Ready-to-use: eliminates trimming, washing, drying and chopping vegetables.

5. Pre-selection of highest quality produce.

6. Maintenance of nutritional content through the retail cold-chain.

7. Hygienic protection of produce from dust, uncontrolled spraying spill-overs, or easy touching and tampering.

Product Characteristics:

1. High eye appeal

2. Pieces sized to consumer preference

3. Long shelf-life

4. Branded

5. Transparent polypropylene bag as packaging material

6. Competitively priced, but with a value added price premium for convenience at the retail outlets

Prices set with three objectives in mind:

1. The pricing is right in order to penetrate the market.

2. The price always cover the costs of production.

3. The price allows for profitability.

Product cost does not vary greatly with size of package, since the form-fill-seal machinery has maximum speed regardless of size. Price is adjusted every day for fruits and vegetables in order to take into account daily variations in the price of the raw material.

Pricing policy is flexible enough to maintain market position once competition intensifies. This will be done by providing for better quality and extra features without necessitating dramatic price reductions which may jeopardize "positioning" as a high quality product.

AP MANI'S MARKET SELECTION AND ROLL-OUT OF PRODUCTS

Geographic Market Selection

The market entry strategy is *Cover Entire Mumbai* which is ready to accept these products.

Supply to more Retailers:

1. Closeness to producers and suppliers for all through the year supplies.

2. Brand-building activities will include:

    (a) In-store customer interactions.

    (b) Free Home Service which also acts as a channel of reaching out to the customer.

    (c) Point-of-purchase materials.

OPERATIONS

Product Potential

The relative simplicity of the technology and its production capacity flexibility permit quick and inexpensive adaptation of the process to new products. The product characteristics that could be modified in the course of business are:

Location and Facilities

Their production line consists of preparation tables, chillers, cutters, washers, spin dryers, electronic scales, automated fill-form and seal machines: cut leaves are packaged in air-filled sealed bags, carton packing machines.

Management

The management team consists of three key positions: There are three directors and they directly deal with the hundred plus employees. The two maternal uncles and Nagesh Nadar are responsible for achieving growth, supervising all operations, negotiating with suppliers and retailers and ordering quality and quantity of raw material necessary to meet orders and standards.

There is no training provided on or before the job. Each employee learns on the job. That is why they prefer taking people who have been referred to by their own employees. The employee acts as a mentor to the new entrant.

Critical Risks

1. Intense competition for quality, freshness and shelf life.

2. Retailers are getting into sourcing as well.

3. Easy to replicate the products offered.

4. Price cutting by competitors.

The firm's *financial objective* is to reach a point where stocks can be offered. The factors that make this possible are the size of the market, lead time of the company over competitors, and its dedication to stay ahead through an aggressive marketing strategy and a solid R&D programme.

Recommendations

1. A.P. Mani must keep a tab on the competitor's product variety and test it for quality, freshness, and shelf life making any necessary modification of their production line quality control measures.

2. It must enter newer markets with differentiated products from its competitors. It also needs to replace its packaging material and have more PR and brand building activities, which convey to the consumers and retailers about how their product is better than their competition.

3. A delicate balance must be maintained between pushing for market share and being the second best choice.

Price Cutting by Competitors

1. To sustain price cutting by competitors, value will be added to the product difficulties encountered in the supply of raw materials.

2. If domestic supplies cannot be met economically, because of bad weather, strikes, etc., raw materials will be purchased through import wholesalers and brokers. The price will be revised accordingly and accepted because of previous efficiencies.

References

Prasad. K, *Entrepreneurship: Concepts and Cases*, 2002, ICFAI University Press, Hyderabad.

Krishna. S, *Small and Medium Enterprises: Concepts and Cases*, 2006, ICFAI University Press, Hyderabad.

Gupta. S, *Entrepreneurial Development: An Introduction*, 2004, ICFAI University Press, Hyderabad.

Kaulgud. A, *Entrepreneurship Management*, 2003, Vikas Publishing House, New Delhi.

Doyle. B & Vincent O'Neill, *Mentoring Entrepreneurs*, 2006, Prentice Hall of India Pvt. Ltd, New Delhi.

17

Case Study: Social Entrepreneurship

Dr. Thomas Mathew*
Dr. Pradip Manjrekar**

This paper reports examine a successful social entrepreneurship of a Indian Christian Education Society. It examines important factors which have facilitated the development of the venture over its 100 year life. The paper is based on a case study of the Francisian Education Society (FES). The authors use multiple sources of data including interviews and a review of relevant documentation to identify both the outcomes of the venture (in substantive terms) and factors associated with its success. The authors report that the venture has provided demonstrable benefits for community by (amongst other things) reducing illiteracy and providing innovative solutions to the problem of long-term education (social outcomes). The paper also develops a descriptive model which identifies key facilitating factors grouped into categories relating to: environment, governance and accountability, resourcing, leader characteristics, process and structure, and communication. The paper has a number of implications for researchers, policy makers and practitioners. It provides exploratory insights for policy makers and other funders who advocate social enterprise, around how they may support such activities. Finally, it highlights some important challenges and opportunities for other non-profit organisations seeking to diversify their activities and revenue streams beyond traditional forms.

INTRODUCTION

This paper provides a detailed analysis of a case of social entrepreneurship widely recognised in India as successful. It seeks to answer the question: What are the factors associated with successful social entrepreneurship? Using Austin, Stevensan and Wei-Skillern's (2006), framework for Social Entrepreneurship, the author suggests a number of factors in the key areas of opportunity, people, financial resources, economic and institutional factors, organisational factors and social value. The paper concludes with a discussion of the implications for practitioners, policymakers and researchers of social entrepreneurship.

Social entrepreneurship is not a new phenomenon in India. It has always been possible to identify examples of nonprofit organisations which have used entrepreneurial strategies to

* Director, St. Francis Institute of Management & Research, Borivili (W), Mumbai.
** Professor, Dr. D.Y. Patil Institute of Management Studies, CBD Belapur, Navi Mumbai.

achieve particular social purposes. However, whilst it may not be new there is evidence that the incidence of social entrepreneurship in India is increasing. Driven by a changing landscape—one that is increasingly characterised by market-driven approaches (Field, 2001; Ryan, 1999), and/or pressing social need it would seem that more non-profit organisations are adapting entrepreneurial approaches and strategies.

There is also some evidence that policy makers in India are becoming increasingly interested in social entrepreneurship. In the past years, the Indian government, for example, has provided funds to a number of nonprofit organisations and communities to establish social enterprises. It is likely that the policy environment, in several Indian states will continue to advance the phenomenon of social entrepreneurship.

As an area of academic interest, social entrepreneurship is still emerging (Masher-Williams, 2006) and there is much that remains to be understood about the phenomena. In particular, the factors or considerations which are critical to successful social entrepreneurship are not well known. The amount of research into social entrepreneurship in India is particularly limited.

This paper aims to develop our understanding of social entrepreneurship, specifically the factors which underpin its success, using a case of social entrepreneurship widely recognised as successful in Mumbai, India. It seeks to answer the key question: what are the factors associated with the success of this particular case of social entrepreneurship? In addressing this issue, the author also seeks to respond to a common criticism that much social entrepreneurship research lacks a systematic and theoretical approach. To this end, the authors use Austin, Stevensan and Wei-Skillern's (2006) analytical Framework for Social Entrepreneurship to guide the research process.

The paper begins with a brief overview of social entrepreneurship. The authors discuss several perspectives on social entrepreneurship, provides a working definition of the concept, and describes the research framework which guides the analysis. They go on to describe the method of inquiry, identifying the case of social entrepreneurship and justifying its selection. In the body of the paper the authors explores common themes in the research to identify and describe these factors which appear to be related to successful social entrepreneurship. They conclude the paper by providing same insights about value of the research framework used in the research and same implications far social entrepreneurship policy, research and practice.

One way of making sense of the various definitions of social entrepreneurship is to group them according to their scope. Broad definitions typically describe social entrepreneurship as innovative activity with a social purpose which may occur in either for profit, government or the nonprofit sectors (Dees, 1998). These definitions of social entrepreneurship include social commercial ventures, corporate social entrepreneurship and nonprofit organisations which adopt commercial tools and knowledge. Narrow definitions, on the other hand, tend to limit the focus of social entrepreneurship to entrepreneurial activity in the non-profit sector (Thompson, 2002).

Another way of approaching definitions of social entrepreneurship is to focus on innovation as the source of value (Alvord, Brown and Letts, 2002; Schumpeter, 1951). Some definitions of social entrepreneurship focus on combining commercial enterprises with social impacts. Social entrepreneurs apply business skills and knowledge (through trading) to generate resources which may then be used to achieve social purposes (Emerson and Twersky, 1996). Other definitions of social entrepreneurship emphasise innovation for social impact.

Social entrepreneurs use innovative approaches to solve intractable social problems; they may pay relatively little attention to economic viability using conventional commercial criteria (Dees, 1998). Others still view social entrepreneurship as a means of initiating large-scale social transformation, well beyond the scope of the initial social problem (Ashoka Foundation, 2000).

Despite their differences, these definitions do share a number of common features. First, they focus on the creation of social value, rather than shareholder value or personal value (Austin, Stevenson and Wei-Skillern, 2006). The key driver of social entrepreneurship relates, at least initially, to solving a particular social problem or set of problems. Secondly, the definitions encompass innovation (Alvord, Brown and Letts, 2002) either in the process by which social value is created, and/or in the outcome of that process.

For the purposes of the paper, the authors do not intend to engage in a debate about the relative merits of various definitions of social entrepreneurship. Rather, they adopts a definition which satisfactorily encompasses both common aspects of social value and innovation. The definition is broad and thus does not limit social entrepreneurship to occurring in a type of organisation or sector. In keeping with the research framework adopted in this study, the author adopts the definition of social entrepreneurship expounded by Austin, Stevenson and Wei-Skillern (2006). Social entrepreneurship then is innovative, social value creating activity that can occur within or across the nonprofit, business or government sectors (Austin, Stevenson and Wei-Skillern (2006).

Theoretical Framework

One of the common criticisms of the social entrepreneurship research, particularly research about the factors associated with its success, is that it lacks a systematic and theoretical focus. In an effort to avoid this criticism, the authors adopt Austin, Stevenson and Wei-Skillern's (2006), analytical Framework for Social Entrepreneurship to guide the research process and to provide the lens through which the factors associated with social entrepreneurship can be viewed.

According to this framework, there are five components of social entrepreneurship. These are: opportunity, human resources, financial resources, contextual factors and the social value proposition. These components are overlapping and interrelated, with social value the central consideration.

Opportunity: According to Austin, Stevenson and Wei-Skillern (2006), is the "initiating point" for social entrepreneurship. It represents the vision of a future desired state, different from the present, and the belief that this state can be achieved via a particular and credible path of change. One of the challenges for social entrepreneurship is ensuring that all parties share a common understanding of the nature of this opportunity (Austin, Stevenson and Wek-Skillern, 2006).

Human Resources and Capital Resources: Are the enabling variables for social entrepreneurship. Like their commercial counterparts, social entrepreneurs must understand the industry in which they are planning to attract resources and start their venture. Given the multiplicity of stakeholders commonly involved in social enterprises, and the restricted and typically short-term nature of funding sources, this skill in dealing with individuals' needs, is especially important (Austin, Stevenson and Wek-Skillern, 2006).

The Contextual Factors: The *context* includes all those factors which are outside the control of management, yet have an effect on the nature and outcome of the opportunity. They "shape the opportunities available to the entrepreneur" (Austin, Stevenson and Wei-Skillem, 2006). Managing and adapting to these contextual factors, and indeed, identifying which contextual factors are relevant, are critical considerations for social entrepreneurs.

The Social Value Proposition: According to Austin, Stevenson and Wei-Skillern (2006), is the "integrating driver of the framework". It represents the substance of the bargain between the entrepreneurial venture and all its resource providers and in the case of social entrepreneurship is primarily about creating social value, or impact for society. To deliver on this social value proposition, the social entrepreneur must ensure that all other components of social entrepreneurship – opportunity, human and capital resources and the context – are in a state of alignment.

Methodology

This study provides an analysis of a particular case of social entrepreneurship in India.

The study is inductive rather than deductive, designed to identify the factors associated with successful social entrepreneurship. Given the exploratory nature of the research, a case study approach is considered most useful (Yin, 1984). The complexity of the phenomena provides additional support for this approach. Case descriptions yield rich information and enable identification and assessment of unexpected patterns, which other methodologies may not reveal (Yin, 1994).

The authors have chosen this particular case of social entrepreneurship because it is one widely recognised as successful. The Francisian Education Society (FES) has been profiled in several reputable books and magazines. Whilst acknowledging the debate about what constitutes 'success' when discussing social enterprises, FES meets most, if not all, of the commonly cited criteria: it has operated for a lengthy period (indeed, more than a decade), it has grown (both in terms of revenue and number of employees) during that time, and it can demonstrate significant social impact.

The authors has used a mix of methods to generate information for the study. They have conducted in-depth interviews with key organisation members. They have consulted published and unpublished articles and reports, as well as archival material in the form of performance reports and other relevant organisational documents and records.

The authors have focused the research on identifying common themes relating to the factors associated with success of the Francisian Education Society. Consistent with the research framework adopted, the authors have sought to identify factors related to the key analytical areas of opportunity, people, financial resources, context and social value. They have also sought to identify other factors which are important, but which may fall outside the analytical model.

Background to the case

The Francisian Education Society (FES) is a Francisian Community (a religious order of Christians) initiative having Head Quarters located at Borivili (West), Mumbai (India) and having several Educational initiatives not only in India but also globally.

Created in 1907, FES has extensive experience in the field of education – ranging from schools to a wide variety of Institutions like Industrial Training Institute (ITI), Art & Design Institute, Engineering College, Management College and also training, employment placement services and enterprise activities.

FES differentiates itself through its unique approach of moulding 'productive citizens' of the future. Here, the key to successful education is rooted in the ancient Indian tradition of a 'Gurukul'. It provides a strong education foundation, while recalibrating student personalities, through Indian practices like yoga and meditation, in the hope that they will enrich themselves and our society.

Diversity is inherent to FES. FES's students showcase assorted backgrounds, individualism, synergistic skill-sets, exceptional abilities, focused drives and singular experiences. As a result of the distinctive experience at Fes—A Fusion of Western thought and Indian influences – the students move to becoming individuals who retain their identities, while looking at the outside world, with a strong knowledge base, conviction of purpose and high standards of excellence.

SOCIAL ENTREPRENEURSHIP – FACTORS ASSOCIATED WITH SUCCESS

The Opportunity

In the case of the FES, the initial opportunity identified by founders in 1903, was to establish a community education enterprise which would create education opportunities for long-term local people in the area at a time when insufficient education were available. FES could see that the opportunity would deliver benefits to individuals (who would gain employment), to the local municipal council, to the community, to government and to the environment. The enterprise, if successful, would also enhance the profile of FES in the community, and bring much needed income into the organisation. However, FES could also' see that success of the enterprise required the active support (and inputs) of these key stakeholder groups.

One of the key factors associated with the success of FES is that key stakeholders have a common understanding of the nature of the opportunity. FES Board of Management and key staff have invested considerable time and energy with key stakeholders, particularly at the outset of the enterprise, articulating the opportunity, describing the enterprise and ensuring stakeholders support.

Another factor associated with FES's success seems to be that it is perceived to be a credible organisation to operate the social enterprise. The organisation is well regarded within its community for its work: The organisation has been operating in the community for more than 100 years, and for much of that time, its focus has been on assisting long-term rural/urban poor education seekers who face multiple barriers into employment, training and enterprise. At the same time, the organisation is known for having an entrepreneurial orientation. The majority of the Board of Management members is of business people, and the organisation has established and operated several other social enterprises.

The enterprise has experienced steady and managed growth. In the period between 1907 and 2007, growth has been steady: staff numbers have increased from X full-time staff to Y, the amount of student enrollment annually has increased to almost A thousand. This growth has been resourced from within the enterprise.

The organisation is currently planning for its next stage of growth, and is negotiating with global universities for collaborations. Growth in the FES has been planned and managed, and the organisation has been able to avoid issues related to unplanned growth.

Human Resources

The social entrepreneur has the capacity to work across many diverse constituencies. From the outset, FES has demonstrated his capacity to work with multiple, often diverse stakeholders. It has a rich network of government, business and community contacts in the area and is involved in a number of local committees and initiatives. FES's philosophy of 'never do anything alone' has underpinned their approach and has been particularly important in terms of mobilising financial and other inputs to the organisation. This capacity to work across stakeholders would appear to be akin to Alvord, Brown and Letts' (2002), notion of bridging capacity.

Related to this, FES has also demonstrated its capacity to understand the perspectives and concerns of those stakeholders whose support is critical for the initiative (akin to Austin, Stevenson and Wei-Skillern's (2006) political and relationship management skills). FES's reputation for fairness and trust may be a significant contributor to this capacity to build and then maintain strategic partnerships.

The social entrepreneur has a long-term commitment to the initiative. FES has maintained its leadership of, and commitment to, education for 100 years. This commitment has been instrumental in enabling the enterprise to address many of the challenges associated with its operation. Some of the most significant internal challenges have related to managing employees. Significant external challenges have related to maintaining relationships with key stakeholders (especially the government). This long-term commitment (which manifests itself in Cox's ability to overcome hurdles and pursue strategies to strengthen the future of the enterprise) is consistent with Alvord, Brown and Letts' (2002) notion of adaptive capacity.

There are others in the organisation, beyond the social entrepreneur FES, whose skills and knowledge are critical to successful social entrepreneurship. Key people within the enterprise are resourceful; able to mobilise assets and other resources within the community. An important aspect of FES success has related to the resourcefulness of key people associated with the organisation. FES has been able to bring key assets and resources into the enterprise, quite often at little or no direct cost to its operation.

Financial Resources

The organisation is financially self-sustaining. FES has funded almost all of its direct and indirect operating costs over its 100 year life. Approximately 80 per cent of FES expenditure goes to wages with the remaining 20 per cent used to cover purchase of materials and equipment, overheads and other expenses. All profits from operations are reinvested in the organisation. Whilst this arrangement may have constrained the organisation's growth somewhat, it has enabled the organisation to avoid risks associated with an undue reliance on external funding sources, and an ongoing preoccupation with sourcing external funds.

From time to time FES has successfully accessed small amounts of funding from a diverse range of partners. On several occasions, FES has secured small grants from various organisations to purchase specific items. These funds have provided several benefits for FES: they have enabled the organisation to purchase particular 'one-off items and served to increase its range of partners.

Context

Contextual forces have been instrumental in creating the entrepreneurial opportunity. In particular, economic and institutional factors at start-up gave impetus to the organisation.

It was adverse contextual conditions in the post independence era which were significant. With uneducated rates above 50% there were insufficient education opportunities for those who wanted to have education and levels of community concern about the impacts of insufficient education were high. Consequently, there was significant demand for, and interest in, potential solutions to the education problem. FES was able to present itself as a sustainable way of creating new education opportunities. Support from government partners was also important. Low education levels in the post independence period meant that government was supportive of a range of initiatives to support education activities.

Social Value Proposition

The deal is relatively simple. The nature of the deal between the partners is relatively straightforward. Whilst there is a formal, written agreement between the key partners, the relationship between the partners emphasises trust, rather than the legal ties (Sahlman, 1996). That is not to say the relationship is without tensions; however, the level of trust or 'goodwill' which exists between the key partners has seen them address and overcome challenges in the relationship.

The enterprise is generating value for all key partners. The venture has produced significant and measurable outcomes (value) for all its key partners during its life. It has provided meaningful education and training to people who were previously uneducated. Finally, it has built the credibility of FES within and beyond its local community by demonstrating that the organisation is innovative, efficient and achievement oriented. The creation of this social value has remained the primary focus of the enterprise.

Additional Factors

In addition to the factors already identified, there are a number of others which emerged through the research process. These additional factors do not fit quite so comfortably within the research framework adopted by the authors, and appear to relate to organisational practices and systems. These additional factors are: participative and democratic, decision-making processes and the level of organisational support for the enterprise. Decision-making process within the enterprise are participative and democratic. This approach to managing the business has been instrumental in promoting teamwork and developing high levels of ownership amongst the stakeholders.

FACTORS ASSOCIATED WITH SUCCESSFUL ENTREPRENEURSHIP: IMPLICATIONS FOR POLICY AND PRACTICE

This exploratory analysis identifies a number of factors associated with successful social entrepreneurship using the Indian case of FES. At the same time, the paper also explores the utility of Austin, Stevenson and Wei-Skillern's (2006), Framework for Social Entrepreneurship in guiding the research process.

The research prompts a number of observations. Firstly, the Framework for Social Entrepreneurship adopted by the authors seems to be an appropriate lens through which to view social entrepreneurship and the factors which are related to its success. In the case of FES, it is definitely useful to organise and analyse those factors around variables relating to the opportunity, the people and financial resources, the context and the social value proposition. However, there are also other factors which do not sit so quite so comfortably within the framework, suggesting that some modification may be useful.

Secondly, although exploratory, the research provides some potential insights and guidance, both for policymakers and practitioners, around the key factors which may be associated with successful entrepreneurship. From the case of FES, these are:

1. *In terms of the opportunity:* That key stakeholders share a common understanding of its nature and view the founding body as a credible organisation to operate the enterprise. Growth should be planned and managed;

2. *In terms of people:* The social entrepreneur demonstrates the capacity to work across, and understand and manage, the interests of diverse constituencies. He or she should also possess a long-term commitment to the initiative and a heightened sense of accountability for its outcomes. In addition to the social entrepreneur, there will be others in the enterprise whose skills, experience and resourcefulness will be closely associated with its success;

3. *In terms of financial resources:* The organisation should be financially self-sustaining;

4. *Key elements of the context:* Especially economic and institutional factors, will shape the opportunity, and

5. The deal creates social value for all key stakeholders.

At the same time, the authors provides a note of caution. The research is exploratory, and concentrates on one particular case of social entrepreneurship in India. As such, it raises as many questions it answers, not the least of which is whether factors associated with the success of FES are similar to those for other cases of successful social entrepreneurship in India. That is a topic for future and more extensive research.

References

Alvord, S., Brown, D. and Letts, C. (2002), "Social entrepreneurship and social transformation: An exploratory study". Hauser Center for Non-profit Organizations working paper no.15.

Ashoka Innovators for the Public (2002), *Selecting leading social entrepreneurs* retrieved from http://www.ashoka.org. in December 2006.

Austin, J. Stevenson, H. and Wei-Skillern, J. (2006), "Social and commercial entrepreneurship: Same, different or both?", *Entrepreneurship Theory and Practice*, January 2006.

Barraket, J. (2006), "Community and social enterprise: What role for government?" retrieved from www.dvc.vie.gov.au in November 2006.

Emerson, J. and Twersky, F (Eds). (1996), "New social entrepreneurs: The success, challenge and lessons of non-profit enterprise creation". San Francisco: Roberts. Foundation, Homeless Economic Development Fund.

Field, C. (2001), *How social entrepreneurs can make a difference* retrieved from http:// e l.newcastle.edu.au/coffee/pubs/workshops/ 1 L200l/sen_field.pdf.

Mosher-Williams, R. (2006), *Much more to do: Issues for further research on social entrepreneurship in Mosher-Williams, R. (2006) (Ed.). Research on social entrepreneurship: Understanding and contributing to an emerging field.* ARNOVA Occasional Paper Series Vol 1. No.3.

Ryan, W. (1999), "The new landscape for non-profits", *Harvard Business Review*, January - February.

Sahlman, W.A. (1996), "Some thoughts on business plans in Sahlman", W.A., Stevenson, H., Roberts, M.J. and Bhide (Eds), The entrepreneurial venture. Boston: *Harvard Business Review*.

Schumpeter, J. A. (1951), *"Essays: On entrepreneurs, innovations, business cycles and the evolution of capitalism"*, ed. Riehard V. Clemence, Cambridge: Addison-Wesley.

Thompson, J. (2002), "The world of the social entrepreneur", *International Journal of Public Sector Management*, 15(5).

18

Micro Entrepreneurship – The Role of Microfinance Self-Help Groups

M. Prasada Rao*

The Indian economy basically is agrarian-based. 741.0 million of the population still depends on agriculture or agri-based rural business sectors. It could be wholesale or retail. The Indian economy, for most past, still revolves around rural or allied products, particularly in the villages and semi-urban center.

The rural entrepreneurship is as diversified as the Indian economy; some are HNIs but the majority is of low-income groups and below the poverty line. The business capital of HNIs is totally self-dependent or offered by banking.

Those are not privileged for self-dependency or access to banking sector due in eligibility (many factors). This inequality leads to the mechanism of microfinance in rural entrepreneurship. Microfinance means "providing finance to small entrepreneur and producers demonstrate that poor people in small amounts".

The larger of the two main models, the Self-Help Group (SHG) Bank Linkage Programme (SGH-BLP) covered about 14 million poor households in March 2006. Today, the Grameen Bank model of Bangladesh is been followed by a number of MFIs and some private banks to offer the small loans to the poor and nearly Rs. 500bn already lend to 25 laks customers through SHGs in the financial year of 2006-07.

By end of this financial year of 2007-08, it is expected to offer loan nearly Rs. 1000bn. The prosperity of rural entrepreneurship is totally depends on MFI system and SHGs functionality. If this continues as planned, in the near future, there will not be a single poor person in rural India and a balanced economy could be possible.

INTRODUCTION

Since ancient times, the Indian economy has had an agrarian base (i.e., consisting of farmers, potters, blacksmiths, goldsmiths, artisans, construction experts, workers, etc.). The per-capita income basically depended on agrarian and its allied products. Even after industrialization,

* Ph.D Scholar, Dr. D. Y. Patil Institute of Management Studies, C.B.D. Belapur, Navi Mumbai.

a substantial percentage of national income was from purely from agricultural products and agri-based industries.

Even now, over 72 per cent of the Indian population depends on agri-based rural business sectors. It could be wholesale or retail. The major part of the Indian economy still revolves around the agrarian sector. The agricultural sector has a proven susceptibility to natural calamities and low productivity. This has led many rural populations to shift their profession (source of income). These unwarranted conditions have forced the rural poor to search for other means of earning.

"Microfinance" entails providing finance to small entrepreneurs and producers demonstrate that poor people in small amounts.

"Microfinance can be defined as any activity that includes the provision of financial services such as credit, savings, and insurance to low-income individuals who fall just above the nationally defined poverty line, and poor individuals who fall below that poverty line, with the goal of creating social value. The creation of social value includes poverty alleviation and the broader impact of improving livelihood opportunities through the provision of capital of micro enterprise, and insurance and savings for risk mitigation and consumption smoothing".

Home to the largest population of poor in the world, India has been a natural candidate for experimenting with microfinance as a tool for poverty alleviation. With a nationalized formal banking sector that has emphasised rural and developmental banking for several decades. Now, India's involvement with small credit targeted primarily at the rural poor is hardly new. However, recent years have generated unprecedented interest in microcredit and microfinance in the form of group-lending without collateral; thanks in part to the remarkable success of institutions like the Grameen Bank in neighbouring Bangladesh and BRI, BancoSol and others in more distant lands. The performance of organizations like SEWA in Western India and SHARE and BASIX in Southern India have convinced many a sceptic that microfinance can indeed make a difference in India as well. Over the past decade, NABARD's "SHG-Bank Linkage Programme" aimed at connecting self-help groups of poor people with banks, has, in fact, created the *largest microfinance network in the world*. The self-help group approach has won enthusiastic supporters among influential policymakers like the Andhra Pradesh CM, Chandrababu Naidu. Even the central government has recognized the advantages of group lending and has adopted the approach in its battle against poverty.

Within India, the microfinance revolution in Western and Southern India have received most attention, both in the media as well as in academic research. The poster boys of Indian microfinance – SHARE, BASIX, SEWA, MYRADA and PRADAN, for instance – have deservingly received attention from academicians, media-persons as well as the government. Andhra Pradesh, in particular, has witnessed a remarkable growth in microfinance activities and its success stories have been widely reported as well. In comparison, Eastern India has not enjoyed the limelight in the stage of microfinance, partly because of the absence of a single very large microfinance institution in the region.

However, Self-Help Groups (SHGs), usually at the behest of certain developmental Non-Government Organizations (NGOs), have quietly mushroomed in most districts of Eastern India – particularly in the state of West Bengal – over the last few years. Millions of poor, predominantly women, are now members of thousands of SHGs. Studies – academic or practitioner-oriented – documenting the extent and impact of these Eastern Indian Microfinance

Institutions (MFIs) have, so far been conspicuous by their absence. Given the lack of an easily accessible data source covering the operation and performance of multiple MFIs and SHGs spread out over a region, it is hardly surprising that much of the extant research on microfinance in India has focused on developing case studies, often covering the well-known success stories. In this paper, we seek to follow a slightly different approach. In an effort to understand the grassroots situation and appreciate the challenges faced by the not-yet-superstar NGO, MFIs, we put together glimpses of a couple of self-help groups (SHGs) and take an in-depth look at an NGO MFI from Eastern India.

The paper is organized in the following manner. The next section provides a brief background of microfinance activities in India. The third section presents brief case studies of two typical MFIs from West Bengal. The financial management and operational challenges of yet another MFI is discussed in the fourth section. The fifth and final section concludes with insights from these case studies and an attempt to generalize the findings.

MICROFINANCE IN INDIA

As mentioned before, microfinance activities in India, particularly microcredit, have had a considerable history in India. Traders and moneylenders have traditionally provided credit to the rural poor, usually at exorbitant rates of interest leading to considerable hardship and impoverishment of borrowers. Over the past few decades government initiatives, both in the form of establishment of a network of Regional Rural Banks (RRBs) and apex institutions like the National Bank of Agriculture and Rural Development (NABARD) charged with the role of distributing credit to the rural and micro-industries, as well as the main poverty alleviation programme, Integrated Rural Development Programme (IRDP), have sought to boost development and poverty alleviation through use of rural and micro-credit. However, most of these banks and programmes have been plagued by mismanagement and misuse of funds and abysmal repayment rates and have failed to emerge as self-sustaining vehicles of microfinance.

Over the last quarter century, a few organizations, outside the purview of the public sector, have succeeded in effective poverty alleviation through micro-credit. Self Employed Women's Association (SEWA) in the western Indian state of Gujarat and Working Women's Forum in the southern state of Tamil Nadu were among the pioneers in this effort. The sector received a major boost in the 1990s with the entry of several Non-Government Organizations (NGOs). Many of these NGOs have been previously functioning in different developmental roles among the poor, and now added microcredit to the list of services they provided. A few others, impressed by the success of microfinance elsewhere, started off as MFIs. Self-Help Groups (SHGs) among the poor, mostly women, have rapidly become a common rural phenomenon in many Indian states. NGOs provide the leadership and management necessary in forming and running such groups in most cases. They also act as the crucial link between these groups and the formal banking system. Presently, well over 500 NGO-MFIs are actively engaged in microfinance intermediation across the country.

NABARD's Bank Linkage Programme, pilot-tested in 1991-92 and launched in full vigour in 1996, has been a major effort to connect thousands of SHGs across the country with the formal banking system. By late 2002, it connected about *half a million* SHGs to the banking system with total loan disbursement of about Rs. 1,026 crores.

In spite of, the impressive rise of microfinance institutions, the scope of further microfinance efforts in India is almost unlimited. Indeed poverty alleviation in India is a Herculean task. India has roughly about 60 million poor households, accounting for over 350 million people, about 35% of the entire population. Even NABARD aims at reaching only 100 million of the poor (less than a third) by 2008. Clearly, a quantum leap in microfinance activities is necessary if it is expected to make a serious impact on the poverty situation in India. There are, of course, other issues connected with microfinance and poverty alleviation. As elsewhere in the world, it is contended that in India too, microfinance often eludes the "poorest of the poor" and it is people above poverty line – barely or comfortably – who can benefit from such microfinancial services. Finally, the distribution of microfinance within India is far from uniform. While Andhra Pradesh probably has the most widespread and developed microfinance sector in India, some of the "Hindi belt" states and the North-East have significantly lower penetration level of microfinance. However, given the lack of studies documenting the penetration rates of microfinance in different parts of India, it is difficult to provide more precise information on the relative spread of microfinance in the different states of India.

Self-Help Groups (SHGs) – voluntary groups of individual savers and borrowers, usually from the same village, have emerged as the fundamental unit of micro-borrowing. Non-banking Financial Corporations (NBFCs) and other non-government organizations (NGOs) typically connect these SHGs to local banks or to the funds provided by wholesale credit suppliers like NABARD or SIDBI (Small Industries Development Bank of India). The SHGs develop a habit of saving among its members for a period of time and then begin making loans to applying members from the collective savings of the group. After a few rounds of successfully repaid loans, an SHG begins borrowing from an outside source (i.e. a bank). Banks usually consider SHGs "bankable" after six months of their existence.

Several alternative models of SHG-NGO-bank relationship have emerged in recent years. One such model is where the bank lends directly to the SHG and the latter further lends it to individual members. As a variant of this model, an NGO may provide training and guidance to the SHG still dealing directly with the bank. This has been the most popular model in the Indian context. Alternatively, the NGO itself may act as an intermediary between the bank and the SHG, borrowing from the bank and lending it to (usually multiple) SHGs. Yet another model involves the bank lending directly to the individual borrower with the NGO and the SHG acquiring an advisory role.

There are several major legal, regulatory and financial challenges for NGOs involved in microfinance activities. Legally, they are usually registered as societies and trusts with no equity capital and consequently can never be "capital adequate" in leveraging debt. Also, these NGOs do not come under any specific control by any regulatory body and their only responsibility is to submit annual accounts to the registrar of societies. This lack of specific regulatory provisions has acted as a mixed blessing in the area – it has allowed for organic growth and spread of NGO MFIs and at the same time has led to lack of financial sustainability for most of these organizations, sometimes with disastrous effects on the goodwill of microfinance at large.

AN INTRODUCTION TO SELF-HELP GROUPS

Self Help Groups (SHGs) form the basic constituent unit of the microfinance movement in India. An SHG is a group of a few individuals – usually poor and often women – who pool their savings into a fund from which they can borrow as and when necessary. Such a group is linked with a bank – a rural, co-operative or commercial bank – where they maintain a group account. Over time, the bank begins to lend to the group as a unit, without collateral, relying on self-monitoring and peer pressure within the group for repayment of these loans.

An SHG consists of five to twenty persons, usually all from different families. Often a group like this is given a name. Each such group has a leader and a deputy leader, elected by the group members. The members decide among themselves the amount of deposit they have to make individually to the group account. The starting monthly individual deposit level is usually low – Rs. 10 or Rs. 20 (about 20-40 US cents). For a group of size 10, this translates to Rs. 100 to 200 (about $2 to $ 4) of group savings per month. On the basis of the resolutions adopted and signed by all members of the group, the manager of a local rural or commercial bank opens a savings bank account. The savings are collected by a certain date (often the 10th of the month) from individual members and deposited in the bank account.

Joining an existing SHG is often a costly affair for an aspiring villager. In order to maintain parity among the members, a new member has to join by depositing the total accumulated individual savings and interest of the group. Besides, the new member has to be accepted by every member of the existing group. Thus, it is often easier for a person not affiliated with an SHG to start a new SHG than joining a pre-existing one.

Loans are then given out to individual members from out of these funds upon application and unanimous resolution drawn at a group meeting. The bank permits withdrawal from the group account on the basis of such resolutions. Such loans, fully funded out of the savings generated by the group members themselves, are called "inter-loans". The repayment periods of loans are usually short, 3-6 months. After regular loan issuance and repayment for six months, the bank considers making a bank loan to the SHG. The maximum loan amount is a multiple (usually 4:1) of the total funds in the group account. This limit is also reached gradually starting from a lower (2:1 or 1:1) figure. Thus, a 10 member SHG with individual monthly deposit level of Rs. 20, completing a six-month successful "inter-loaning", accumulates total savings of Rs. 1,200 (part of which may be lent out to individual members) and is eligible for a maximum bank loan of Rs. 4,800.

Self-Help Groups are almost always formed with outside assistance. Developmental NGOs, often with considerable history of working in a particular area for projects like literacy, sanitation etc., take to organizing SHGs, bringing together people, explaining the concept to them, attending and helping coordinate a few of the initial group meetings, helping them maintain accounts and linking them with the banks. Of late, some of the rural banks themselves are being designated as Self-Help Promoting Institutions (SHPIs) and they help in the formation and 'nursing' of SHGs.

While most of the SHG formation/nursing processes have initially been in non-government hands, the developmental potential of the SHG-based microfinance process has not gone unnoticed by the government. In recent years, government developmental programmes have also sought to target the poor through the SHGs. The most important of the government programmes using the SHG approach is the *Swarnajayanti Gram Swarojgar Yojana* (SGSY) launched in 1999.

Government involvement in microfinance has, however, not been an unmixed blessing. Politicizing of the subsidy allotment among SHGs has become a big problem. Qualification for government subsidy is easily influenced by panchayat members. Thus, panchayats are now competing with NGOs and rural banks in forming SHGs. While the panchayat-formed

SHGs have the lure of government grants, they are often open to political pressure and misuse of funds by the recommending panchayats and/or political parties. Besides, the NGO-formed SHGs have the benefit of honest and expert counseling from the nursing NGOs. Thus the quality of NGO-formed groups are usually superior to those formed by the local government (Panchayats) and villagers are often keen to join the former. These age-old problems of government initiatives in poverty reduction, unless stemmed quickly, can actually harm the movement by eroding the fundamental precepts of self-help and empowerment of the poor.

A GLIMPSE OF AN NGO MICROFINANCE INSTITUTION

A large number of SHGs in India are incubated and nurtured by Non-Government Organizations (NGOs) working for developmental and humanitarian causes. A look at their functioning and efficiency is essential for gaining a complete understanding of the microfinance sector. Here, we focus on one such NGO, Bagaria Relief and Welfare Ambulance Society (BRWAS), and examine the different developmental and managerial aspects of its functioning. BRWAS is a larger than median-sized NGO and has been fairly successful so far.

CONCLUSION AND FUTURE WORK

In this paper, we have sought to provide a clinical view of the microfinance activities in India. We have attempted to provide a glimpse of the Self-Help Group (SHG)-based microfinance system by providing brief case studies of two SHGs in the district of Andhra Pradesh and a more detailed description of an NGO microfinance institution operating in the southern states.

The picture that emerges from these case studies is that the SHG-based system is indeed making a difference in the lives of the poor by providing much needed credit. There are, however, considerable differences among the SHGs and these differences affect their performances and successes. NGO, MFIs are playing a major role in forming and nurturing these SHGs.

Case studies, by their very natures, are restricted in universality of their results. It is our intention to accumulate survey information from a large number of MFIs in the near future so as to develop a rigorous empirical study of the different features of microfinance in Eastern India. In our opinion, developing and analyzing a large database that would allow us to better understand these essential constituents of the microfinance revolution should be a major subject of future research in this area.

NABARD's SHG-Bank Linkage Programme – Facts and Figures

NABARD started its SHG-Bank Linkage programme on a pilot basis in 1992 and in right earnest in 1996. The emphasis on linking the self-help groups of rural poor to the formal banking system was made in the mid-80s in the Asia and Pacific Regional Agricultural Credit Association and the SHG-Bank Linkage emerged as a result of that. The RBI included the programme in its "priority sector lending" and in 1999, the Government of India recognized in its Budget. A few studies commissioned by NABARD on the tenth anniversary of the launching of the programme in 2002 attempted an assessment of the programme. The findings indicate that the programme has emerged as the largest microfinance network in the world with some impressive statistics.

As of March 2002, the programme covered 461,478 SHGs with total cumulative lending of Rs 1,026 cores (US $ 218.27 million). The accumulated savings in SHGs exceeds Rs 875 crores (US $ 186.31 million) by unofficial estimates. 90% of SHGs financed were exclusive women groups. 444 banks (121 RRBs, 209

Contd...

cooperatives banks, all 27 public sector banks and 17 private banks) with a total of 17,085 branches participated in the programme providing credit to about 7.8 million poor households in 488 districts. Average loan sizes are Rs 22,240 (US $ 463) per SHG and 1,300 (US $27) per member. Today, the programme is estimated to cover well over 500,000 SHGs with cumulative loans exceeding Rs. 1,200 crore reaching over 8 million households.

Source: Kropp and Suran (2002) and Seibel and Dave (2002).

References

Mario B. Lamberte (2006), *Building Inclusive Rural Financial Markets in Central Asia*, Research on Central Asian countries submitted to Asian Development Bank.

Harper, Malcolm, 2002, *"Promotion of Self-Help Groups under the SHG Bank Linkage Programme in India"*, Paper presented at the Seminar on SHG-bank Linkage Programme at New Delhi, November 25-26, 2002.

Kropp, Erhard, W. and B.S. Suran, 2002, *Linking Banks and (Financial) Self Help Groups in India -An Assessment*, Paper presented at the Seminar on SHG-bank Linkage Programme at New Delhi, November 25-26, 2002.

19

Indian Retail Industry: A Study

Rajesh Sharma*

The retail industry is one of the largest industrial sectors in the world, contributing US$ 225 billion to the global economy, out of which the share of organized retail is 3.2%. A.T. Kearney Inc. places India, the fifth most favourite destination on the global retail development index.

As on date in India, organized retail accounts for only 4%, and is projected to grow 25% - 30% per annum to reach an astounding figure of INR 1,000 billion by 2010. This retail scenario includes malls, hypermarkets, supermarkets and departmental stores.

Less than a decade ago, in several cities there is a total of approximately 55 million sq ft of malls in various stages of completion, covering more than 300 malls all over the country. More than half of them are in Mumbai and Delhi. By 2010, approximately 600 malls are likely to be operational in India.

The mushrooming of malls is not restricted to metros alone, small cities and towns are also picking up this trend in rapid pace. This retail boom so far concentrated in the metros has started to percolate down to smaller cities and towns. This phenomenon is the direct result of the emergence of avenues to do summer jobs for students, double-income nuclear families, boom in IT-sector and India being viewed as the hub for BPO and lately, for KPO.

The mall sector growth, the glass and metal façade, glistening exterior is being seen as a clear indicator of the economic prosperity in India. The boom in the retail sector symbolizes India's transition from a stagnant, so-called developing economy to an emerging economic superpower.

Eager to cash in this "loot-n-scoot" situation real estate developers too jumped in to this 'great mall bandwagon'. Some of big and established developers have quickly acquired the skill of constructing the malls, but it seems that new entrants to the scene lack long-term vision. Malls are essentially public spaces and are basically weather controlled. Good roads and other civic facilities are crucial for large mall formats. Uninterrupted power supply is a major problem for metros like Mumbai and Delhi. A press release from shows that there will be shortage of almost 5700 MHz electricity in Mumbai in the coming months. These super structures can be a major burden on the ever exhausting electric energy pool. To solve this problem, these malls will have to relay on other energy sources like diesel-powered generators, which will cause significant pollution. In most of the suburban areas of Mumbai, the daily exodus of shoppers to various malls causes excruciating delays on the roads.

* Student, MBA in Hospitality Management, Kohinoor IMI School of Hospitality Management, Khandala, Maharashtra.

India, is a country with largest young population, of over 870 million people below the age of 45 and 300 million odd belonging to the middle class segment – the real consumers, the rapid growth in the retail sector and mall culture are very evidents. But the concern and question here is, does India have enough infrastructures to support this rapidly growing number of malls? The objective of this research is to shed some light on this question.

OBJECTIVE

A brief study to understand the need for planning of the upcoming retail structure and a visionary approach from Retail Entrepreneurs.

METHOD

- *Approach – Inductive*

  Interviews were conducted to generally as certain the expectations of people who are at the age group of 18 to 65 who visit quite often the mall and hypermarkets. Data are collected also from the people those who are residing near the malls which are situated in suburban areas of Mumbai.

- *Methodology:* Opinion survey using the interview schedule.

- *Data collection technique:* Convenient random sampling. Structured interviews of about 50 people.

- *Data clusters/Sampling strata:* The sample can be classified as a combination people from various professional and cultural back ground who were chosen depending on the availability and willingness to share the information.

- *Sample size:* 50.

- *Variables under study:* Civic and infrastructural expectations of the consumers.

- *Statistical tools:* Arithmetic mean.

- *Limitation:* Sampling errors (subjectivity of the respondent), sample size and time constraint.

- *Scope of further study:* Other dimensions of the picture, like sustainability and profitability of the too many malls in the same locality, which are designed and constructed in haste.

The following questionnaire is designed to gauge the outlook of people of different age groups residing in Mumbai about retail outlets and their experiences while visiting any mall.

The sample size of survey is 50.

Q1. Traffic jam, noise pollution, congestion are the most significant inconveniences you face due to the emergence of malls, supermarkets, shopping arcade, etc.

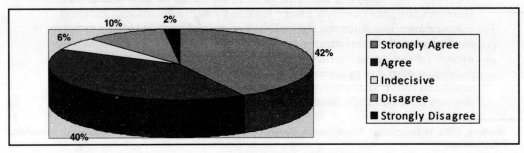

More than 80% of the interviewees agreed that, sudden increase of crowd pulled towards the area causes greater inconvenience to movement of traffic, even though malls are of great convenience while shopping is concerned.

12% of the people think that emergence of malls is not the cause of inconvenience out of 2% strongly disagree.

6% were indecisive and were not able to give their judgments on the statement.

Q2. According to you, which factor should be mandatory for malls, supermarkets, etc., to have?

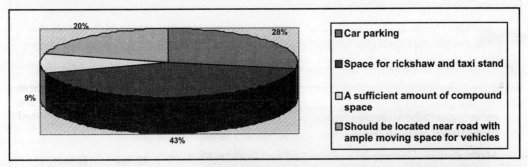

43% of the people say that they need rickshaw and taxi facilities quiet often when shopping at malls and find it very inconvenient if these facilities are not available.

28% people say that they travel to malls by their personal vehicles hence, need ample car parking space so to avoid inconvenience in finding car parking in the nearby area of the mall, especially on weekends and it will also ensure smooth flow of traffic at the entrance of the mall.

Q3. In your opinion, which is the most suitable place for malls, supermarkets, hypermarkets, etc., to be constructed?

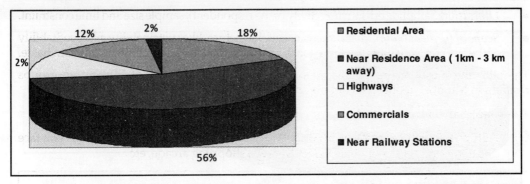

For any commercial structure, the right location is the main priority. Right location coupled with proper infrastructure can solve most of the inconveniences due to the emergence of the malls. Out of 50 people interviewed, 27 voted for malls near the residential area (1km to 3km).

Q4.   Where do you prefer shopping for your groceries?

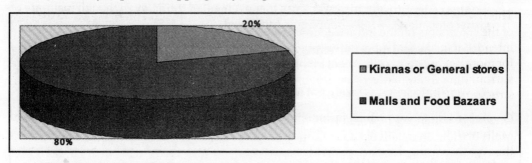

Irrespective of general stores and kiranas available at every corner of the street, 80% of the people surveyed preferred going for shopping in malls and organized food bazaars.

Q5.   Are a large number of malls, supermarkets, hypermarkets etc., needed in Mumbai?

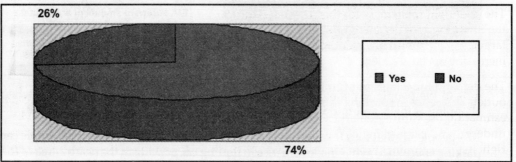

An increase in the working young people at the age group of 20 to 25 with higher disposable income due to the emergence of BPO boom and nuclear double income families have altered the whole concept of shopping and consumer behaviour in India.

Q6.   Do you think the government should have a strict regulation before allocating place for malls, supermarkets, hypermarkets, etc.?

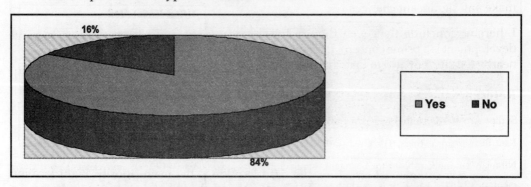

The government, being a statutory body has the power to regulate the retail sector where licensing is a concern. In fact, the law should have necessary elements to avoid any inconvenience to people in that locality or any damage to the environment.

CONCLUSION AND RECOMMENDATIONS

This research is focused on the mushrooming of the malls and hypermarkets and expectations of the consumers on the infrastructure and other facilities around them. This research is not intended to make any substantive conclusion from such limited data. However, there is scope for more research and refinement in the areas like power shortage and water supply in these surrounding areas, since these resources are highly consumed by malls and other super structures. The following are some of the recommendations.

One major difference between Indian malls and malls abroad is inadequate parking space. Malls in India are relatively a new concept and mall developers may not be able to visualize the ever-increasing demand for parking space. By providing extended space for underground and basement parking, multi-storied parking lots, more compound area for the movement of traffic and proper direction for the customers become possible. Also, the government should push the promoters of the malls and hypermarkets to submit traffic plans to reduce the threat of ever increasing traffic congestion around the proposed locality.

The underlying statement for this research is not negating the retail sector but understanding the importance of organized retail and the need for its growth. The research is specifically targeted to the suburban areas of Mumbai where the organized retail outlets are growing at an increasing speed.

The demand for estates in Mumbai is ever increasing and therefore, to get a place for retail outlets and space for parking is difficult. Thus, it is essential to have the right structural plan estimating the future demand wherein one can have the vertical growth of structure like underground car parking or one floor for car parking or having a defined compound place right in the beginning. From the research made, I can analyze that people do enjoy shopping in malls but due to unplanned structure, not only the shoppers but also the people within the locality and commuters passing through face inconvenience. The retail sector is booming and defining new standards for shopping and increasing in terms of revenue. The main reason for the emergence of malls is to give customers a better and convenient way for shopping hence, this becomes an implied responsibility for an organized retailer. It is also vital to comprehend the future demand because once a structure is built, it becomes difficult and expensive to make any significant changes.

I, hereby, conclude that even though the importance of malls is growing, sustainable development is a prime concern. It is not only important to understand the convenience of the nearby locality, but also to take into account the future demand of such localities.

References

Sudipt Arora, The United News of India (2005 March), The Mall Mania in India.

Raju Bist, *The Asia Times*, The Great India Mall Boom (2005 June).

Niranjan Mudholkar, Need for Stringent Regulations, *Times Journal for Construction and Design* (April 2006).

Shailesh Madhur, *Retailing Trends in India* , (2006, February).

Amelia Gentleman, *International Herald Tribune*, India's Malls Pulls the People Who are Buying (2006).

Zubair Ahmed, *BBC News*, Mumbai, India Ready for Shopping Mall Boom.

20

Innovative Idea-based Entrepreneurship in Services in Mumbai: A Case Study

Sameera Khan*
Dr. Pradip Manjrekar**

GROWING DOMINANCE OF THE SERVICE SECTOR IN THE INDIAN ECONOMY

Conceptual Understanding of Service Sector

The segment of the economy that provides services to its customer/consumers is known as service sector. From cutting the grass to providing super-specialty health care to exporting cutting-edge software packages to nirvana offered by enlightened gurus, service industries in India play an integral part in the daily activities of one billion people of the country. The services offered would include professional, legal and technical expertise, public utilities, and education, financial services, and government services, spiritual services by various religious groups and social services by NGOs.

Definition of Service Sector

The U. S. Department of Commerce's Bureau of Economic Analysis (BEA) broadly defines service industries as those providing products that cannot be stored and are consumed at the place and time of purchase. Generally, these services include only the performance of actions on behalf of the customers and have little, if any, tangible substance. For example, a Chartered Accountant doing the statutory audit and filing the Returns.

Growth of Service Sector

Post-1991 Liberalisation, Privatization and Globalization (LPG) the service sector share of contribution to India's GDP has been steadily raising from a meagre 36.67% in 1985-86 to about 53% in 2006-07.

An examination of the above data implies transition of the Indian economy from traditional agro-centric to services dominated implying better standards of living for the people. In the light of the above analysis, *one important factor emerging is that sunny days are ahead for service sector*. Innovative entrepreneurship in services supported by venture capitalists, angel

* M.Phil Scholar, Padmashree Dr. D.Y. Patil University, Navi Mumbai.
** Professor, Dr. D.Y. Patil Institute of Management Studies, CBD Belapur, Navi Mumbai.

financiers and given the pro-growth and developments policies pursued by the government and reasonable political stability places India as Rapidly Developing Economy (RDE), next only to China in the world.

INNOVATIVE IDEAS AND ENTREPRENEURSHIP

Importance of Bright Ideas

The intellectuals, thinkers, academics, and business pundits all agree on the importance of good ideas to future business survival – and that of the individual and society. Michael Eisner, Chief Executive of Disney, commented: *"The pursuit of ideas is the only one that matters. You can always find people to do almost everything else."*

Ideas are like diamonds in the dust—lying around unappreciated until an entrepreneur has the insight to spot them, pick them up and turn them into profitable business ventures.

Apart from rationality and analysis the spark for must of the business ideas come from "intuition". When you are in a situation where you can "smell' that something is wrong/right "the sixth sense" is playing its subtle role.

The inspiration for new ideas, unfortunately, stems from mostly adverse conditions, such as threat of closure/extinction/breakdown/huge losses and a strong urge to survive/grow/expand in the face of cut-throat competition. "Necessity breeds invention" is a timeless cliché. It would be apt to cite an illustration by a government-owned service providing organization, which introduced innovative practices to keep the competitors at bay.

Illustration: The Kerala Postal Department has tied-up with REVA—a Bangalore based eco-friendly car producer to deliver speed post articles in and around Thiruvananthapuram. Besides, these cars would drive up to the doorsteps of people living in narrow lanes. On an average, each battery powered car will cover 60 kilometres daily delivering around 5000 parcels. Postal officials claim the schemes introduced by the department recently have drawn in more customers. Hence, they say, innovative ideas like the introduction of electric cars are needed to improve customer services. The postal department also hopes these innovative value added services will give the private courier companies a run for their money.

Innovative Entrepreneurs

Entrepreneurship and Innovation go hand in hand. In fact, they are two sides of the same coin. In today's market-driven economy the mantra is "Innovate or Die". Economists predict, the Indian economy in an accelerated transition next phase/avatar will be an Entrepreneurial Economy driven by entrepreneurial ventures/practices based on Innovative products, services, logistics and initiatives. Entrepreneurs are the prime movers of an economy and innovation is the specific tool of entrepreneurs, the means by which they exploit change as an opportunity for a different business or a different service.

INTRODUCTION

Entrepreneurship is the practice of starting new organizations, particularly new businesses, generally in response to identified opportunities. Entrepreneurship is often a difficult undertaking, as a vast majority of new businesses fail. Entrepreneurial activities are substantially different, depending on the type of organization that is being started. Entrepreneurship ranges in scale from solo projects (even involving the entrepreneur only part-time) to major undertakings creating many job opportunities. Many "high-profile" entrepreneurial ventures seek venture capital or angel funding in order to raise capital to build the business. Angel investors generally seek returns of 20-30% and more extensive involvement in the business. Many kinds of organizations now exist to support would-be entrepreneurs, including specialized government agencies, business incubators, science parks, and some NGOs.

The understanding of entrepreneurship owes much to the work of economist Joseph Schumpeter and the Austrian economists such as Ludwig von Mises and Friedrich von Hayek. In Schumpeter (1950), an entrepreneur is a person who is willing and able to convert a new idea or invention into a successful innovation. Entrepreneurship forces "creative destruction" across markets and industries, simultaneously creating new products and business models. In this way, creative destruction is largely responsible for the dynamism of industries and long-run economic growth. Despite Schumpeter's early 20th century contributions, the traditional microeconomic theory of economics has had little room for entrepreneurs in its theoretical frameworks (instead assuming that resources would find each other through a price system).

Entrepreneurs have many of the same character traits as leaders. Similar to the early great man theories of leadership; trait-based theories of entrepreneurship are now increasingly being called into question. Entrepreneurs are often contrasted with managers and administrators who are said to be more methodical and less prone to risk-taking. Although such person-centric models of entrepreneurship have shown to be of questionable validity, a vast but clearly dated literature studying the entrepreneurial personality found that certain traits seem to be associated with entrepreneurs.

OBJECTIVES

Context

The Indian economy has been steadily growing at 8 to 8.5% for the last three years and economists expect that the momentum of growth to continue in the next few years. This growth has been made visible with soaring income levels, increased Foreign Direct Investment (FDI), and mega acquisitions by Indian companies and the rising standard of living of the people. As a spin-off effect the demand for essential commodities, energy, real estate, luxury goods and so on have multiplied.

The new generation kids armed with abundant disposable income and a consumeristic life-style, chanting the mantra 'more is less', have an insatiable appetite for new goods and services hitherto unheard of. It is in this context of assured market, entrepreneurs with innovative ideas and ability to 'think out of the box' and create new products and services come-into fill the void.

Therefore, the primary objectives of the study are:

1. To know the overwhelming importance of innovative ideas for the success of business enterprise in services.

2. To determine at least two motivating factors that lead individual's entrepreneurial growth.

3. To understand the role and influence of family members in the transformation of ideas from seed stage to successful business models.

4. To find out relationship for entrepreneurship with job satisfaction.

5. To understand the relation between education level and risk appetite.

RESEARCH QUESTIONS

The above objectives give raise to the following questions.

i) How important is an innovative idea for the success of entrepreneurial ventures in services sector?

ii) What are the two motivating factors that drive people to take to entrepreneurship in services?

iii) How important is the support of parent/spouse in the seed stage?

iv) What is the role of banks/specialized institutions in promoting entrepreneurship?

v) Why do the entrepreneurs hesitate to take partners?

vi) Do the successful entrepreneurs have any social commitment?

vii) Is there any relation between job satisfaction/dissatisfaction on entrepreneurship?

viii) What is relation between education and attitude towards undertaking risk?

ix) How useful this study can be for young entrepreneurs sitting on the edge?

x) What is the value addition of this study to the available body of knowledge?

SCOPE AND LIMITATIONS

The scope of the present study in the first place, falls in the area of unearthing the need for new products/services in the market. Secondly, having understood the real need, the entrepreneur creates a new service or product in order to satisfy the demand and earns a profit.

As the study is exploratory in nature, that is, to understand how idea-based entrepreneurs in services industry have made it big. Five successful entrepreneurs have been profiled adapting the method of structured interview. The method is subject to certain inherent limitations such as interviewer bias, respondent bias, lack of subject knowledge on the part of the interviewed, concealing of important facts and so on. Inferences have been drawn based on five samples adapting case study approach. Will they truly, represent the universe? This is another limiting factor.

Nevertheless, the wealth of learning derived from these five cases aspires to be a pioneering attempt at what could become a phenomenon even if a few thousand from the 34% under the age group of 20 from one billion people.

RESEARCH METHODOLOGY

Data Collection: The data needed for this study has been obtained from secondary sources as well as primary sources.

Secondary Sources: The secondary data have been obtained from the following sources:

- Reference Books
- Magazines and Journals
- Newspapers
- Internet Websites

Primary Sources: We have set three parameters for selection of entrepreneurs for case study method. They are:

1. Innovative idea-based services.
2. Middle class background.
3. Should be a first generation entrepreneur.

On the basis of the above parameters, Eve entrepreneurs were carefully chosen from a pool of entrepreneurs. Three of them were men and two women. They were contacted by email. Academic purpose of the study was made known to them.

In consultation with the guide, it was decided to adapt structured interview (open-ended) as a method of data collection to obtain qualitative data. Interview schedule was prepared and sent to all the four respondents by email in order to save time on interview and avoid errors. Appointments were taken over phone/email.

The researcher met the respondent face-to-face as fixed earlier. The interview was conducted as per the interview schedule in English and the response was recorded on a tape recorder.

Later on, the researcher typed the interview questions and answers on computer and sent them back to the respondent to ensure accuracy of data content and meaning. Discrepancies, if any, were corrected. Thereafter, as a proof of validation the respondent was asked to affix his/her signature along with organization seal on the document. They have been preserved with the researcher.

Sample Size

Qualitative data were collected from a sample size of two case studies.

REVIEW OF LITERATURE

In this section of study, the researcher shows in a nutshell, previous studies of researches, papers, information posted on different websites on the subject.

In the panel discussion titled, "How can innovation and entrepreneurship help India succeed in global markets" held to coincide with the launch of the Indian Edition of knowledge@Wharton the panelists said, "Lots of opportunities exist for innovation and entrepreneurship to thrive in India, especially in areas such as, technology, health care, education, rural marketing and social services".

Dr. J. S. Gandhi and Dr. Ganesan, noted economists trace the steady increase in the services sector contribution to GDP in the Indian economy at the expense of manufacturing sector. The exponential growth of this sector would transform the Indian economy into a developed economy provided the momentum is sustained, they hold.

Incisive studies by Dr. David C. McClelland and his associates have led to a much clearer understanding of the characteristics of entrepreneurs.

According to Anand Saxena, a supportive family is the bedrock upon which lives and careers of entrepreneurs are built. This could not be more true anywhere than in the case of first generation entrepreneurs who are the prime targets of our study.

The researcher, in order to learn the role of commercial banks, specialized financial institutions and dedicated entrepreneurship development institutes set up by the government of India/ sponsored by apex financial institutions visited the official websites. Notable among them are: Entrepreneurship Development Institute of India, Ahmedabad; Institute for Entrepreneurship Development, Guwahati; Indira Gandhi Institute of Development Research, Mumbai; State Bank of India, Small Industries Development Bank of India, Maharashtra Knowledge Corporation and NASSCOM.

CASE STUDY 1

Innovation in Services Marketing

Role of Family: Wilson D' Abreo hails from a middle-class service family in the extended suburbs of Mumbai. His wife is a school teacher. In the year 1994, this first generation entrepreneur took the bold decision of starting 'MicroIan Computer' at Andheri (East), the Silicon Valley of Mumbai.

Being aware of the risk-averse mind of his parents, he did not discuss with them his idea of starting an enterprise of his own. Whereas, he confided everything with his wife. Together with her, he gave shape to his idea. She, being a teacher having regular monthly income took upon herself the financial burden of running the family in the absence of husband's income. This relieved him of his financial obligation to the family and gave an opportunity to invest all his time and energy to translate his idea into a business venture. He gives full credit to his wife for her unstinted support and co-operation.

His peers gave full encouragement, support and necessary advice at the seed stage. He candidly admits that a couple of them were skeptical and openly questioned his decision to give-up a secure, salaried job.

Education: He has successfully completed his Diploma in Electronics & Radio Engineering and Diploma in Sound and Television Engineering from a reputed Catholic educational institution in Mumbai.

Job Experience: His first work assignment was at Zenith India Limited. He joined the company as 'Trainee Engineer' and eight years down the line went on to become 'Service Manager' Bombay branch. He hasn't worked in any other place. He says this is due to learning opportunities, good work environment and high job satisfaction at Zenith.

It was during this period at Zenith, that the entrepreneurial bug bit him. By the end of his 7 year, he was seriously exploring markets and evaluating business opportunities for sales and service of computers. However, he humbly admits he secured enough knowledge and honed his business skills during the several in-house marketing programmes that he attended and live market exposure at Zenith Computers.

Market Survey: Putting to use his experience and market knowledge gained at Zenith Computer, he did a sample market survey going door to door. Again all by himself, his survey revealed a huge marketing opportunity for computer maintenance waiting to be tapped and the market promising to grow in the future.

Innovative Idea to Business Enterprise Teething Stages: His initial investment was Rs. 5000 from his savings. This, he needed to pay one month rent in advance to the landlord for the room taken on rental basis. He did not require much investment. As he proudly claims, this is due to his innovative strategy of taking service/maintenance contracts in the beginning, for which the contract amount was received in advance. In the early days, he did not employ anyone. He went door-to-door seeking, obtaining contract and doing maintenance work all by himself. He was the owner and worker. Over a period of time, this strategy brought in huge savings which was ploughed back into business and utilized as seed capital for conducting business of purchase of parts, assembly and sale of computers under the company's logo MLC. Since then there has been no turning back in the business.

Role of Institutions: Mr. Wilson claims he never sought any help, monetary or otherwise, either from banks/financial institutions like SIDBI or specialized entrepreneur development institutes at any time of business.

He has also not taken/attended any entrepreneurial course run by different entrepreneurship development institutes spread across the country. With the changing face of market and technology, he says that he needs to attend at least on a part-time basis, a few sector-specific programmes in the near future. He is aware of the worth of attending the programmes.

Preference to go alone rather than seeking Partnership: According to him, as of now, the business is quite satisfactory and smooth. Often, he thought of taking someone as partner to share the burdens. Based on his observation over the years, he is convinced that partnership is as option not an its demerits outweigh the merits. Now and in the future, he would do business of his own. As a fall out of this decision, in the administration, he has inducted his close relatives in key positions. "They are loyal and take field decisions in the best interests of the company", he says.

Strategy to keep Customer Loyalty: Claims Wilson, "During my 13 years of business I haven't lost a single customer." A tall claim indeed. Asked about his USP, he attributes it to his "customer-focus, and one-to-one relations, efficient service on time and honesty in dealings". He intends to extend this brand image by opening a new branch at Vasai.

Another Innovative Idea ready to take off: Also on the anvil, his next innovative child 'One-stop-maintenance-stores' at Andheri (E). This store, to be designed on lines of super market will be providing maintenance/service of computers and accessories of all brands and types.

Social Commitment: Not to forget his obligation, Wilson sponsors a child's education expenses for one year. This, he has been doing for the last 5 years. Besides, he regularly donates to CRY and UNICEF. He looks forward to doing more in the coming years.

Motivating Factors: The chief factors that motivated Wilson to take the plunge in his own words "my desire to be my own boss, work for me rather than work for someone else. My confidence that I could contribute to my family and society by being on my own more than that I could have done in the employment of somebody else".

His Recipe for Success: Innovative ideas, honesty and simplicity. A good business idea is a must for business. It is the first thing you need. Simplicity endears you to customers. But it is honesty in dealings that wins and sustains customer loyalty and builds long-term relations with customers says Wilson. Aspiring entrepreneurs better take note.

CASE STUDY 2

Consulting Services by Leading Entrepreneur

Profile: Futurz HR Solutions has been in the business of People Consulting and Services for about two years now. We are actively consulting with top notch companies providing Staffing Solutions and HR Services. Futurz is a leader in the employment services industry, offering customers a continuum of services to meet their needs throughout the employment and business cycle. The company specializes in permanent, temporary and contract recruitment; employee assessment; training; career transition; organizational consulting; and professional financial services. Futurz nationwide network enables the company to meet the needs of its customers, including small and medium size enterprises in all industry sectors, as well as the world's largest multinational corporation. The focus of Futurz work is on raising productivity through improved quality, efficiency and cost-reduction, enabling customers to concentrate on their core business activities.

History: Founded in 2005 to offer, permanent staffing business initially for IT, BPO & Finance Verticals located @ prime location in Mumbai, Malad, with a 5000 sq ft carpet area office. Now, Futurz offers RPO, Staffing Solutions, Talent Acquisition & Permanent Staffing, and Training & Learning Solutions in India and since then we have been growing more than 100% year over year, We bought our own building at Malad with 10000 sq.

The Entrepreneur: Farhan Azmi is the Director of **FuturZ HR Solutions Pvt. Ltd.** In addition to his day-to-day leadership responsibilities, Farhan plays a key role in leading and shaping the market in the region. Farhan started FuturZ HR in 2005 specialising in the provision of recruitment services to the financial services and the BPO sector. His career developed with the group through team leadership, business management and overall strategic management and development of finance and professional services business across India and the United Kingdom. Prior to FuturZ, Farhan spent three years developing his knowledge and expertise of the financial services and the BPO sector.

Farhan is a Graduate from Mumbai

At the age of 22, he has reached a mark where people recognize him in this corporate world as "Mr Commitment" in terms of getting the task done. His goal in life is to become the best recruitment service provider globally.

Corporate Social Responsibility: **FuturZ HR Solutions Pvt. Ltd.** understands "We have an obligation to the community, to operate in a socially responsible manner. We believe that corporate social responsibility is best achieved by embedding the following into all operational aspects of our business: (a) our core values; (b) our corporate codes of ethics; and (c) policies, procedures and practices that deliver benefits to our people, community and environment and that result in responsible and ethical business conduct. We commit to the ongoing continued improvement of business policies, practices and strategies that impact and/or result in productive and positive outcomes in all areas."

Recruitment: The Top Priority Issues facing Executives: FuturZ Temporary Staffing division provides a total staffing solution to clients. FuturZ helps its clients to manage their short and long-term objectives by establishing a co-employment relationship & taking full responsibility for all compliances, administration, and HR activities related to all employees on assignment.

FuturZ works on three models for the temporary staffing vertical:

Temping: Identifying and recruiting candidates based on the clients requirement and thereon managing the employees in terms of other requirements e.g. joining, Induction and onboarding.

Payrolling: Transitioning pre-identified employees of the clients onto FuturZ roles & managing the HR, administrator & regulatory compliances.

Settlement: FuturZ will save time of its clients for settlement of pre-identified employees who have resigned from the services and avoid interfaces with other existing operations.

Also some of these below services to our clients

Services Offering

- Just-in-time recruitment
- Temporary to permanent recruitment
- Complete outplacement
- Quality just-in-time staff for all requirements
- Domain-specialist consultants with first-hand
- Experience and knowledge of the sectors they represent
- Tailored solutions based on our specific clients' requirements
- End-to-end back end support for our clients
- Highly cost effective staffing solutions
- Headcount flexibility
- Statutory compliance
- Strong database of candidates

DATA ANALYSIS/INTERPRETATION/FINDINGS

OBJECTIVE NO. 1

To know the overwhelming importance of innovative ideas for the success of business in services.

Case study no.1 – WILSON – innovative ideas are very important

Case study no.2 – FARHAN AZMI – strongly believes in innovative ideas

Innovative idea is certainly not the be all and end all. Most ideas could do is to give an impetus for a flying start in the transition of and innovative idea into a commercially viable venture.

There are a host of other factors that aid or hinder, which deserve due attention. The study brings out three such aiding factors that would certainly give an impetus for giving a flying start: Belief in one's idea, good communication skills and well thought out strategy. The hindering factors are internal to the entrepreneur himself/herself.

OBJECTIVE NO. 2

To determine at least two motivating factors that lead individual's entrepreneurial growth.

Case 1

- Strong desire to be on my own
- Strong belief in idea and ability

Case 2

- Desire to be my own boss
- Flexible working hours and mobility in operations

Result/Interpretation

The desire to be one's own boss is the chief motivator in one out of two cases. In one case, it is the need to be on my own idea; the second motivator varies, like: intellectual challenge and satisfaction, confidence.

FINDINGS

Joseph Schumpter, noted researcher in the area of entrepreneurship stated, way back in 1930 that there are primarily three factors that motivate a person to become an entrepreneur. They are: (i) the desire for power and independence, (ii) the will to succeed, and (iii) the satisfaction of getting things done. The present exploratory study on the entrepreneurs' reinforces Prof. Schumpter's views that: (i) desire for money and freedom to do what they like; (ii) hard work and determination to succeed; and (iii) sense of accomplishment and satisfaction. These three important motivators prompt entrepreneurs even in the 21st century to take to entrepreneurship.

OBJECTIVE NO. 3

To understand the role and influence of family members in the transformation of ideas from the seed stage to successful business models.

Entrepreneurs from both the case strongly agree to this objective.

Findings

There have been many researchers on the topic of the importance of entrepreneurship. Which shown that family support is important for entrepreneur.

OBJECTIVE NO. 4

To find out the relationship of entrepreneurship with job satisfaction.

Interpretation

Out of the two, one people who had high or very high job satisfaction too embraced entrepreneurship. This goes to prove that job dissatisfaction is not one of the reasons for people taking to entrepreneurship. People having high job satisfaction also do take to entrepreneurship.

OBJECTIVE NO. 5

To understand the relation between education level and risk appetite.

Interpretation

It is the very evident that the professionally qualified reduced risks to as low as they could, whereas graduates undertook moderately risky ventures. The least educated took recourse to higher risk ventures. The risk appetite among the professionally educated is low.

CONCLUSION

People with entrepreneurial talent propel economic growth with innovative ideas, products and services that are found in every society at the infant stage of business. Family support, peers' encouragement and easy availability of institutional finance provide a conducive environment for entrepreneurship to grow and flourish. In today's knowledge economy, in addition to the conventional entrepreneurial characteristics, the new-age entrepreneur needs to hone his skills in risk-management, marketing, finance and is also duty bound to make some worthwhile contributions to society.

Inspiration and Motivation

This twenty-first century is being touted as the new entrepreneurial era because of hectic entrepreneurship specifically in innovative service ideas. The case studies, in this study of five first generation entrepreneurs and their remarkable success is sure to inspire and motivate many young men and women to undertake entrepreneurship and replicate their success.

Innovative Ideas as a Cutting-edge Magic Tool to Fight Relentless Competition and Sustain Vibrant Growth

The case studies presented in this investigation, amply demonstrate how critical innovative ideas for the success of entrepreneurial ventures. This is an important lesson to be noted how innovation in different spheres of business, education and life in various hues and colours could facilitate/drive sustainable competitive advantage and rapid growth for the country in an increasingly competitive environment.

Innovation as Core Competency

This study highlights the growing recognition that innovation is the core competency for success, sustaining growth and the new wealth in today's knowledge economy.

21

Global Business of Auto Ancillary: A Case Study – An Entrepreneurial Perspective

Rhizu Krishna*
Dr. Pradip Manjrekar**
Dr. R.B. Smarta***

The Indian Auto Ancillary Industry is expanding at a very fast rate. Entrepreneurial opportunities exist for exporting various auto components across the globe.

In the present paper, the authors have taken the example of auto components and successfully identified for the export markets for them. This type of work could be useful for any potential entrepreneur.

INTRODUCTION

Global business is the most powerful and definite force in the development of modern civilization. Fuelled by scientific research and development, the evolution of global Business is synonymous with man's struggle to improve condition of life on the planet, will and desire to create altogether new ways of communicating, working, creating, living, thinking and continues to transform where we are. Global business is so deeply embedded in the human psyche and our desire to exercise control over the environment, that global business is an essential element of virtually every facet of life. As such the way it is managed and practiced is a matter of critical importance having far reaching implications for international consumers, business and society at large. Global business and its knowledge management has established themselves as the engines of the new international economy bringing improvements in overseas production and quality with the rapid rise of information intensive marketing system, supply chain management, international marketing research and development.

Global business in Auto Ancillary has reached staggering proportions. Earlier, the major producers of auto ancillary were Western countries and Western MNC's. However, since, 1990 the picture is changing dramatically and the Indian auto ancillary industry has made a massive mark in this area globally. Now, global auto component manufactures are sourcing

---
* Ph.D. Student, S.N.D.T. University, Mumbai.
** Ph.D. Guide, Padmashree Dr. D.Y. Patil University, Navi Mumbai.
*** Ph.D. Guide, S.N.D.T. University, Mumbai.

their requirements from India in a big way. This provides an opportunity to entrepreneurs to export their auto components.

- The automotive industry is the industry involved in the design, development, manufacture, marketing and sale of motor vehicles.

- In 2006, more than 69 million motor vehicles, including cars and commercial vehicles were produced worldwide.

- In year 2006, 16 million new automobiles were sold in the US, 15 million in Western Europe, 7 million in China and 1 million in India.

- In 2007, the markets in Canada, USA, Western Europe and Japan are stagnating, while those in South America (especially Brazil) and Asia (South Korea and India) are growing.

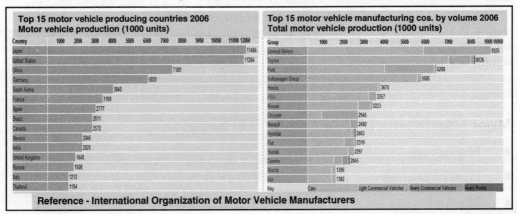

Reference - International Organization of Motor Vehicle Manufacturers

INDIAN AUTO ANCILLARY INDUSTRY

The Indian automotive components industry's annual turnover (for FY 2003) was US$ 6.73 billion (global industry of US $737 billion). With a compounded growth rate of 20-25 %, the growth in India's auto components exports is much faster than that of the domestic market (10-14%).

The auto ancillary industry caters to three broad categories of the market:

- Original Equipment Manufacturers (OEM) or vehicle manufacturers that comprises of 25% total demand.

- Replacement market, which comprises 65% of the total demand.

- Export market, which comprises primarily of international tier I suppliers and constitutes 10% of total demand.

The auto ancillary industry can be further divided into six main segments:

- ***Engine Parts:*** Engine assembly, fall into three broad categories: Core engine parts; fuel delivery system; and others. These also include products such as, Pistons, Piston Rings, Engine Valves, Carburettors and Diesel-based Fuel Delivery Systems.

- ***Electrical Parts:*** The main products in this category include starter motors, generators, spark plugs and distributors.

- *Drive Transmission and Steering Parts:* Gears, wheels, steering systems, axles and clutches are the important components in this category.

- *Suspension and Braking Parts:* These include Brakes, Leaf Springs, Shock Absorbers.

- *Equipment:* This includes headlights, dashboard Instruments.

- *Others:* Sheet metal components and plastic molded parts are two of the major components in this category.

Automobile Components Manufacturers Association (ACMA)

The Automotive Component Manufacturers Association of India (ACMA), with a membership of over 365 companies, has been the Indian auto component industry's spokesman for the last 38 years. ACMA has a membership of over 365 companies that contribute 90% of the total output in the organized sector. The Association's active involvement in trade promotion, technology upgradation, quality enhancement and collection and dissemination of information have made it a vital catalyst for the progress of the industry. ACMA is represented on a number of panels, committees and councils of the Government of India through which it helps in the formulation of policies pertaining to the Indian automotive industry.

Major Manufactures of Auto Ancillaries in India

- Bharat Forge

- Lumax Industries

- Rico Auto

- Sundaram Clayton

- Jai Auto Engineering Works

- Windsor Exports

- Chennai Auto Ancillary Industrial Infrastructure Upgradation Company (CAAIIUC)

Duroshox

Situated in Pune, India, Duroshox began business in 1986 as an ancillary to Kinetic Engineering Limited. Pune is the engineering hub and the automotive capital of India and houses the plants of several automotive manufacturers.

The demand for its products has led to a period of expansion and today the company is catering to the engineering product requirements of some of the leading vehicle manufacturers in India, Europe and the USA. With over a hundred different types of products under its belt, the company has the solution for many engineering product requirements.

The company believes in action. For the sake of timely accomplishment, the people at Duroshox are ever willing to walk that extra mile with a single focus of serving their customers better. Duroshox is an ISO 9001 certified company and also in the process of implementing TS 16949 quality systems.

Duroshox's People

The company's internal structure is designed to focus on its key functions: Production, quality assurance, finance, administration, corporate management, sales and global marketing. The firm's workforce comprises of over 115 individuals working with a common goal of continuous improvement & constantly striving to exceed customer expectations.

The people in our organization are the key to innovation and success. Just as we are dedicated for growing our business, we are dedicated for growing their careers with trainings and development opportunities.

Duroshox's R&D

Duroshox has devoted a significant investment in time and resource for research and development (R&D).

Strengths of Duroshox's R&D

- Customer's requirements (Time and Quality)
- Rapid route selection
- Process innovation
- Product development
- Industrial scale-up

Features and Benefits

- Flexibility and reliability
- Continuous and confidential information
- Quick response in feasibility study and samples preparation
- Fast evaluation of multi-step organic synthesis
- Complete process development flow

Duroshox Regulatory Compliance Capabilities

TS 16949 quality systems.

Audited by global and domestic customer and internal audit team.

Constantly reviewing and upgrading and standards according to new guidelines and latest requirements of internationally recognized bodies.

Objectives of the Present Study

- To find markets globally for their products
    1. Shock Absorbers
    2. Auto Electrical

- To identify the companies in these markets i.e., the US and Europe who consume these components.

Methodology

- By surfing the Internet.

- By sending enquiries through e-mails to companies consuming these components.

- By literature survey.

Discussion

	Discussed Questions	Proposed Answers
1.	Where are the companies consuming the two selected auto ancillary products generally located?	Companies consuming these products are predominantly situated in the U.S. and Europe. These companies are mainly large ones having large consumption, i.e.: • General Motors (US) • Ford Motor Company (US) • Chrysler LLC (US) • BMW (Germany) • Volkswagen AG (Germany) • PSA Peugeot Citroën (France) • Renault SA (France) • Fiat Group SpA (Italy) • Daimler AG (Germany)
2.	Where do the above companies normally import from?	These companies normally import from China, Israel and Australia auto component manufacturers. However, the Duroshox auto ancillary manufacturer, as mentioned above supplies to auto companies in the U.S. and Europe.

CONCLUSION

The auto ancillary industry is a growing industry. The growth and achievement of the Indian auto industry during the last five decades has been phenomenal and has been rated as one of the highest among the developing countries. It has more scope for exports. Auto ancillary industry and auto ancillary exports are a good option for new upcoming entrepreneurs, provided the auto ancillary has excellent features (international certifications, R&D, Quality Control) and the pricing is very competitive.

References

Sak Onkvisit and John J. Shaw, *International Marketing*, Prentice Hall of India (P) Ltd., New Delhi, 1999.

William F. Glueck, *Business Policy and Strategic Management*, McGraw Hill 1980.

Francis Cherumilam, *International Business*, Wheeler Publishing, New Delhi, 1998.

Eric Wiklund, *International Marketing, Marketing Exports Pay off*, McGraw Hill, New York, 1986.

International Organization of Motor Vehicle Manufacturers.

www.dir.indiamart.com

www.indianindustry.com/automobile

www.auto.indiamart.com

www.researchandmarkets.com

www.mgmt.purdue.edu

www.globalautoindustry.com

22

Corporate Entrepreneurship: The Creation of New Businesses within a Firm – A Case Study of Mahesh Tutorials

Shrenik Kotecha*
Dr. Pradip Manjrekar**

Corporate entrepreneurship, which refers to the efforts of corporations to generate new business, has, until recently, received far less attention. Indeed, to those who view large firms as bureaucratic and inhospitable to creativity and innovation, the term "corporate entrepreneurship" is an oxymoron.

The 1950s and 1960s image of the corporate executive in the conservative grey flannel suit was replaced in the 1980s and 1990s as an overly compensated short-term thinker, unwilling to innovate and take risks. And in the post-Enron era, the word "corporate" followed by the word "entrepreneurship" conjures up dark images of greedy corporate executives who find creative and innovative ways, whether legal or not, to line their pockets with millions of dollars at the expense of shareholders, employees and the public at large.

However, ironically, we can still see trends of a growing interest in the use of corporate entrepreneurship by corporations to enhance the innovative abilities of their employees and, at the same time, increase corporate success through the creation of new corporate ventures. In certain conditions, corporate managers have to take more risk and have to venture into entrepreneurial activities. Certain studies show that many corporations struggle to manage the inherent contradictions of corporate entrepreneurship, due to tensions between the notions of individual initiative on the one hand and conventional corporate management on the other. While corporate entrepreneurship offers a number of merits and is at times a strategic necessity, it also throws up a number of issues, the most important being the risk of strategic misalignment and the risk of competitive advantage erosion. Success of these ventures, therefore, would depend on the organization's ability to nurture an environment conducive to a peaceful co-existence of entrepreneurship and traditional management.

* Director, Mahesh Tutorials.
* Professor & Head, Research & Extension Centre, Dr. D.Y. Patil Institute of Management Studies, Navi Mumbai.

This paper, through literature review, attempts to explore the meaning and domain of corporate entrepreneurship, the need for entrepreneurial activity within an organization, conditions that favour corporate entrepreneurship, synergy between corporate entrepreneurship and strategic management, strategic benefits of corporate entrepreneurship and issues inherent to corporate entrepreneurship.

INTRODUCTION

Corporate entrepreneurship is an evolving area of research. Today, there is no universally acceptable definition of corporate entrepreneurship (Gautam & Verma, 1997). Authors use many terms to refer to different aspects of corporate entrepreneurship: Intrapreneurship (Kuratko *et al*, 1990), internal corporate entrepreneurship (Schollhammer, 1982), corporate ventures (Ellis and Taylor, 1987; MacMillan *et al*., 1986), venture management (Veciana, 1996), new ventures (Roberts, 1980) and, internal corporate venturing (Burgelman, 1984).

Despite this growing interest in corporate entrepreneurship, there appears to be nothing near a consensus on what it is. Some scholars emphasizing its analogue to new business creation by individual entrepreneurs, view corporate entrepreneurship as a concept that is limited to new venture creation within existing organisations (Burgelman, 1984). Others argue that the concept of corporate entrepreneurship should encompass the struggle of large firms to renew them by carrying out new combinations of resources that alter the relationships between them and their environments (Baumol, 1986; Burgelman, 1983). According to Zahra (1991), corporate entrepreneurship refers to the process of creating new business within established firms to improve organisational profitability and enhance a firm's competitive position or the strategic renewal of existing business.

Burgelman (1984), conceptualised the definition of corporate entrepreneurship as a process of "extending the firm's domain of competence and corresponding opportunity set through internally generated new resource combinations". The term "new resource combinations" is interpreted to be synonymous with innovation in the Schumpeterian sense. Thus, corporate entrepreneurship is conceived of as the effort to extend an organisation's competitive advantage through internally generated innovations that significantly alter the balance of competition within an industry or create entirely new industries.

According to Sathe (1989), corporate entrepreneurship is a process of organisational renewal that has two distincts but related dimensions: Innovation and venturing, and strategic stress creating new business through market developments on by undertaking product, process, technological and administrative innovations.

DIFFERENT FLAVOURS OF CORPORATE ENTREPRENEURSHIP

The concept of Corporate Entrepreneurship, initially called "Intrapreneuring" is essentially "start-up" entrepreneurship turned inward. The literature available in this area, loosely identifies four types of corporate entrepreneurship, one of which, if not properly applied, may artificially stretch the notion of Entrepreneurship beyond the original definition first proffered by Schumpeter. These four types of corporate entrepreneurship are: Corporate Venturing, Intrapreneuring, Organizational Transformation, and Industry Rule Breaking.

(a) Corporate Venturing

Corporate venturing involves starting a business within a business, usually emanating from a core competency or process. A bank, for example, which has a core competency in transaction processing, turns this into a separate business and offers transaction processing to other companies who need mass processing of information.

In some organizations, functions like product development are tasked with being the people responsible for new venture creation. Ventures usually involve the creation, nurturing, and development of a new business that comes from within the old business, but represents a significantly new product or market opportunity. Unlike simple line extensions, ventures require vast amounts of new learning on the part of the organization.

New, but not totally foreign competencies are required, or current competencies are leveraged in a completely new way.

For example, Mott's, a subsidiary of Cadbury Schweppes, embarked on a journey to develop a more creative, innovative and entrepreneurial culture. Mott's, a conservative and successful organization, agreed to double shareholder value every three years. This tremendously aggressive goal couldn't be reached by developing new businesses and new markets. Mott's had a superb back office set-up honed over the years to support their field sales force. One idea emanating from a Mott's corporate intrapreneur was the idea of Mott's selling this back office competency to smaller companies whose current back office support was either poor or absent. Mott's would then be in a completely new business, that of outsourcing by leveraging a core competency.

Thermo-Electron provides another example of venturing. They attempted to take their laser technology, which had been historically used in medical, military, and industrial markets, to the beauty/cosmetic market. They designed a laser, which was purpose-built to painlessly and effectively remove facial and body hair from women in a salon setting. While their core competency was laser technology, this market was totally new and required tremendous learning on the part of the company.

(b) Intrapreneuring

Intrapreneuring, first espoused by Pinchot, is an attempt to take the mindset and behaviours that external entrepreneurs have, and inculcate these characteristics into their employees. Sometimes, the company wants every employee to act like an entrepreneur, but a more typical approach involves the targeting of a subset of managers to act as corporate entrepreneurs. Companies usually want this cadre of corporate entrepreneurs to identify and develop spin-ups (innovations in current businesses that can lead to substantial growth opportunities) or to create an environment where more innovation and entrepreneurial behavior is evidenced.

Siemens-Nixdorf, a former subsidiary of the giant Siemens AG, located in Germany, provides an excellent example of intrapreneuring in 1995; they embarked on a two year process which attempted to systematically create corporate entrepreneurs out of 300 line managers inside the Siemens Nixdorf (SNI) division.

Gerhard Schulmeyer, the President of Siemens US, embarked on an organization-wide change programme to turn a rather staid, conservative, risk-averse culture into a more opportunistic, market-focused, fast, flexible organization. His goal was to compete more effectively with the likes of HP, IBM, Arthur Andersen and the small aggressive boutique IT vendors increasingly present in the marketplace. Schulmeyer brought in new board members from the outside and a number of internal change efforts when Babson was approached to design and deliver a corporate entrepreneurship programme to these 300 unit managers. SNI's goal was to turn 300 unit mangers into intrapreneurs who would be close to their markets and be skilled in spotting high potential new business opportunities. In addition, they were expected to infect others in the organization with a newly found entrepreneurial attitude.

The Siemens and Mott's examples are rooted in the idea that a company needs to develop a critical mass of internal entrepreneurs who are intimately and closely tied to new or emerging markets and technologies. These intrapreneurs are then accountable for identifying and pursuing, or encouraging the pursuit of, new business opportunities or innovations in current businesses.

(c) Organizational Transformation

Organizational Transformation is another variation or flavour of corporate entrepreneurship concept especially if the transformation results in the development of new business opportunities. This type of entrepreneurship only fits the original Schumpeterian definition if the transformation involves innovation, a new arrangement or combination of resources, and results in the creation of sustainable economic value. Clearly, some transformations meet these requirements, while others do not. Transforming an organization by de-layering, cost- cutting, re-engineering, downsizing, and using the latest technology do not guarantee that the organization will recognize or capture new opportunities.

Sun Financial Group, a large international insurance/financial services organization, found itself under increasing pressure to cut costs and improve profitability. They were not asking for entrepreneurship per se, only creative cost cutting. Ian Kennedy, a middle manager at their Annuity Service Center, was told to do more with less. Cut costs or be cut. He put a design team together who came up with a new way of re-arranging his department and resources into cross trained, self-directed work teams so that they could more effectively and efficiently serve their agents and the end customer. Ian did not start out trying to be entrepreneurial. But, his rearrangement of resources in a new and different pattern resulted in the ability of the company to process significantly more business while at the same time, drastically reduce the cost per policy. The truly entrepreneurial part of this rearrangement was their ability to increase the speed of the application and vetting process for the company's insurance policies. It then gave them a competitive edge, a new core capability resulting in significantly more business. This rearrangement of resources required no investment. In fact, it saved money. Thus, this manager changed an internal process that resulted in a new value proposition for the agent and the end customer.

(d) Industry Rule-Bending

Industry Rule Bending is another type of transformation but focuses on changing the rules of competitive engagement. Stopford and Baden Fuller label this behaviour as "frame-breaking change". Toyota, for example, changed the rules of the game in the automobile industry by producing low cost automobiles with exceptionally high quality. As a result, US and European auto manufacturers were forced by Toyota and other Japanese automakers to follow suit. Thus, Toyota not only transformed itself, but also helped to start a wholesale transformation of the industry.

Many new e-commerce companies have earned dizzying market capitalizations in the same way. Amazon.com changed the way books are sold. Callyx and Corolla utilize the Internet and catalog sales to ship flowers directly from the grower to the customer. Flowers no longer spend time in a flower shop ageing. These two examples highlight the changing rules of competition. In fact, they have cut out an entire segment of the typical industry business system or model.

NEED FOR CORPORATE ENTREPRENEURSHIP

Not all companies need embrace a concept of corporate entrepreneurship. Some companies are doing quite well running their businesses in a planned, effective, and efficient manner. But some companies need a jolt, an infusion of creativity, especially if they are operating in rapidly changing or turbulent environments. Because rapidly changing environments are by definition unpredictable, planning becomes a fairly imprecise and blunt weapon. If you can't plan for an unpredictable future, then you have to prepare for it by building an organization that is opportunity focused. Start-ups are already built for or around an opportunity that arises. They were probably built because someone saw an opportunity, and that someone quickly put people and resources together in order to capture that opportunity. Speed and flexibility are what allows start-ups and small entrepreneurial companies to send chills down the spines of their large bureaucratic brethren.

Therefore, it is the large, slow moving, bureaucratic organization operating in an increasingly turbulent environment that needs to do the most amount of entrepreneurial soul searching. These are the companies that must build themselves to be more opportunity-focused in both mind and body, in both vision and structure. The companies who are coming to us for help in corporate entrepreneurship have at least seen the problem. They realize that opportunities are passing them by and the little guys are getting them.

DOMAIN OF CORPORATE ENTREPRENEURSHIP

Corporate entrepreneurship activities can be internally or externally oriented (MacMillan *et al*, 1986; Veciana, 1996). Internal activities are typified as the development within a large organisation of internal markets and relatively small and independent units designed to create internal test-markets or expand improved or innovative staff services, technologies, or production methods within the organisation. These activities may cover product, process, and administrative innovations at various levels of the firm (Zahra, 1991). Schollhammer (1982), proposed that internal entrepreneurship expresses itself in a variety of modes on strategies—administrative (management of research and development), opportunistic (search and exploitation), imitative (internalisation of an external development, technical or organisational), acquisitive (acquisitions and mergers, divestments) and incubative (formation of semi-autonomous units within existing organisations). External entrepreneurship can be defined as the first phenomenon that consists of the process of combining resources dispersed in the environment by individual entrepreneurs with his or her own unique resources to create a new resource combination independent of all others (Gautam & Verma, 1997). External efforts entail mergers, joint ventures, corporate venture; venture nurturing, venture spin-off and others.

Corporate entrepreneurship can also be formal or informal. Informal efforts occur autonomously, with or without the blessing of the official organization. Such informal activities result from individual creativity or pursuit of self-interest, and some of these efforts eventually receive the firm's formal recognition and thus become an integral part of the business concept. According to Zahra (1991), corporate entrepreneurship must incorporate both formal and informal aspects of corporate venturing, as follows: "corporate entrepreneurship refers to formal and informal activities aimed at creating new business in established companies through product and process innovations and market developments". These activities may take place at the corporate, division (business), functional, or project levels, with the unifying objective of improving a firm's competitive position and financial performance (Morris *et al*, 1988).

In light of these manifestations, it is evident that corporate entrepreneurship is not confined to a particular business size or a particular stage in an organisation's life cycle, such as the start-up phase. In a competitive environment, entrepreneurship is an essential element in the long-range success of every business organisation, small or large, new or long established.

SYNERGY BETWEEN CORPORATE ENTREPRENEURSHIP AND STRATEGIC MANAGEMENT

The strategy literature identifies three types of corporate entrepreneurship. One is the creation of new business within an existing organization—corporate venturing or intrapreneurship (Burgelman, 1983; Kuratko *et al*., 1990; Guth & Ginsberg, 1990). Another is the more pervasive activity associated with the transformation or renewal of existing organisations (Stopford & Fuller, 1994). The third is where the enterprise changes the rules of competition for its industry in the manner suggested by Schumpeter and implied by Stevensen and Gumpert (1985).

Changes in the pattern of resource deployment, transform the firm into something significantly different from what it was before i.e., something 'new'. This transformation of the firm from the old to the new reflects entrepreneurial behaviour. Corporate venturing, or new business development within an existing firm, is only one of the possible ways to achieve strategic renewal. Strategic renewal involves the creation of new wealth through new combinations of resources. This includes actions such as refocusing a business competitively, making major changes in marketing or distribution, redirecting product development, and reshaping operations (Guth and Ginsberg, 1990).

According to Burgelman (1983), relatively little is know about the process through which large, complex firms engage in corporate entrepreneurship. To Burgelman, the corporate entrepreneurship refers to the process whereby firms engage in diversification through internal development. Such diversification requires new resource combinations to extend the firm's activities in areas unrelated, or marginally related, to its current domain of competence and corresponding opportunity set. In the Schumpeterian sense, diversification through internal development is the corporate analogue to the process of individual entrepreneurship (Russell, 1995). Corporate entrepreneurship, typically, is the result of the inter-locking entrepreneurial activities of multiple participants.

The role of entrepreneurial activity is to provide the required diversity. Order, in strategy, can be achieved through planning and structuring. Diversity, in strategy, depends on experimentation and selection. The task of strategic management is to maintain an appropriate balance between these fundamentally different processes. These insights have implications for the design of organisational arrangements and for the development of strategic managerial skills. Miller and Friesen (1982), created a distinction between the concepts of corporate entrepreneurship and an entrepreneurial strategy. An entrepreneurial strategy is defined as the frequent and persistent effort to establish competitive advantage through innovation, while corporate entrepreneurship can describe any attempt, even if infrequent, to implement innovation. Corporate entrepreneurship is to a great extent, a social process in which innovations are socially constructed through a series of trial-and-error learning episodes (Van de Ven, 1986).

CONDITIONS THAT FAVOUR CORPORATE ENTREPRENEURSHIP

Some of the internal and external factors that facilitate a successful CE culture in an organization are as follows:

(a) *Dynamism and Competitiveness of the Environment of the Corporation:* Dynamic and competitive environments shorten the life of competitive advantages and force corporations to engage into constant innovation. It is undeniable that with the twin forces of globalization and digital revolution, the potential for radical change in any industry is greater now than ever before.

(b) *The Values and Traits of the Top Management Team:* Cultural orientations such as authorizing the expression of unorthodox ideas and perceiving change positively are correlated with the adoption of an entrepreneurial posture. These values can be seen in abundance in **HCL Technologies** founder Shiv Nadar who provided the early support to Rajendra Pawar and Vijay Thadani to set up **NIIT**, which became a pioneer in the field of IT education in India.

(c) *The Culture and Structure of the Corporation:* A corporation structured as a learning organization is more likely to be conducive to CE than any other structure. The learning organization is based on equality, open information, little hierarchy, and a culture that encourages adaptability and participation, enabling ideas to bubble up from anywhere that can help an organization seize opportunities and handle crises.

(d) *The Level of Performance of Organization:* There are diverse perspectives possible on this. For some organizations, poor corporate performance could lead to conservatism. Others perceive crisis as an excellent innovation opportunity. For instance, **New York Times Company**, when faced with an onslaught from dotcoms offering free content to readers, responded by seeding and funding a new media business unit to counter the threat.

(e) *Right Selection Mechanisms:* These selection mechanisms should ensure strategic alignment of CE initiatives while preserving their operational autonomy. This could take the form of explicit programme goals, norms and procedures, standardized project evaluation criteria and methods or formal approval instances. Such processes reduce the risks inherent to CE by insuring that the various selected initiatives fall within an acceptable scope, that they are reasonably resource consuming and that they do not generate excessive conflict.

(f) *Right Retention Mechanisms:* Corporate entrepreneurs are key resources whose exit can damage the corporation's human and social capital. Research has established corporate entrepreneurs in large organizations considered the non-pecuniary motives more important. Therefore, managers should monitor the motivations and expectations of each corporate entrepreneur and appropriately tailor the rewards and incentives.

(g) **Right Structure for the Corporate Venture:** The choice of structure for a new venture depends on a number of factors, the most fundamental being how close the activities are to the core of the business. Other factors include the level and urgency of the venturing activity, the nature and number of ventures to be established, and the corporate culture and experience. Based on the balance between the desire to learn new competencies and the need to leverage existing competencies, one can identify four possible structures from the figure below.

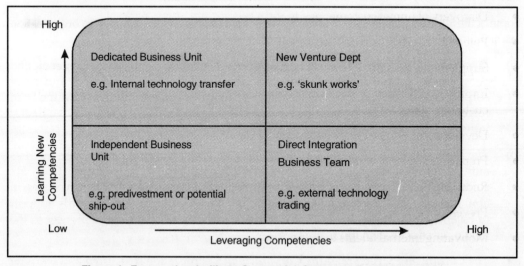

Figure 1: Factors that facilitate Successful Corporate Entrepreneurship

BENEFITS OF CORPORATE ENTREPRENEURSHIP

It has been observed that about 80% of all new ventures fail within the first five years (cited in Kanter, 1990). So, what do the firms stand to gain by pursuing risky CE ventures?

(a) **Testing the Waters:** CE initiatives by virtue of being small, get thoroughly sieved before big investments are made. Corporates can decide whether to exercise or extinguish the initiatives at an early stage, thereby improving the pay-off from its various strategic choices.

(b) **Cost Effectiveness:** Almost all CE initiatives require very less up-front investment and use far less resources than a regular development project. Also, by pursuing multiple ventures, the firm can diversify its risk.

(c) **Flexibility and Manageability:** Managing a small team of people would be far easier than managing organizational entities. Also, resource endowments made to the CE initiatives are highly flexible.

(d) **Synergy between Internal and External Ventures:** For today's corporations, traditional internal expansions, efficiency improvements and "synergistic" acquisitions are no longer sufficient sources of growth. The new challenge is to search for emerging "white space" opportunities that would meet the unmet needs of customers in emerging markets". The value created for the firm is maximum when there is perfect synergy between the internal and external ventures of the firm.

(e) **Turning around Underutilized Resources:** At Cadbury Schweppes, the IT division was extracted from an existing division, thereby forming a separate business unit to supply the internal needs of the Cadbury-CocaCola-Schweppes group. With the mechanisms in place for operation as a trading entity, ITnet Limited began to seek and develop external clients, who now account for a significant portion of its revenues.

In a nutshell, the strategic benefits of corporate entrepreneurship are:

● Discovery of unmet customer needs and unserved emerging markets.

● Potentially high return on investment, if succeeded.

● Supplements to internal research and product/service development investments.

● Improved efficiency of the value chain management, in particular, supply chain and customer relationships.

● Development of new business relationships.

● Preparing potential candidates for strategic alliance or acquisition.

● Reducing the risk of missing a new turn in technological development.

● Preventing competitors from acquiring a breakthrough technology.

● Motivating internal talents to outperform outside ventures.

ISSUES INHERENT TO CORPORATE ENTREPRENEURSHIP

The major obstacles encountered by CE initiatives are related to Systems, Structures, Strategic Direction, Procedures and Policies, People and Culture.

(a) **Risk of Strategic Misalignment:** Corporate Entrepreneurship comes along with increased autonomy for individuals involved. But these personal projects may be tangential to the key strategic alignments of the corporation.

(b) **Loss of Focus and Erosion of Corporate Identity:** Corporate Entrepreneurship, which encourages the pursuit of a large number of related and unrelated initiatives, is the antithesis of focus and coherence. Corporate Entrepreneurship diverts valuable resources away from the core business: technical and financial resources, and the time and energy of highly skilled managers and technologists. The opportunity driven behavior of Corporate Entrepreneurs encourages them to venture outside the domain of activities and competencies of the corporation and to care little about synergy and relatedness. This exposes the corporation to the liabilities of unrelated diversification.

(c) **Control Risk:** A large number of small CE projects lead to spreading of managers' attention. The natural tendency of CE projects to 'hide out' from the limelight magnifies the risk further. This may lead to failure of the CE initiatives. Firms like Xerox and Salomon have experienced the painful consequences of uncontrolled divergence.

(d) **Risk of Competitive Advantage Erosion:** When the corporation starts relying on individuals to foster innovation, it indirectly favours the development of highly-mobile resources. With easily available venture capital, there are a lot of opportunities for corporate entrepreneurs outside the corporation. The high degree of formalization and control required to limit uncontrolled divergence will compel Corporate Entrepreneurs to go outside the corporation in search of a more supportive environment; reciprocally, an internal environment that is well adapted to the requirements of Corporate Entrepreneurs and provides them with sufficient autonomy, increases the risk of uncontrolled divergence.

(e)   *Mismanagement by Corporate Managers:* Corporate Entrepreneurship is an open-ended process, liable to many changes and re-orientations as it grows. Such emergent processes cannot be managed in the same fashion as regular projects and most corporate managers are unaware of how to handle CE initiatives.

(f)   *Early Withdrawal:* Several studies on Corporate Entrepreneurship indicate that most of the initiatives have been declared failures and are wound up in a hurry. The reasons for this move may be circumstantial (change in top management), a shift in strategic priorities or top management's inability to properly measure the Corporate Entrepreneur's benefits.

(g)   *Lack of Proper Support:* In most cases, Corporate Entrepreneurs are born in the middle of a hostile corporate environment. The absence of supportive colleagues and superiors acts as a damper on the creativity and daringness of the would-be entrepreneurs. In the absence of these proper support and incentives, dispersed CE programmes tend to die out.

CONCLUSION

Because CE constitutes a "contradiction in terms" it raises, independently of the context and modality of its implementation, a number of complex and interrelated issues. Case studies show that most corporations have a hard time managing the inherent contradictions of CE. Yet, more and more corporations would like to elicit entrepreneurial behaviours from their employees and are thinking of CE as a potentially effective corporate development tool. In these conditions, it becomes legitimate to try and realistically appraise CE by determining whether and how the issues it raises can be dealt with.

From a corporate strategy standpoint, CE raises critical issues since it reinforces the risk of strategic misalignment and the risk of competitive erosion. Because it relies on autonomous behaviour, CE exposes the corporation to the liabilities of uncontrolled divergence i.e., loss of direction, poor exploitation of unique resources, waste, high failure risk and loss of managerial control. Because it relies on individuals qua individuals, CE exposes the corporation to the liabilities of individualization, i.e. the progressive erosion of its competitive advantage as a result of the increasing mobility and decreasing appropriability of its resources.

Are these strategic risks acceptable? Does CE remain a valuable instrument of corporate development? The answer these questions is conditional. It depends on corporate managers' risk perception and control ability which are themselves influenced by various internal and external factors. In certain conditions – a dynamic environment, a strong growth imperative or a foreseeable decline in performance – corporate managers have to take more risk and will be more willing to engage into entrepreneurial activities. In conditions of high uncertainty and tight time-to-market requirements, the traditional high commitment/strong focus recipe becomes risky while CE, because of its flexibility and the diversity it generates, becomes, by comparison, a low cost/low risk option.

Strategic risks will be more acceptable if they can be contained. Selection mechanisms in the broadest sense play a key role in the unfolding of CE and their primary goal is to reduce the risk of uncontrolled divergence. They should be designed to simultaneously respect strategic alignment and operational autonomy requirements and to reflect changing priorities and learning. Sophisticated and customized retention mechanisms will help reduce the mobility of corporate entrepreneurs and the downside of individualization. Finally, risk acceptance ©can contribute to reduce both the cost of uncontrolled divergence and the mobility of corporate entrepreneurs.

References

Ansoff, H.I., 1965, *Corporate strategy: an analytical approach to business policy for growth and expansion*, New York: McGraw Hill.

Block, Z. and Macmillan, I.C., 1993, *Corporate venturing: creating new businesses within the firm*, Boston: Harvard Business School Press.

Bouchard, Véronique, 2001, *Exploring Corporate Entrepreneurship: A Corporate Strategy Perspective*, European Entrepreneurial Learning.

Burgelman, Robert, A., 1983, "A Process Model of Internal Corporate Venturing in the Diversified Major Firm", *Administrative Science Quarterly*.

Clark, Jon, 1995, "Learning through Corporate Ventures", *Managing Innovation*, pp. 279-309.

23

Corporate Entrepreneurship in Family-owned Business in India – A Case Study of Electrocon Group of Companies

P.K. Srivastava*
Dr. Pradip Manjrekar**

Corporate entrepreneurship is the process by which individuals inside organizations pursue opportunities without regard to the resources they currently control.[1] There is a growing interest in the use of Corporate Entrepreneurship by enterprises across the globe. Corporates are using it as a means to enhance the abilities of the people in the organization to encourage them to put forth their innovative views and ideas to develop new business and ensure corporate growth.

The Family-owned Business in India is a very old institution and most of the private sector earlier comprised of the family-owned business. Over the years, they have followed the concept of Corporate Entrepreneurship, though they may not have ever termed it so. The economic environment of India (with the license raj and quotas) and the philosophy of the family-owned business (of being fair to all) have ensured that the younger generation, from the family and also kids of trusted workers, were encouraged to set up new ventures with support from the main business in terms of skills, finance and use of the family influence. Diversification was not necessarily in keeping with the core business of the family. Most of these new ventures have proved to be very profitable and the families have accepted them as the main ventures of the group for e.g., Bajaj groups and Bajaj Auto.[2]

What was the strategy followed by these Family-owned Business of India while introducing several new ventures and ensuring that the survival rate was always as high as 75%?[3] Are there lessons for the world to learn from the India Family-owned Business in Corporate Entrepreneurship?

***Keywords:** Corporate Entrepreneurship, Family-owned Business, Entrepreneurship, Survival, Growth.*

* MD, Electrocon Group of Companies, Belapur, Navi Mumbai.
** Professor & Head, Research and Extension Centre, Dr. D.Y. Patil Institute of Management Studies, Navi Mumbai.

CONTEXT

Industry across the globe has been for some time been downsizing and restructuring in order to stay with core competencies and avail of economies of scale. Globally, big companies have hived off small units and ancillary units in order to concentrate on few business ventures. They have used up the sales proceeds to expand a few of the business ventures to large international size operation. The aim being, to have their presence in as many countries as possible and to operate at competitive costs.

Managements, today, are thinking again about growth and expansion beyond core competencies and venturing into niche areas without thinking about economies of scale or cost advantages. But growth does not come as naturally or as automatically as it once did. The innovation of products, services and processes and the formation of new business enterprises are crucially important to every economy. Innovation and new business development can be initiated by independent individuals or by existing enterprises. Revitalisation of industry and the creation of new jobs must increasingly depend on the development of new products and new markets to satisfy unrecognized and unmet public and personal needs.

The Indian economy has been blessed with a large number of family-owned business houses. In these institutions, the importance of a family member has been very strong and the distinguishing line between family and business has been very thin. The family is business and the business is family. In order to keep with their principle of fairness to all and peace in family at all cost, family-owned businesses in India have always encouraged the younger members in the family to venture into new field of business. The younger generation has also always been encouraged to pursue higher education and training abroad which has helped them to have alternative perspective to the existing business in the family. The family members have encouraged the younger generation to re-look into the existing business in order to improve their profitability.

Business scholars and consultants have been aping the west in their business policies and have been advising family-owned business houses to concentrate on core competencies and consolidate their business ventures. Is this aping necessary? Or does India have a point to showcase to the world with their family-owned businesses that have in their own way and for their survival always used corporate entrepreneurship? The strategies may not have been very crisp but the concept has always been there. Strategy provides a good starting point for the examination of corporate entrepreneurship. With a clear strategic intent, the core competence of the corporation can be effectively leveraged to create new business. Strategies in entrepreneurship do not automatically lead to successful new business. Proper organizational context must be created and the right process installed.

WHO IS AN ENTREPRENEUR?

An entrepreneur is a person who undertakes and operates a new venture, and assumes some accountability for the inherent risks.

The will to spot opportunities and take risks in order to realize them is part of a person's overall makeup, which is partly innate and partly a product of his upbringing.

Entrepreneurs from family-owned businesses have a very good opportunity to learn about business right from the time they are in their cradles.[1]

The best way to learn how to be an entrepreneur is to work at the side of a successful one.

By bring born in a family that operates a business gives the younger member of the family an opportunity to observe not only the best in the family but also from the professionals appointed in the business and learn from them.

Risk-taking and opportunism go along with frugality. Really good entrepreneurs squeeze as much as possible out of limited amounts of cash. They leverage the money of others, and never invent the wheel when a good, cheap one is available in the marketplace. By keeping the rate at which they burn cash low, entrepreneurs can try a lot of ideas.

The Marwaris and other families in business in India have proved to the world their strength when it comes to money management. Indian businessmen have left far behind the fabled Jewish people in money management. Frugality comes naturally to Indian businessmen due to a constant crunch of resources.[2]

Entrepreneurship as practiced by the individual is often associated with such characteristics as risk taking, innovation and proactive pursuit of opportunities. Entrepreneurs build companies that are specifically crafted to exploit a particular opportunity. This gives them an advantage over older companies that were designed in response to challenges of the past and must change to adapt of today's requirements. Entrepreneurs can build new companies. They can also rejuvenate existing companies via buyouts and turnarounds. They can also build new companies inside existing companies, which can be called corporate entrepreneurship.

WHAT IS CORPORATE ENTREPRENEURSHIP?

Corporate Entrepreneurship (CE) is the process by which individuals inside organizations pursue opportunities without regard to the resources they currently control.[3] An entrepreneurial manager links up discrete pieces of new technical knowledge that would provide a solution to a customer problem and matches this technical capability with the satisfaction of a market and garners resources and skills needed to take the venture to the next stage. This process leads to the birth of new businesses and to the transformation of companies through a renewal of their key ideas.[4]

Researchers have used a variety of labels to describe the first two Corporate Entrepreneurship phenomena.

Corporate entrepreneurial efforts that lead to the creation of new business organisations within the corporate organisation are called corporate venturing. They may follow from or lead to innovations that exploit new markets, or new product offerings, or both. If corporate venturing activities result in the creation of semi-autonomous or autonomous organisational

---

[1] Ritu Bhattacharyya, Are Leaders made or are they Born: A Study of Business Houses in Pune, Pune University, MPhil. 1996, Chapter 5.

[2] Ritu Bhattacharyya, Are Leaders made or are they Born: A Study of Business Houses in Pune, Pune University, MPhil. 1996, Chapter 9.

[3] Stevenson, H., H. Irving Grousbeck, M.J. Roberts and Amar V. Bhide. New Business Ventures and the Entrepreneur. 5th ed., Richard D. Irwin, 1999.

[4] Guth, W.D. and Ginsberg A. 1990. *Corporate Entrepreneurship. Strategic Management Journal*, (Special Issue 11): 5-15.

entities that reside outside the existing organisational domain, it is called External Corporate Venturing. If corporate venturing activities result in the creation of organisational entities that reside within an existing organisational domain, it is called Internal Corporate Venturing.

The process of transformation of corporations through a renewal of their key ideas has been called strategic renewal, strategic change, revival and transformation, organisation renewal. Strategic Renewal refers to the corporate entrepreneurial efforts that result in significant changes in an organisation's business or corporate level strategy or structure. These changes alter pre-existing relationships within the organisation or between the organisations and its external environment and in most cases will involve some sorts of innovation.

Innovation of products, services and processes and the formation of new business enterprises are crucially important to every economy. Innovation and new business development can be initiated by independent individuals or by existing enterprises. The first is referred to as (independent) entrepreneurship, the latter as corporate entrepreneurship.

Thus, corporate entrepreneurship as the process whereby an individual or a group of individuals, in association with an existing organisation, create a new organisation or instigate renewal or innovation within that organisation. Corporate entrepreneurship is often defined as a process that goes on inside an existing firm and that may lead to new business ventures, the development of new products, services or processes and the renewal of strategies and competitive postures. As such, it can be seen as the sum of a company's innovation, venturing and renewal efforts.

Corporate entrepreneurship refers to the effort of corporations to generate new business. Corporate entrepreneurship is in the national interest because corporate and independent entrepreneurs complement and compete with one another thus improving national competitiveness in business.

ENTREPRENEURSHIP IN INDIA

India is the second among all nations in Total Entrepreneurship Activity as per the Global Entrepreneurship Monitor Report, 2002. The climate of entrepreneurship in India is excellent. Young, upwardly mobile middle class with an eagerness to consume are engaging in entrepreneurial activities in multiple sectors, including telecom, wired and wireless networks, devices and services, online and offline retail sectors, traditional and digital entertainment, financial services, infrastructure, insurance and healthcare.

FAMILY-OWNED BUSINESS IN INDIA

The concept of the family-owned business is as old as that of commercial enterprise itself India-family-owned businesses have survived multiple generations and have continued to make significant contributions to the economy. Family-owned businesses have played and will continue to play a central role in the growth and development of the country. Family-owned businesses have existed in India since as long ago as recorded history. With time, the contribution of family businesses has gone beyond simply paying taxes and employing people. During the last 100 years or so, Indian family-owned businesses have made significant contributions to the economy. Family businesses have done an excellent job of keeping the spirit of enterprise alive especially through the 40 years of quasi-socialism. The spirit survived onerous taxation and repeated government attempts to undo supposed 'concentration' of economic power.

FAMILY-OWNED BUSINESS AND ENTREPRENEURSHIP

The connection between entrepreneurship and family business is very strong. An entrepreneur is often defined as someone who specializes in making judgmental decisions about the coordination of scarce resources, is institution-free, deals with the factors of risk, and has influence over the flow of information. Entrepreneurs are generally referred to as individuals but families are vital and supportive environments for entrepreneurial growth and development. Entrepreneurship is the start and heart of most family managed businesses. Family-owned business has always been a result of very strong entrepreneurial activities.[5]

According to Rahul Bajaj, Chairman of the Bajaj Group of companies, if a professionally managed firm means one that is managed by those who hold no equity in the enterprise, there is "no reason to believe that a non-owner is more competent than an owner. In fact, a lot of studies done recently in the U.S. show that family-owned businesses are doing better than non-family managed companies". What is relevant in a competitive economy is that the company has to be efficiently managed. Bajaj believes that while family-managed companies have advantages, such as commitment and continuity.[6]

FAMILY-OWNED BUSINESS AND CORPORATE ENTREPRENEURSHIP

Family-owned businesses in India have been practicing corporate entrepreneurship in their businesses for a long time. The structure of any family-owned business in India shows many different fields of business, some as auxiliary to the main business and some very different form the main business of the group. This type of network of many businesses in the group is due to a number of factors like:

1. *Government Policies:* Successive government of India have, for at-least 40 years, when they subscribed to socialist believes, have treated the private enterprise as an institution of profit making and creation of wealth inequality. The private enterprise that comprised mainly of family-owned businesses was governed by high restriction. Every enterprise has to be sanctioned through a license right from setting up an industry to the amount they manufactured and sold in the market. Since licenses were not given for increasing capacities the only way to grow was to take licenses for which every industry that were available. This resulted in fragmented growth. This was basically an expansion strategy and not a corporate growth strategy, the limiting factor being the government policies. All the family-owned businesses can be an example. The Birlas have their holding companies though the Birlas were best known for their jute mills to begin with, they then diversified into all fields of business from cement to textiles to metal to name a few. The same is the case with the Tatas, the Goderjs, the Walchands, the Doshis, etc.

2. *Family Policies:* Family-owned businesses in India have always worked on the principle of equality and fairness. Due to this, every member of the family must get an equal share in the dynasty/business. Since the government restriction result in small company, the equal distribution among all the sons of the family results in small fragments of the

---

5 Ritu Bhattacharyya, *Succession Process in Family-owned Business in India*, Pune University, PhD. 2001.
6 Bajaj Group Chairman Rahul Bajaj on *Family-owned Enterprises, the U.S. Auto Industry and Global Pollution*, Published: November 16, 2006 in Knowledge@Wharton.

business which render the business uneconomical. Therefore, the patriarch of the family-owned business always encouraged every male member who was old enough to be a part of the business to start some new venture, for which the license was available. The family recourses monetary and others were made available to the family member. The business was never a separate entity but always the part of the group.

3. *Keeping the Family together:* Indians, by tradition, have always been people of very strong family orientation. Thus, when young members of the extended family (sons of brothers, sisters, cousins) decided to join the business they were always encouraged to do so, after a few years of training they were also encouraged to start new business ventures of their interest or for which again licenses were available. The business always operated as a part of the group and the group made all resources available for the same.

4. *Encouraging Trusted Employees:* Family-owned businesses have been known to be very supportive towards their employees especially those who have stayed with them for long. Loyalty has been rewarded in various forms, it may be in the form of treating him and his family as part of the family or taking their children/into the folds of the family viz providing of education and opportunities to join the business group or set up any new business within the group. They may also motivated by being encouraged to open up new ventures with the group and be their own bosses with benefits like total buy back or using their contacts to get them a good market.

5. *The New Generation:* Family-owned businesses have always encouraged the younger generation to seek professional higher education at the best universities in the world. This has given them an exposure to think differently from what the others in the business are doing. Similarly, these youngsters are encouraged to take up jobs in foreign countries after their studies in order to learn the new management practices in these countries and try and apply what they learn in the family business. These youngsters thus learn the global perspectives and come home to apply the same to either improve the existing business or to start new ventures that they feel have high potential internationally.

6. *Change:* Change is the order of the day. All business houses know that with time, the requirements of the market are likely to change and in order to keep the profitability high, the business group needs to venture into new businesses or new processes and Indian family-owned businesses have always been able quick to avail of these business opportunities.

7. *Taxation and other Policies:* Since the Government of India has very strict taxation policies, most family-owned businesses try and keep the size of the business small, since small businesses are given several benefits. When the demand exceeds the size, a new business is set up at a new place with a new family member in charge of the same. The government reserves certain types of business for the Small Scale Sector and provides several benefits to those businesses. Therefore, when the business falls in the small-scale sector, the businessmen have no choice to open small-sized firms and when they have a bigger market, they tend to have several small firms.

THE STRATEGY FOR MANAGEMENT

Conceptually, the strategic planning processes and the resulting strategies of family businesses differ significantly from the processes and strategies of non-family firms. These differences exist because in family-owned businesses, the basic strategy is growth and survival. Most family-owned businesses have six characteristics that contribute to successful business strategy.

These characteristics found in family-owned businesses provide the foundation for leveraging the competitive advantages and core competencies of the business:

1. *Long-term Vision:* Because of long-term ownership, family-owned businesses can develop business strategies based on a long-term vision and commitment rather than short-term profitability.

2. *Loyalty:* With this long-term commitment, family businesses establish customer loyalty, as well as the loyalty of key employees who see the benefit of the long-term commitment of the family to the business.

3. *Lower Cost of Capital:* Not only are family businesses able to take a long-term perspective, they also have the advantage of a lower cost of capital for doing business. This is primarily the result of the reinvestment of profits back into the business rather than the payment of dividends to stockholders in the corporation.

4. *Working with a Small Group:* Family-owned businesses work with a small group of family members and some trusted employees. They keep their strategies very well-guarded and ensure that work is done quickly and with the least possible fuss.

5. *Flexibility:* Family-owned businesses are usually managed by the owners, who can make decisions quickly and decisively. Family-owned businesses often have the flexibility and speed to out-maneuver the competition.

6. *Customer Service:* Because ownership and management are closely tied together, family-owned businesses are often driven to serve customers with whom they have personal relationships at the top-executive levels.

THE ASPECT OF CORPORATE ENTREPRENEURSHIP IN FAMILY-OWNED BUSINESS

The three aspects that signify corporate entrepreneurship are:

1. The birth of new businesses within an existing firm,

2. The transformation of existing firms through the renewal or reshaping of the key ideas on which they are built, and

3. Innovation.[7]

When one looks closely at the Indian business scenario, one notice that the family-owned businesses of Indian have always followed the three aspects to survive at all time. They have floated a number of new enterprises when the economic atmosphere did not allow them to expand their business. They did it to sustain themselves the family and to keep the business in good financial health.

When liberalisation came, family-owned businesses realized that they were again in a position where their survival was at stake. They then took on to transforming the existing business with the help of family members, consultants and professionals. Sometimes a complete transformation took place and companies adopted ideologies that never figured in their scheme in order to face the completion and survive. Many family-owned businesses gave up their old ideologies and also the old management to adopt newer ways to conduct business.

---

[7] Pramodita Sharma, James J. Chrisman, Towards a Reconciliation of the Definitional Issues in the field of Corporate Entrepreneurship, *Entrepreneurship Theory and Practice*, 1999.

Liberalisation automatically brought with it a lot of innovative ideas and practices. Innovation came more as a survival technique than an expansion technique in family-owned businesses in India. Innovative techniques were used to make companies in the group more competitive and make them competitive in the global market without using the amount of resources available with the foreign competitors. Innovative ideas were used to find out where Indian companies could make a niche for themselves in the global scenario with their shortage of resources and technology and family-owned businesses were the first to invest in these fields.

Though family-owned businesses have been doing all this, they have never termed it as Corporate Entrepreneurship. It may be coined in different forms as Good Entrepreneurship, Survival Techniques, Social Entrepreneurship, Growth Strategies, Family and Business Management, Sustainable Growth Techniques etc. But the history of family-owned businesses is the story of continuous Corporate Entrepreneurship at a time the world had not heard of it. Indian family-owned businesses have been following it and have been very successful. The failure rate of a new venture or an innovation in family-owned business in India is very small, only 18% of all new ventures set up by family-owned businesses fail.[8] This by itself is a very big achievement, and the global business community has to learn for the Indian lesson as to how the success rate is so high.

CONCLUSION

In conclusion, it is felt that a proper research into the strategies followed by family-owned business is necessary. The areas of great interest to scholars as well as to businessmen should be to study how over the year family-owned businesses have been able to:

- Endure a number of different ventures,

- Keep them successful and profitable,

- Ensure that all the business ventures work in the interest of the group,

- Ensure all ventures in the group are closely knit,

- All ventures follow same policies and cultures and there is no conflict of interest, and

- Cost of operations is among the lowest in the world.

The study of these few aspects would give the business world a very new and unique technique of management that would help businesses to flourish and would work as a very good motivational tool to the employees.

References

Stevenson, Robert and Grousbeck, 1989, The New *Business Venture and the Entrepreneur*, Irwin.

Ritu Bhattacharyya, *Succession Process in Family-owned Business in India*, Pune University, PhD. 2001.

Ritu Bhattacharyya, *Are Leaders made or are they Born: A Study of Business Houses in Pune*, Pune University, MPhil. 1996, Chapter 2.

---

[8] Ritu Bhattacharyya, *Are Leaders made or are they Born: A Study of Business Houses in Pune*, Pune University, MPhil. 1996, Chapter 6.

Stevenson, H., H. Irving Grousbeck, M.J. Roberts and Amar V. Bhide, *New Business Ventures and the Entrepreneur*, 5th ed., Richard D. Irwin, 1999.

Guth, W.D. and Ginsberg A., 1990, Corporate Entrepreneurship, *Strategic Management Journal*, (Special Issue 11): 5-15.

Pramodita Sharma, James J. Chrisman, Toward a Reconciliation of the Definitional Issues in the field of Corporate Entrepreneurship, *Entrepreneurship Theory and Practice*, 1999.

Bajaj Group Chairman Rahul Bajaj on Family-owned Enterprises, the U.S. Auto Industry and Global Pollution, Published: November 16, 2006 in Knowledge@Wharton.

24

An Exploratory Study of Malaysian Students' Attitudes and Perceptions towards Entrepreneurship

Sudarsan Jayasingh*

Small businesses, small and medium-sized enterprises and new start-up ventures play a vital role in the economic development of a country. There has been limited research on entrepreneurship in Malaysia. This study may provide some insight into the general perceptions of Malaysian towards entrepreneurship. This is to understand why entrepreneurship is rarely taken seriously as career choice. This study too will help to identify opportunities and potential obstructions that prospective entrepreneurs may believe they may experience.

INTRODUCTION

Fostering entrepreneurship among students has become an important topic in universities and governments' as well as in research. As a number of studies show, student interest in entrepreneurship as a career choice is growing, while interest in professional employment in businesses is declining (Venesaar, Kolbre and Piliste, 2006).

Heinecke & Marsh (2003), in their book, *The Entrepreneur*, describe an entrepreneur as a person who gauges the risks and rewards of a business and works quickly to initiate, organize and manage a particular opportunity, idea or concept. He stressed that the entrepreneur will often risk more, work harder and demand more of himself or herself than any ordinary businessperson. Shefsky (1994), defines the word entrepreneur by looking at the word in its three parts entre, pre and neur and tracing them to their Latin roots. "Entre" means enter, "pre" means before, and "neur" means nerve center.

Recent studies have emphasised the need for entrepreneurial attitude and intention as factors determining entrepreneurial behaviour (Fayolle & Gailly, 2005). These factors can be considerably influenced by entrepreneurship education. Attitudes are defined by cognitive psychology as the predisposition to respond in a generally favourable or unfavourable manner with respect to the object of the attitude (Ajzen, 1987). The attitudinal approach has been utilised in many fields including in evaluating entrepreneurship education.

---

* Faculty, School of Business, Swinburne University of Technology Sarawak, Kuching, Sarawak.

There has been limited research on entrepreneurship in Malaysia. This study may give some insight of the general perceptions of Malaysian towards entrepreneurship. This is to understand why entrepreneurship is rarely taken seriously as career choice. This study too will help to identify opportunities and potential obstructions that prospective entrepreneurs may believe they may experience.

In a survey by The Small Business Service (SBS) Household Survey of Entrepreneurship 2003 in United Kingdom, up to 93 per cent of respondents in UK admire people who start their own business. Surprisingly, only 64 per cent would encourage their friends or family to involve themselves in the business. (SBS, 2003).

Among the barriers towards entrepreneurship identified in the survey are difficulties getting the finance from financial institutions, fear of getting in debt, fear of losing security and incomes, good promotional prospects for current job and lack of business opportunity.

The development of entrepreneurship, as both concept and activity, has been growing in importance in Malaysia. The importance of entrepreneurship to Malaysia's economy is shown by the various policies and supporting mechanisms that were created for entrepreneurs and future entrepreneurs, including funding, physical infrastructure and business advisory services. In Malaysia, small businesses contribute about 30% to the nation's Gross Domestic Products (GDP) and 51% of the employment. The establishment of the Ministry of Entrepreneur Development and Cooperatives (MECD) in 1995, clearly shows the importance placed upon the issue of entrepreneurship and entrepreneur development.

ENTREPRENEURSHIP EDUCATION IN MALAYSIA

The Malaysian government has encouraged a very strong mobilisation in entrepreneurship education. There are several types of activities which have been supported by the Malaysian government that started with the Young Entrepreneurs Programme at school, introduction of small business studies in the Kemahiran Hidup (Living Skills subject) syllabus for the secondary school students and this too includes the entrepreneurship studies in local university.

On entrepreneurship education at the tertiary level, to date most of the local universities such as Universiti Teknologi Mara (UiTM), Multimedia University (MMU), Universiti Malaya (UM) have subjects like entrepreneurship and small business management as part of the business management course. Universiti Tenaga Nasional (Uniten) and Universiti Utara Malaysia (UUM), also offer a bachelor's degree in entrepreneurship studies.

RESEARCH METHODOLOGY

The interview questionnaires were designed in such a way to find out the Malaysian students' attitudes and perceptions towards entrepreneurship. This study also designed to find out the number of respondents who would consider entrepreneurship as a career and to examine the perceived potential obstruction (barrier towards entrepreneurship). The method of survey was conducted through the questionnaire survey. The sample size is 100 final year undergraduate students, 93 responded to the survey.

RESEARCH FINDINGS

Perceptions and Attitudes towards Entrepreneurship

To measure the overall entrepreneurial activity of students, we asked them whether or not they had recently set up a business or were at the time of the survey setting up a business, or whether they are thinking to be an entrepreneur. 76% of the respondents have an intention to be active in entrepreneurship. Only 8% had abandoned the thought of starting a business.

Attributes of Entrepreneur

Respondents were asked for the opinions/perspective the attributes of entrepreneurs. The most frequently mentioned attributes of an entrepreneur such as, innovative, creative, risk taker, ambitious, hardworking, visionary and courageous. Generally, the terms entrepreneurs' attributes are perceived as positive rather than negative.

Table 1: Attributes of Entrepreneur

Attribute	Frequency
Innovative	16
Creative	21
Risk taker	34
Ambitious	20
Motivated	19
Visionary	9
Dedicated	9
Hardworking	40
Opportunity	2
Smart/Knowledgeable	25
Courageous	33
Positive	8
Leadership	1
No Response	13

The attributes of hardworking are among top of the list attributes of an entrepreneur. This may suggest that those respondents might perceive an entrepreneur is the person who will go the extra mile in pursuing their careers compared with being in employment.

Career Intention

The respondents were asked on their career preferences in terms on working for others as an employee, being an entrepreneur by owning own business or others. The definition of 'Other' for this question is varied and wide open. Some respondents noted it as not sure, a few respondents chose to involve in politics and quite a number chose retirement.

Table 2: Respondents' Career Intentions

Career Intention	Employee	Business	Others	Total Respondents
Next 1 – 2 Years	82	11	0	93
Next 5 Years	35	57	1	93
Future	14	63	16	93

Only 11 respondents chose to run their own business in next 1-2 years. However, the students group may not be concerned in short-term planning with the possibility of starting a business because the event is too remote. Rather, they would rather focus on the direction that their studies and/or internship training should take to prepare them for a career. Hence, they may be more concerned to practise what they were taught at universities, and get more work experience before deciding to be entrepreneurs.

Major Obstacles to start own Business

Among the obstacles cited across the groups are: lack of capital, lack of knowledge and experience, lack of support from families, friends and society and no business opportunity or lack of ideas.

Table 3: Most Frequent Obstacles towards Entrepreneurial Activities

Reasons	Frequency
Lack of Capital	31
Lack of Experience	24
Lack of Knowledge	13
Looking for Network	0
Still Studying	21

Lack of resources in terms of capital was chosen by 33 per cent of respondents. The second most cited obstacle is the lack of experience and knowledge.

CONCLUSION AND SUGGESTIONS

This study has found that the Malaysian students viewed entrepreneurship favourably in positive perceptions. Most of the respondents have the intention to be entrepreneurs and be involved in business in the near future without any specific timeframe. Very few saw themselves continuing as employees.

An understanding of business start-up obstacles can enable policy makers (governments) to develop entrepreneurship programmes that can better prepare a prospective entrepreneur a successful entrepreneurial venture. The results from the survey indicate that the three major common obstacles to entrepreneurial ventures are perceptions of money, risks and skills. The objective of any entrepreneurship programmes should be to encourage the launch of new entrepreneurial ventures.

In the future, in-depth studies of factors contributing to Malaysia's students attitudes and perceptions towards entrepreneurship can be conducted with larger samples to make generalization as accurate as possible.

References

Ajzen, I. 1991, Theory of Planned Behaviour, *Organizational Behaviour and Human Decisions Processes*, 50, 2, 179-211.

Fayolle, A. & Gailly, B. (2005), *Using the Theory of Planned Behaviour to Assess Entrepreneurship Teaching Programmes*, Louvain School of Management, Center for Research in Change, Innovation and Strategy (CRECIS), retrieved on 05.03.2007 from http://www.crecis.be

Heinecke, W. & Marsh, J. (2003), *The Entrepreneur – 25 Golden Rules for the Global Business Manager*, Singapore: John Wiley & Sons (Asia).

Linan, F., Rodriguez-Cohard, J., Rueda-Cantuche, J. 2005, *Factors affecting Entrepreneurial Intention Levels*, 45th Congress of the European Regional Science Association, Amsterdam, 23-25 August, 2005.

SBS Small Business Service, Department of Trade and Industry. (2003), *The Small Business Service (SBS) Household Survey of Entrepreneurship* 2003, London, United Kingdom, Retrieved April 20, 2005, from, http://www.sbs.gov.uk

Venesaar. U, Kolbre E and Piliste T, (2006), *Students' Attitudes and Intentions towards Entrepreneurship at Tallinn University of Technology*, Working paper, School of Economics and Business Administration, Tallinn University of Technology.

25

The Impact of State Policy Initiatives towards Entrepreneurship Development

Sudeep Chatterjee*

The paper attempts to analyse the impact of state policy initiatives towards entrepreneurship development. The author argues on the hypothesis that Governments can play a more proactive role in developing entrepreneurs through its policy initiatives.

The paper comprehensively studies of the role of the Government of India in entrepreneurship development and the impact of public policy on entrepreneurship, its competitiveness and success.

The paper analyses the different entrepreneurial categories including the Small and Medium Enterprises (SME), cooperatives, economic clusters and Micro credit funded Self-Help Groups (SHG) besides the large companies, to see the impact of the different policy initiatives.

The author argues that path breaking initiatives taken by governments whether at the state level or the centre alone can foster a climate for entrepreneurial development to fasten India's transition from a developing to a developed nation. Alien environments abroad, have in fact facilitated overseas Indian entrepreneurs to achieve greater success in comparison to entrepreneurs operating within the country.

Finally, drawing from the examples of remarkable Indian entrepreneurial success stories the author posits that most Indians can flourish as entrepreneurs provided there is a supportive environment.

The paper concludes that only proper policy initiatives for entrepreneurship development can sustain the economic growth of the country and help in the creation of wealth.

Keywords: *Entrepreneurship, SME- Small and Medium Enterprise, SHG-Self-Help Groups, Micro credit, Liberalisation, Public policy, Economic clusters*

---

* Assistant Professor, Institute of Engineering & Management, Kolkata.

INTRODUCTION

Entrepreneur is a person who creates an enterprise and the process of creation is called entrepreneurship. The word entrepreneur is derived from the French word *enterprendre*, which means 'to undertake.'

According to D C McClelland, "Entrepreneurship is doing things in a new and better way and the decision-making under the condition of uncertainty". Benjamin Higgins has defined "Entrepreneurship as the function of foreseeing investment and production opportunity, organising an enterprise to undertake a new production process, raising capital, hiring labour, arranging for the supply of raw materials, and selecting managers for the day-to-day operations of the enterprise".

India, in its history of more than sixty years, since its independence has produced many successful entrepreneurs. A large number of overseas Indians have also achieved remarkable success like Laxmi Niwas Mittal who is known as the steel king of the world and is probably the richest Indian.

Entrepreneurship development today has assumed special significance, since it is a key to economic development. Entrepreneurs are the seeds of industrial development and lead to greater employment opportunities to the unemployed youth, increase in per capita income, higher standard of living, increased individual saving, revenue to the government in the form of income tax, sales tax, duties, and lead to balanced regional development. India, in particular, needs entrepreneurs for two main reasons, to capitalise on new opportunities like IT, BPO, Biotechnology among others and for the creation of wealth.

A recent Mckinsey & Co., NASSCOM report has projected that India needs at least 8000 new businesses to achieve its target of building a $87 billion IT sector by 2008. Similarly, by 2015, 110-130 million Indians citizens will need jobs including about 80-100 million first job seekers, which is seven times Australia's population. Added to this is the disguised unemployment of over half of the 230 million employed in the rural sector. Since, Government jobs are scarce and old economy players are downsizing, there are lesser opportunities to employ in the future and only new entrepreneurs can create these new jobs and opportunities.

The importance of small and medium enterprises for increasing the GDP growth rate of India has been realised and the thrust on this area has begun. However, there is no defined meaning of the term. SME and continues to be nebulous in India, broadly including the erstwhile SSI segment but not the services and trade.

Governments, whether the previous NDA or the present UPA have taken certain steps which maybe helpful for development of entrepreneurship. However, we need to look closely at other emerging economies like China, Brazil, South Africa and definitely the developed countries of Europe, Japan and the US to replicate their public policies on entrepreneurship.

RESEARCH QUESTION

The paper hopes to comprehensively analyse the impact of policy initiatives by the Indian government, and attempts to gauge how successful the state has been in creating the supportive environment for entrepreneurship development. The author argues on the hypothesis that a more proactive role by the government can develop more entrepreneurs.

Research Methodology

This is a working research paper which studies the policy initiatives of the state with the empirical support of examples. The secondary data source of websites, books and published research have been referred to collate information.

Understanding Different Entrepreneurs

We aim to study some category of entrepreneurs as mentioned below:

a) Large Entrepreneurs

History is witness to the great entrepreneurial spirit that drove entrepreneurs like the Tatas to create a giant steel plant in a remote part of backward Bihar, which is now known as Jamshedpur. Here was created a totally new township to offset the zero infrastructure available and Tata Steel was born. India has produced many other Indian MNCs (Indian companies with multinational operations), which have excelled. Some companies like Marico Industries, Ranbaxy, Videocon, Dr. Reddy's Laboratories, Godrej Consumers among others are totally homegrown and at some time started off as small enterprises. However, Reliance Industries Ltd. and Bharti Airtel are examples of rapid growth of first generation entrepreneurs. These companies have faced the license and quota raj, administrative apathy, excessive regulations and restrictive policy decisions yet used innovative techniques to grow into large companies. Today, there are more than 7,500 listed companies, which are categorised as large enterprises.

b) Small and Medium Entrepreneurs (SME)

SMEs play a major role in the socio-economic development of a country like India. A growing nation like India needs to nurture its SMEs to grow into large corporations. 50% of India's GDP comes from SME produce and 40% of India's industrial output comes from SMEs. This sector provides the second largest employment after agriculture. In India, the SSI is a part of the SME sector and realising its employment generating capacity, the Government in 2005 introduced the SMEDB (Small and Medium Enterprises Development Bill) which among other things, includes medium enterprises (units with investments above the SSI limit) into the SME sector in keeping with global practices. The government has suggested that PSU banks set their own targets for funding SME in order to achieve a minimum 20% year on growth in credit to SMEs, so as to double the flow of credit from Rs. 67,000 crore in 2004-05 to Rs. 135,200 crore to the SME sector by 2009-10 (5 years).

SIDBI (Small Industries Development Bank of India) has started a dedicated rating agency for SME sector called SMERA (SME Rating Agency) SME Rating Agency of India Ltd. in association with Dun & Bradstreet (D&B), Credit information Bureau (I) Ltd and leading public and private sector banks to enable SMEs to avail of credit at lower interest rates and minimum collaterals. SMEs employment generating capacity has been felt across the globe in G-8 countries like Canada, US, Japan as the well as the Asian Tigers like Taiwan, Korea and China.

c) Co-operatives

The cooperatives have proven to be viable option to provide direct and indirect employment to thousands of people. Dr. Verghese Kurien created the concept of AMUL co-operative which led to the economic upliftment of milk producers of Anand district in rural Gujarat. Besides, women co-operatives like Lijjat papad have given gainful employment to hundreds.

d) Economic Cluster Entrepreneurs

Economic clusters are present in Moradabad for brass, Aligarh for locks, Meerut for sports goods etc., where quality, scale of production sourcing raw materials are problems. UNIDO, a UN body has supported the clusters to move up the value chain. As per UNIDO, there are 388 clusters, 4,90,000 enterprises, employing 7.5 million people and an output of Rs.160000 crores. Most economic clusters have grown in strength and today need help in the form of common R&D facilities, information centres, and help in buying the latest equipments. Marketing, especially International is much needed to tap the export market.

e) Micro credit based Self-Help Groups (SHG)

India is the world's seventh largest country in land area and the second largest in population; around 64% of the population lives in the rural areas depending on agriculture as a source of livelihood. There is a high level of disguised unemployment, illiteracy and poverty in the rural areas. The agricultural sector has seen a poor growth rate of under 3.5% and with a population explosion, there is massive unemployment and as much as 75% of the poor are in rural areas. In this scenario, we have NABARD which has played a crucial role in starting SHG in different rural pockets like Kachhighati in Aurangabad district where watershed Development programme was introduced and a mere loan of Rs. 25,000 from NABARD and contribution of Rs. 50 by each SHG member led to the purchase of 10 goats for the ten members. Today, each member has 4-5 goats and earn about Rs. 1000. Even the SBI has targeted women to start SHG and lend Rs.1800 crores and have a repayment record of 99%. Its activities are spread over Andhra Pradesh, Kerala, Gujarat, Maharashtra and Uttar Pradesh and income generation activities include fish farming, vermicompost making, spice trading, pottery making, dairy farming, bamboo craft and wood carving. The loan amount ranges from Rs.14, 000 to Rs. 3.5 lakh. The earliest example of micro finance initiative in the private sector dates back to 1974, when Ms. Ela Bhat of SEWA (Self-Employed Women's Association) provided banking service to the rural poor in the unorganised sector in Ahmedabad, through its bank Shri Mahila SEWA Sahakari Bank.

AN ANALYSIS OF THE STATE POLICY INITIATIVES ON ENTREPRENEURSHIP

1. *Business Environment:* The Business environment of a country has a positive relationship with development of entrepreneurship. The political environment, industrial policy, licensing policy, foreign exchange regulations, banking policy, technological development and social change form the framework within which an enterprise has to work.

    The business environment can be broadly categorised as:

    ❖ *Political:* Policy decisions on equity and debt financing, skills development through training and education, policy on support services like business advisory including techno-commercial studies, incubators and EDP.

THE SUPPORT SYSTEM OF THE STATE (GOVERNMENT)

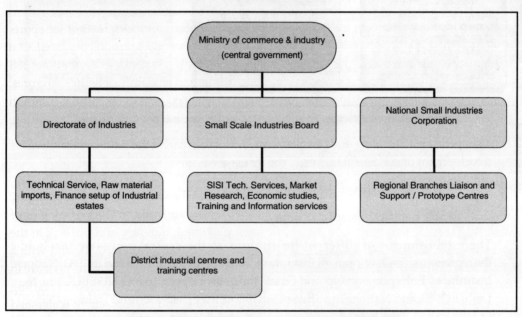

Figure 1: State Policy Initiatives on Entrepreneurship

❖ *Economic:* Economic, Labour policies, Trade and tariff, Incentives and Subsidies.

❖ *Social:* Family support, attitudes and motivation to become an entrepreneur.

❖ *Technological:* Training, efficiency, productivity and competitiveness, R&D, level of infrastructure.

❖ *Legal:* Laws for Taxation, Rules and regulations for running an enterprise, competition/Free markets.

❖ *Cultural:* Values and Aspirations of the cultures and subcultures and its mindset.

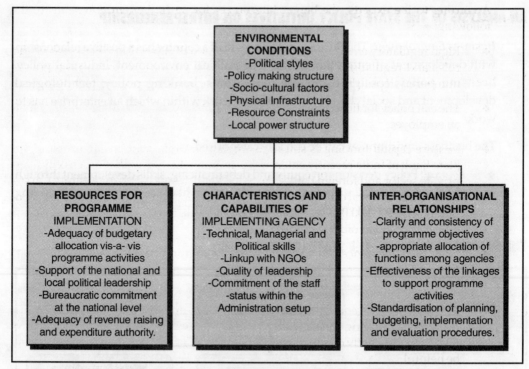

Figure 2: Factors affecting Implementation of Entrepreneurial Development

2. *Entrepreneurial Training and Development:* Towards creating the right environment for development of successful business, the thrust areas are:

    ❖   Ensure entrepreneurs possess the right skills,

    ❖   Enable networking and exchange.

    The establishment of different institutions at the central and state levels like Entrepreneurship Development Institute of India (EDII) in Ahmedabad in 1983, National Institute of Entrepreneurship and Small Business Development (NIESBUD) in New Delhi in 1983, and National Institute of Small Industry Extension and Training (NISIET) in Hyderabad have helped in co-ordination and development of Small and Medium Entrepreneurial (SME) activities in India.

3. *Banking and Finance*

    ❖   Entrepreneurs should find it easy to start a business: Indian process is slow whereas in US, a Venture Capitalist (VC) or angel investor is brought in early on, professional multifunctional management team would drive the business and early partnerships would be explored to scale up business.

    ❖   Ensure entrepreneurs have access to smart capital.

    ❖   Involve the public sector banks like SBI and other private sector banks like ICICI banks in having structured SME funding procedures and also offer micro credit.

According to the experts, the bigger hindrances for an Indian entrepreneur are the following:

❖ Rigid regulatory environment puts off the keenest of entrepreneurs whereas simple rules and regulations are much more effective worldwide. India has twice the number of steps to be completed before starting an enterprise compared to China.

❖ The exit policy for firms is very complicated. Unlike China, it is difficult to terminate an employee.

❖ Venture capital funding is still in its infancy in India, with its largest bank, the State Bank of India recently entering VC funding. Earlier, we have seen only a few private sector and foreign banks like ICICI Ventures and Citibank Venture Capital offering seed capital during the incubation period for the start-ups. I-flex Solutions Ltd. received $ 4,00,000 seed funds from Citibank. However, most PSU banks are risk averse and avoid VC funding.

❖ High NPA incidence has stymied further bank funding especially for the SME. Japanese model of credit guarantee system could be a solution besides securitisation of bad loans by asset reconstruction Companies.

❖ The difficulty of equity markets to help start-up ventures to tap funds. The confidence building measures by industry associations like CII, ASSOCHAM, FICCI, etc., to jointly conduct road shows for IPO's from these new ventures could be helpful.

❖ Since banks give loan on the risk perception basis, they should develop expertise in funding SME, with recruitment of people in the loan department familiar with domain knowledge of the different SMEs. Further credit risk rating models can help banks price their loans competitively.

❖ Taxation is stiff and this can be improved by giving tax holidays to new ventures especially those coming up in backward zones.

❖ Marketing deficiency is prevalent among cluster entrepreneurs and the other SME. Offering common consultancy and advisory service in both domestic and export marketing can offset this.

❖ Increasing competitiveness both domestically and globally with WTO guidance on opening of marketing and removal of quotas. Government support on R&D and bringing of new technology can offset some of these concerns. However, the Indian ventures are also challenging China on the cost front by improving productivity, etc.

❖ Lack of skills and competency to manage the rapid changes in the environment. The different bodies like District Industries Centres, Entrepreneurship Development Institute of India (EDII), IIMs, SP Jain Institute, Indian Institute of Entrepreneurship and National Institute of Small Industry Extension and Training (NISIET) and finally, National Productivity Council (NPC) can equip the entrepreneurs to face the challenges better.

❖ Non-availability of raw materials at competitive prices. Since the market is highly fragmented, the government should have a policy to help the SME and cluster entrepreneurs, by collective procurements to avail of volume discounts.

❖ Infrastructural bottlenecks can be improved with more warehousing, adequate power supply, better roads and improved communication.

❖ Inconsistency of policy decisions lead to sudden changes whenever a new party comes to power. A general consensus among political parties would help to have long-term policies firmly in place.

❖ Quality control facilities poor. The government can have common quality control facilities in accordance with international standards.

❖ Rural SHG usually ignorant about government departments. More publicity is required about the facilities that can be availed by them under micro credit funding.

❖ Micro finance has only reached a mere 2% of the county's 60 million poor families and as of now, all PSU banks are going slow on lending to the very poor. However, NABARD has a target of starting one million SHG by the year 2008.

Inspiring Examples of Indian Entrepreneurial Success

(a) *Reliance Industries Ltd.:* The story of Dhirubhai Ambani is epitomised as the ultimate entrepreneurial success story of independent India wherein a man made a journey from obscurity to fame. He was born to Jamunaben and Hirachand G. Ambani, a lowly paid schoolteacher in 1932, in Chorwad, a village the in Saurashtra region of Gujarat.

At the age of seventeen, he went to Aden in 1949 and took his first job as a gas station attendant earning a monthly salary of Rs. 300.

On his return to Mumbai in 1958, he started spice trading of ginger and turmeric under a firm Reliance Commercial Co-operation, floated with a capital of Rs.15,000. In 1959, he switched business to yarn trade. Eventually, he bought up a mill at Naroda, Gujarat in 1966. In 1977, the company went public and 58,000 investors, mostly first timers in shares purchased his shares and history was made. Finally, at the time of his passing away in 2002, Reliance had become a Fortune 500 company.

(b) *Infosys Technology Ltd.:* This is a story of six technocrats from IIT, who in 1981 started Infosys with a capital of Rs.10,000 at Mr. Narayan Murthy's house in Pune. Principally led by Narayan Murthy, the six showed enormous courage in starting as small time techno-entrepreneurs. Today, this company has created the largest stakeholder wealth in this country and its revenue exceeds $2 million and has 50,000 employees. This IT giant has a worldwide presence and has proved for all entrepreneurs what it means to dream big.

(c) *Amul Ltd.:* Amul is the best example of the success of the co-operative movement in India. As a part of the White Revolution movement, Dr. Verghese Kurien started this co-operative in Anand, Gujarat and transformed the lives of thousands of farmers and rural folk who joined this dairy business.

(d) *Calvin Kare:* This is the story of C.K. Ranganathan from the rural Cuddalore district of Tamil Nadu. He managed to manufacture a shampoo in his home and used to sell it loose in the rural areas on his bicycle. He went on to form this company and challenged MNC companies like HLL and P&G. Today, his products include shampoos, Talcum powder, pickles and other FMCG products and have an all-India market.

(e) ***Nirma:*** Karsanbhai Patel's life story is one of an average lower middle-class man, working as a chemist in Gujarat Mineral Development Corporation on a meagre salary. He dared to dream and experimented in his kitchen on a low cost washing powder. He recognised a need for an affordable product and named it Nirma after his daughter Nilanjana who expired subsequently. This product took on the might of the MNC behemoth HLL, as he sold his product in small plain pouches door to door, on his bicycle. As the word-of-mouth spread, so did his customers and sales. Eventually, Nirma captured 35% market share and has become a classic case of marketing success for an entrepreneur, directly employing 14,000 people.

(f) ***Biocon:*** Started in Bangalore by a first generation women entrepreneur Ms. Kiran Mazumdar Shaw, BIOCON has created the largest New Age company in Biotechnology. After its public issue two years back, this company has catapulted its CEO to the richest women entrepreneur in India.

Relevance

India is an emerging economy and happens to be one of the fastest growing economies in the world. India had a 9% plus GDP growth rate for 2006. However, the country is still plagued by poverty, unemployment and a lowly rank of 127 on the Human Development index. It is our contention that if the entrepreneurship culture can spread within India and produce profitable business ventures then it could help to boost our economy. To aid this process, the government should develop crystallised policy initiatives for entrepreneurship development and enhance their competitiveness and success.

Limitation

This study is merely exploratory in nature and secondary data sources like newspaper articles, published conference papers and websites have been scanned for data. The government policy makers or the departments directly associated with entrepreneurship could not be interviewed for their opinions.

Observations on State Policy Initiatives

The findings of this paper strongly support the argument that the Indian policy on entrepreneurs has improved considerable in the last decade with the liberalisation process and the increased integration with the world economy. However, the pace has been slow and to give impetus to the entrepreneurship movement, much more needs to be done. Based on the observations, the author has a few suggestions as mentioned below:

- In comparison to other countries like China and South Korea, the Indian government has not introduced enough incentive programmes and schemes to support the growth and development of start-ups in the incubation stage.

- The Small and Medium Enterprise can transform into large scale companies through the catalytic process provided by the government policy on tax holidays, venture capital funding, corporatisation and other innovative methods.

- Bureaucratic red-tape and numerous permissions required to start an enterprise should be simplified to a single window and have friendly assistance centres.

- The rampant corruption at all levels for getting licence and permits kills the spirit behind entrepreneurship and the government should strengthen the anti-corruption departments.

- Inadequate and delayed bank credit for SMEs and lack of incentives for angels and venture capitals to fund start ups during the incubation period act as a major deterrence. The government should introduce steps to ease these problems.

- SME definition should spell out in clear terms whether services and trade are included as is the global practice.

Result

It appears that policy decisions have not succeeded in creating an enabling environment due to the following:

- Rampant corruption, bureaucratic delays, inspector raj.

- Taxation system is unfriendly. The short-term loss of tax revenue for faster development is in the interest of the country.

- Infrastructure is very poor and need for SEZ level facilities.

- Political inertia on changes in policy.

It is suggested that further research can be undertaken to see why the Indian Entrepreneurs seem to do better when they start a business aboard.

CONCLUSION

Globalisation and liberalisation have no doubt created tremendous opportunities for the growth of entrepreneurs, but in its wake, they have brought in greater competitiveness and challenges.

However, we notice that India can't progress until large areas of backward rural India increase their very low per capita income, move out of illiteracy and access business information and ideas through small-scale entrepreneurship.

The role of Small and Medium Entrepreneurs would be vital and the government policies should be clear-cut to promote the establishment of new ventures. The importance of nurturing cluster entrepreneurs by government initiatives would also strengthen this marginal segment.

The enormous success of micro financing through Grameen Bank initiatives in neighbouring Bangladesh by Dr Khan Nobel laureate, has shown what could be successfully replicated in India. The rural poor who make up Bharat need all the governmental support to become the backbone of India's path to entrepreneurial success.

In conclusion, what needs to be done is to have integrated programmes where concrete public policy decisions are made to make our entrepreneurs more competitive and successful.

References

Charantimath, Poornima M. (2006), *Entrepreneurship Development Small Business Enterprises*, New Delhi, Pearson Education, chapters 1 & 4.

Chopra V.K (2005), *Micro Finance & Self Help Group - Role & Issues*, paper published at BanCon, 2005.

Desai, Vasant (2005), *Dynamics of Entrepreneurial Development and Management*, Mumbai, Himalaya Publishing House, Units 1& 2.

Ghosh, Parijat, Karamchandani, Ashish and Arboleda, Pedro (2006), "The New Frontiers of Entrepreneurship", *The Strategist, Business Standard*, June 20, 2006.

Javeri, B.L. (2005), *Small and Medium Enterprises (SMEs): The thrust sector*, paper published at BanCon, 2005.

Kumar, Sharad (2005), *Micro finance; Strength of rural sector in India*, paper published at BanCon, 2005.

Mohan Kumar, G. (2005), *Small and Medium Enterprises-Support for Higher Growth*, paper published at Bancon, 2005.

www.sidbi.com

www.ssi.nic.in

www.laghu-udyog.com

26

Encouraging Entrepreneurs in Agricultural Production: A Strategy for Increasing Agricultural Growth in India

Sudhanshu Kumar*
Vijay Laxmi Pandey**

INTRODUCTION

Market makers or the entrepreneurs in our discussion are the people who reorganize existing economic activity in an innovative and valuable way. They are the risk-takers who can improve the way agriculture is carried out in our country. In India, farmers need to be more entrepreneurial as there is the need of those people to be involved in the agriculture who take it as if, it were not a subsistence activity but can be made a profitable business. This will improve the growth rate of agriculture, which has been a major concern, as it has always grown at a rate lower than that of GDP and after 1990 has failed to achieve the targeted growth rate (Figure 1). There is a need to bring change in the thinking that agriculture is a stagnant activity, designed to produce basic necessities for the local market or export traditional commodities or import substitution, to international competition. In the present study, we are going to look into the biggest hurdle in the way of the entrepreneurs: infrastructure and the marketing facility.

It has been observed that agriculture has become relatively unrewarding due to unfavourable price regime and low value addition. According to NSS Situational Assessment Survey of Farmers (2003), conducted for Indian farmers, 40% of the farm households would like to quit farming to take up some other career, 27% of the households don't like farming because of its not being profitable. One of the prime reasons is that they are unable to get appropriate return for their farm produce due to unavailability of efficient market. Such a situation has led to abandoning of farming by the skilled people and increasing migration from the rural areas. The situation is likely to get worse in the wake of agriculture trade liberalization if immediate corrective measures are not taken. Therefore, we need to increase the growth rate of agriculture by not only producing efficiently but also marketing the produce efficiently in which entrepreneurs have to play a larger role.

In the current scenario, we need to focus on two factors: How to produce more? And, how to manage this plenty of produce efficiently so that our grass root level entrepreneurs, i.e., farmers, derive benefit from this? There is a need to shift agriculture from being just a farm activity to

---

* Ph.D. Student, Indira Gandhi Institute of Development Research, Mumbai.
** Faculty, Indira Gandhi Institute of Development Research, Mumbai.

agribusiness, which provides a link between agriculture, livestock, fishery, forestry and development of upstream and downstream agriculture-based industries. To achieve marketing efficiency, better physical and institutional infrastructure facilities are must. With this background, this paper intends to address how to encourage farmers to be part of agri-bussiness. One of the important factors of agri-business is efficient marketing.

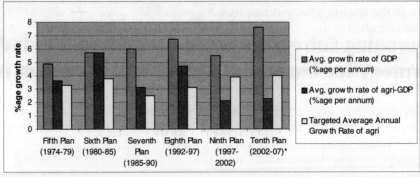

(*Source:* Central Statistical Organisation)

Figure 1: Average Growth Rate of Agriculture and GDP

POTENTIAL OF AGRICULTURAL MARKETING IN INDIA

India has certain advantages, which need to be leveraged, like very good natural resource endowment for agricultural production, large tract of fertile land, 9-10 months of good sunshine and above all bio-diversity in agriculture production, i.e. it can produce various products of demand with easily available labour and abundance of resources.

Despite having the potential, Indian agriculture has failed to achieve higher growth rate. The Economic Outlook (2007-2008)[1] points out, "India is quite favourably placed both in terms of arable land and irrigated land. However, when it comes to yield per acre, India does not compare well with China, the developed economies and in some cases with other developing economies as well. Nor does it compare well for several crops in terms of the gains in yield increases over time. Clearly, India has considerable potential gains to be realized in agriculture".

Traditional excuses (irrigation facility, smaller farm sizes, lower mechanisation, etc.) for lower growth rate of Indian agriculture is not true, as China has shown growth rate of more than 4% in recent years compared to the Indian growth rate of 2.7%. Even though, on all the parameters of traditional factors, India is in a position better than China (as evident from Table 1).

Table 1: Comparative Statistics of India and China

	INDIA	CHINA
Arable Land (Million hectare)	161	130
Irrigated Land (Million hectare)	55.8 (33%)	54.5 (35%)
Average Farm Size (In hectare)	1.4	0.4
Farm Mechanisation (Tractors per 1000 hectare)	15.7	7

(*Source:* Economic Outlook for 2007-08, Data are for year 2003)

---

[1] By Economic Advisory Committee to Prime Minister headed by C. Rangarajan.

The major sources of agriculture related discrepancy between India and China are: diverging productivity levels of different crops (technological factor) and the differential mix of crop and non-crop segments in the overall composition of the farm sector (management factor).

The agricultural sector in China today is more diversified, which raises the income of the farmers, in the sense that profitable horticulture, animal husbandry and fisheries contribute about 45% of the total agricultural output whereas in India, it is less than 30% of the total agricultural output.

The major reasons for their success are: technological improvements from extensive research and development, investment in rural infrastructure and liberalized agricultural policy adopted to promote the competitive advantage.

In the current scenario, with stagnated productivity level of cereals, the future growth of agriculture lies in its diversification, success of which depends on market efficiency for these products. For which, apart from R&D, roads, storage, post-harvest management and market facility, the skill level of those who are involved are major concern. A revealing study by "Transport Corporation of India" for long-distance movement of trucks has found that the average distance travelled by a truck; which is a major mode of carrying agricultural produce from farm to port, airport to market in India, is 350 km/day, whereas it is about 1000 km/day in China and the US. It makes production of horticulture produce and other items, which are highly perishable, economically non-viable in remote areas, though they have huge potential for producing these commodities.

Due to stagnation in the earlier crop pattern, the alternative lies in crop diversification. But due to poor post harvest management and lack of proper marketing facility, there is always a question whether we are able to reap the potential benefit from crop diversification. In the absence of linkages between production and available huge market, bumper crop in a season in a locality lead to fall in prices, which benefits the consumer but not the farmer, who produces it. Since, it is rare for local demand to keep pace with supply for horticulture products, milk and poultry and the growers have no access to market where potential demand exists. And it discourages the skilled people to engage in the activity. There is the need to have a pan-Indian market with improved storage facility, processing and packaging and good transportation facility. As a study by ICRISAT[2] suggested that free movement of trade within the country, density of road and availability of market facility has a measurable effect on increasing agricultural productivity.

DATA AND METHODOLOGY

For understanding how efficient is the market for farm producers especially for the diversified products, we have taken the difference in two prices, Wholesale Price[3] and Farm Harvest Price[4] as proxy. We have selected two crops one from cereals and one from cash crop, as wheat is procured by government agency at minimum support price[5] and the other potato[6]. We have chosen major producer states on the basis of area of production[7]. Data over the period 1990 to 2001

---

[2] International Crop Research Institute for the Semi-Arid Tropics.
[3] Wholesale price indicates the price a most efficient consumer pays. The most efficient consumers are those who are able to purchase items at the lowest market price, which is the wholesale price here.
[4] Farm harvest price is the price what farmer gets for his crop at the time of harvest.
[5] Announced by the government on the basis of cost of cultivation.
[6] Part of horticulture.
[7] CMIE: Report on agriculture.

was taken for the two prices from the publications of ministry of agriculture for prices. We have found correlation co-efficient between WSP and FHP, to understand that over the period how much of the prices received by farmers is defined by the wholesale prices. For considering situation of infrastructure, we have taken available state-wise relative infrastructure index, which consider various factors affecting infrastructure.

RESULTS AND DISCUSSION

Difference in the prices shows a cyclical fluctuation over time. With the frequent negative values for wheat, i.e., farm harvest price is more than the wholesale price, is at par with the fact that these crops are highly supported by the government for their procurement. Thus, it is the government that bears the difference. But in the case of potato, it is mostly positive except for Karnataka, which is due to the fact that the government does not support markets for potato by direct procurement. Data from year 1990 to 2001 show a positive correlation between the two prices, which is very high in the case of wheat but varying low value in the case of cash crop potato (Table 1&2). High value of correlation shows that any movement in the wholesale price affects the farmers' price. For the same states (Bihar and UP), the correlation co-efficient for two commodities show different pattern, very high value for wheat, whereas very low value for potato.

On the basis of relative infrastructure index, these states are at very low ranks (Table 4). It indicates that the functioning mechanism of market in the period is not favourable for the producers of the cash crop, as the price they get is not largely determined by the prevailing market price. Wheat draws high degree of support for procurement from government, which may be a reason for high correlation between the prices, whereas there is no support in terms of procurement for potato. From these data, it can be inferred up to some extent that the infrastructure support available for wheat is not there for the promotion of potato. This indicates a need for more institutional and physical support for efficient market to achieve crop diversification in such a way that farmers are able to achieve proper price[8] for their produce.

Table 2: Correlation Coefficient for Wheat (1990-2001)

MAJOR STATES (By Area of production)	WHEAT (Correlation between FHP & WSP)
Bihar	0.8324
Haryana	0.8606
Madhya Pradesh	0.8834
Gujarat	0.9261
Punjab	0.9267
Rajasthan	0.8982
Uttar Pradesh	0.9024

---

[8] Which will reduce the gap between Whole Sale Price and Farm Harvest Price.

Table 3: Correlation Coefficient for Potato (1990-2001)

MAJOR STATES (By Area of production)	POTATO (Correlation between FHP & WSP)
Bihar	0.3918
Karnataka	0.6815
Maharashtra	0.7068
Uttar Pradesh	0.2385
West Bengal	0.2759

Table 4: State-wise Relative Index of Infrastructure in India[9] (During 1980-81 & 1996-97)[10]

States	1980-81	1996-97	States	1980-81	1996-97
Andhra Pradesh	98.09 (8)	93.06 (11)	Madhya Pradesh	62.15 (17)	74.08 (17)
Assam	77.71 (15)	75.57 (16)	Maharashtra	120.1 (6)	111.29 (6)
Bihar	83.53 (13)	77.84 915)	Orissa	81.46 (14)	98.88 (9)
Gujarat	122.99 (5)	121.79 (5)	Punjab	207.31 (1)	185.59 (1)
Haryana	145.52 (4)	137.24 (4)	Rajasthan	74.45 (16)	83.92 (13)
Himachal Pradesh	83.54 (12)	102.49 (8)	Tamil Nadu	158.61 (2)	138.91 (3)
Jammu & Kashmir	88.66 (11)	81.27 (14)	Uttar Pradesh	97.7 (9)	103.81 (7)
Karnataka	94.81 (10)	94.32 (10)	West Bengal	110.6 (7)	90.76 (12)
Kerala	158.05 (3)	155.38 (2)	India	100	100

SITUATION OF AGRICULTURAL MARKETS IN INDIA AND IMPROVING THEIR EFFICIENCY

Agricultural markets in various states in India are regulated and managed under the Agricultural Produce Markets Act enacted by the respective state governments with the objective of improving the institutional and physical infrastructure at the level of primary wholesale markets for farm products. Since the regulated markets had limited success, the Central Government came out with the Model Act (2003), that encourages the development of competitive agricultural marketing, deregulates the marketing system to promote private investment in marketing infrastructure. But there is no uniformity in enacting and amending the APMC Act on the guidelines of new central Act[11] and it is at different stages in different states, even among the major states, Bihar and Kerala have not taken any step to amend the existing Act. Marketing efficiency depends on the various factors affecting the value chain from production to marketing for a certain commodity. With the huge amount of retail investment by major businesses, there will be increased demand for ensured supply, which needs better agricultural produce management; like nationwide distribution infrastructure, increased storage capacity and lower government intervention by allowing private sector to procure, trade and store without restriction.

Infrastructure: Infrastructure in rural areas in India, though improving, is still in primitive stage. Frequent power outages, poor roads and with large number of illiterate population incapable of understanding the new signals and training, poses a challenge to the competent entrepreneur to carry out agribusiness in the rural areas. Marketing infrastructure is important

---

[9] (Source: indiastat.com)
[10] Value in parenthesis indicate the ranking in the respective years.
[11] Marketing is a state subject.

not only for functioning of market and their expansion but also for transfer of signals, which leads to market efficiency (Acharya, 1994) and Ahmed (1995), in their studies, about the impact of investment in rural infrastructure, concluded that improved infrastructure is a primary driving force under every condition for commercialization.

There is considerable regional variation in the availability of different infrastructure in the country (Table 4), due to which, the farmers in the states with poor infrastructure though with huge potential of producing, don't get adequate market signals and remains cut-off from new developments in the market. This poses a major obstacle in developing an efficient pan-Indian market. From Table 4, it is evident that at two different time points, there is not much change in the relative positioning of top six states i.e., figures may be different but pattern is more or less same.

Physical Infrastructure: Roads, railways, electrification, storage facility, telecommunication, grading, packing and processing requires huge initial capital investment and institutional infrastructures usually require limited initial capital investment but substantial operational and maintenance cost. The Expert Committee on Agricultural marketing estimated an investment requirement of Rs. 2,68,700 crore during the current decade for improving these infrastructures. The Government cannot provide the entire investment by itself as it has limited resources available, while, public debt and other government liabilities are increasing; there is the need of private investment. To attract private investment, the government needs to develop basic infrastructures: roads, electricity and a conducive regulatory framework. The report of the task force on Agricultural Reforms (2001), suggested that the credit flow to agricultural sector need to be substantially stepped up to meet increasing demand for capital expenditure for developing marketing infrastructure and for pledging finance, which enables those involved in the farming to take advantage of favourable prices and improve their net margins. In this regard, we need to leverage the potential of a phenomenal outreach of branches of commercial banks and Regional Rural Banks, to transform agriculture into agribusiness.

SHG & PRIs: Given the small size of the marketed surplus with individual farmers, and the fact that they constitute 54% of the total marketed surplus, to gain the benefits of economies of scale in marketing and improved marketing technology, farmers should be promoted to make small groups or associations based on similar interest. It has been established that peer group formation reduces the risk of default leading to easier access of credit (Aghion *et al.*, 2000). So apart from the strengthening the bargaining power of small farmer, formation of Self-help Groups will also help in promoting better credit facility.

Panchayati Raj institutions can play very important role in making agro-marketing more efficient by undertaking various activities. They can act as a link between market players and farmers by ensuring the smoother flow of information. They are the best medium to approach the farmers for making them aware about good agricultural practices and for market extension. For this, all panchayats need to be linked with the various agencies of market at district, state and national level through the Internet and telephones.

Promotion of GAP: According to the Food and Agricultural Organisation, "Good Agricultural Practices (GAP) is the application of available knowledge to address environmental, economic and social sustainability for on-farm production and post-production processes, resulting in production of safe and healthy food and non-food agricultural products". For capturing the huge world market, GAP is becoming the pre-requisite. Though, in India, it is at the very initial stage, we should encourage to ensure food safety from farm to the consumers' plate. In this regard, Panchayti Raj institutions can play a crucial role in promoting GAP at producer level.

Forward/Future Trading in Agriculture: With the increasing risk of production and price variability for the agricultural producers in the agricultural market, risk management has become an important strategy for the producers, either farmer or processor. One of the means of decreasing risk is through the use of the commodity futures exchange market. Though in a nascent stage in India, market-driven price stabilization mechanisms and risk management system in agriculture, through future trades in organized exchanges is seen as a tool for ensuring stable income to farmers and continuous supply of inputs to the agri-business activities. In order to derive benefit from future trading, we need to make commodity market more efficient at par with the world standard. In India, most of the commodity exchanges are associations of members who retain trading rights and ownership, which are integrated in the membership right, there is the need to segregate the ownership and trading rights.

We need to promote farmers participation in the future markets, by strengthening the regional commodity market. Banks with rural branches should be allowed to play a bigger role in the development of commodity market. With a huge network of branches of commercial banks and regional rural banks in rural areas, they have greater exposure to agriculture. And hence, they can play a valuable role in assisting the farmers, as farmers in the remote areas are not in a position to hedge their price risks for their crops on commodity future exchanges. Through these banks, they can participate directly in this form of market. For this, there is the need to improve the collateral value of the goods, and credit flow to commodity market by ensuring efficient monitoring authority to inspect and certify delivery of the traded items on time.

CONCLUSION

The future growth of agriculture lies in the crop diversification, and to take its advantage, farmers need to be more entrepreneurial. There is need of those people to be involved in the agriculture who take it as if it were not a subsistence activity but a profitable business. To encourage and motivate agricultural entrepreneurs, there is a need to have better marketing infrastructure based on improved both physical and institutional infrastructure. As the study suggests that in the absence of support from the government, farmers are unable to get sufficient price for their produce. Without efficient marketing, the farmers are unable to reap the benefit of crop diversification due to mismatch between demand and supply. In addition, there is the need to have enough storage capacity to minimise the post-harvest losses.

Farmers as entrepreneurs should be skilled at selecting the commodities to be produced based on the competitive advantages that we have in certain commodities. There is the need of market-led production to provide maximum benefits to the farmers and hence, attracting skilled individuals to participate in this agri-business venture. This is totally lacking in all the regions of the country and therefore, information pertaining to demand and supply, price fetched in various seasons, quality of items required, quantity and its time of availability in the market has to be made available to the growers through local newspapers, radios and televisions in their local languages.

There is a need to create a network with viable marketing channels covering all the linkages from villages to the global level. To create a sustainable market linkage for rural products, we should promote formation of Self-Help Groups (SHGs) by involving the local communities through village level empowerment for both continued supply of the inputs for the agribusiness and also for capturing the rural market. Panchayati Raj institutions have to play a larger role in ensuring the smoother flow of information by acting as a link between the market and the farmers. Providing quality education to the farmers is necessary, which will help them in adopting the new developments easily. Thus, with the new development, we need an integrated approach from basic infrastructure to developing and opening of the markets for the agricultural growth.

References

Acharya, S.S. (1994), *"Marketing Environment for Farm Products - Emerging Issues and Challenges"*, *Indian Journal of Agricultural Marketing*, 8(2): 162-75, July- September.

Ahmed, R. (1995), *Investment in Rural Infrastructure: Commercialisation in Bangladesh* in Von Braun, Jochim and Eileen Kennedy (Ed.) Agricultural Commercialisation, Economic development and Nutrition, IFPRI, Washington: The John Hopkins University.

De Aghion, Beatriz Armendariz, Ggollier, Christian Gollier, *"Peer Group Formation in an Adverse Selection Model"*, *The Economic Journal*, Volume 110, Number 465, July 2000, pp. 632-643(12).

Economic Advisory Council to Prime Minister of India", *Economic Outlook for 2007-08"*.

Food and Agriculture Organisation of the United Nations (2007), *"FAOSTAT–Agriculture, Online database"*.

Jairatt M.S., Kamboj. P, (2005), *"Some Constraints to Indian Agriculture Commodity Futures"*, *Indian Journal of Agricultural Marketing*, 19(2).

Encouraging Entrepreneurs in Agriculture Production: A strategy for increasing agriculture growth in India.

Ministry of Agriculture and Co-operation (2004), *Agricultural Statistics*, Government of India, New Delhi.

M. Von Oppen, P. Parthasarthy Rao, K. V. Subba Rao, *Impact of Market Access on Agricultural Productivity in India*, ICRISAT, Andhra Pradesh, India.

National Sample Survey (2003), *Situation Assessment Survey of Indian Farmers.*

Transport Corporation of India (2007), *Road Transport Service Efficiency Study.*

27

Relationship Building in Small Businesses in Maharashtra's 3 Cities - The Case of Linking Personal Selling with Collectivism

Sulbha Raorane*
Ashiya Shaikh*
Dr. Pradip Manjrekar**

This paper examines the link between personal selling and collectivism found in small clothing and shoe retailers in three major cities (Pune, Nasik and Aurangabad) of Maharashtra. The results of the study show a strong link between choice of personal selling as a promotional tool and the collectivist orientation on the part of the retailers. The main conclusion of this paper therefore, is that where there is a definitive link between personal selling and collectivism in small clothing and shoe retailers, there also needs to be an understanding on the part of these retailers of how to most effectively use personal selling in their business.

INTRODUCTION

In today's highly technical and fast paced market, consumers are increasingly becoming aware of the need to gather more information regarding products and services before they make a final purchase decision. This information is often available mainly through the form of sales personnel, who act as communicators of a company's market offerings and are seen as somewhat more reliable as the less personal forms of promotion tools such as print and broadcast advertising. Due to the direct contact that a salesperson has with current and potential customers, personal selling is being perceived as a critical contributor to a firm's business success (Brooksbank, 1995). To a small firm, which may find that its promotional efforts go relatively unnoticed in the mass of media communication already in the market, personal selling may be a way to differentiate themselves or to build and maintain effective customer-firm relationships that will continue in the future (Manning and Reece, 1998). Satisfied customers often recommend the business to other potential customers, adding a

---

* Faculty, St. Francis Institute of Management Studies & Research Borivli (W), Mumbai.
** Professor & Head - Research & Extension Centre, Dr. D. Y. Patil Institute of Management Studies, CBD Belapur, Navi Mumbai.

certain amount of extra value to the sale itself, or highlight other product or service needs that the firm may not have easily identified without the two-way communication that personal selling brings (Manning and Reece, 1998). A number of studies have examined why retailers choose promotional tools such as personal selling, identifying several reasons such as the nature of the business (Greenley and Shipley, 1992), the target audience (Nowak, Cameron and Krugman, 1993), the cost effectiveness of the tool (Jackson, Hawkes and Hertel, 1979) and the media attributes (Otnes and Faber, 1989). However, few studies look at the cultural influence behind promotional tool choice (Fam and Merilees, 1998). This study aims to establish the main cultural influence that drives small retailers to focus on personal selling as an important promotional tool for their business and looks at clothing and shoe retailers across three major cities (Pune, Nasik and Aurangabad). The research examines the choice of the personal communication method and seeks to illustrate a connection between this form of promotional tool use and the cultural nature of the retailers who employ it. Small, independent retailers have been chosen because they have been "the numerically dominant retail form in many cities for a very long-time" (Smith and Sparks, 2000, p.205).

BACKGROUND LITERATURE

Personal Selling

Personal selling can be defined as "a seller's presentation conducted on a face-to-face basis with a buyer" where advertising and other promotional tools are largely a non-personal sales presentation paid for by an identified sponsor, usually directed to a large number of potential customers (Marks, 1997). The main attribute of personal selling is that there is essentially a two-way communication flow between the seller and the potential buyer (Manning and Reece, 1998). The ability on the part of the customers to check their understanding of the product or service offered and request further information from the sales person highlights the difference between other promotional tools and the personal selling method (Marks, 1997). These factors show that personal selling as a promotional communication method is inherently more flexible in its ability to be tailored to an individual consumer, can have a greater impact on that consumer and has the advantage of being able to impart a much more complex message to potential customers.

Personal Selling as a Promotional Tool

Personal selling is regarded as an important promotional tool because the appearance of salespersons, knowledge of products and friendliness are equally effective compared to the other promotional tools available when communicating information regarding a firm and the products and services it offers. The use of personal selling as a promotional tool is important for retailers as salespersons can be used to convince the consumers that the more expensive products possess attributes which justify their premium prices (Fam and Merrilees, 1998). For small retailers, where the very nature of being a small business often precludes them from being able to match the cheaper product or service offerings of larger firms (Smith and Sparks, 2000), the use of personal selling via experienced and approachable salespeople can help create a more friendly and helpful shopping environment for the consumer, which gives the impression that the retailer cares about their current and potential customers. These retailers desire to cultivate a friendly relationship with members of the community and consider that this can be achieved by working closely with their target markets. These retailers are deemed to possess cultural values such as collectivism, a community-based value that encourages relationship building amongst its members (Fam and Merrilees, 1998).

Personal Selling and Small Retailers

Smith and Sparks (2000), believe that small retailers have an inherent sense of self-preservation that causes them to work very hard at their businesses to succeed. The authors state that this may be manifested in a small retailer's greater understanding of the local market and an appreciation of the service requirements of customers. This underlies the idea that small retailers would find the promotion tool of personal selling as greatly suited to their needs in maintaining this understanding of the retail market that they operate in. Competitive pressures such as poor site location and reduced customer flow due to increased activity by larger competitors who are able to offer more products and services at lower prices, highlights the need for small retailers to establish a distinctive competence to differentiate itself from the competition, and personal selling may be the most obvious way of doing this.

COLLECTIVISM

Hofstede (1980), describes collectivism as one of the core cultural values that influence the form of social arrangements, customs and practices of society and he believes that collectivism belies the value of harmony in interpersonal relationships. In essence, collectivism is said to indicate a closely-knit, social framework, that is built on trust and sharing between its members (Hofstede, 1980). Teamwork and an enhanced sense of belonging are highly prized by members of a collectivist society (Fam and Merrilees, 1998) and collectivists are encouraged to work as a team and therefore strive for team recognition (Hofstede, 1980). Fam and Merrilees suggest a link between the cultural disposition of retailers and their perceptions of the different promotional tools available, and that collectivism in a retailer's cultural environment indicated a preference for the personal selling promotional tool.

Collectivism and Personal Selling

Fam and Merrilees (1998), believe that a high score on the collectivism index means that a retailer's preference for interpersonal promotional tools such as personal selling will be increased. Personal selling on the whole is more flexible than other promotion tools as two-way communication is an integral part of its use. Salespersons are able to customise a sales message according to the needs and interests of the customers (Boone and Kurtz, 1992). Customers can also use the salesperson as a source of information and reliability (Hawes, Rao and Baker, 1993). These attributes of personal selling make it an important tool in bridging the buyer/seller gap in collectivist societies. To date however, most literatures have focused on the construct for cross-cultural comparison suggested by Hofstede (1980), where a country of highly collectivist culture would be compared with one of a strong individualistic nature (Money, Gilly and Graham 1998; Aaker and Maheswaran, 1997) with the assumption that most citizens of Eastern countries are collectivist and those of Western countries individualistic. Bond (1991), questions this idea by suggesting that there may be differences in the levels of collectivism within a particular country. The focus of this study, therefore, is to identify how the different levels of collectivism affect promotional tool choice by clothing and shoes retailers in New Zealand, Portugal and Hungary, and if, as suggested by Fam and Merrilees (1998), the more collective a retailer, the more likely they are to choose interpersonal promotional tools, such as personal selling, over the other tools available.

HYPOTHESIZED RELATIONSHIPS

According to Smith and Sparks (2000), retailing is no longer a nice, cosy business environment and small retailers are finding it necessary to differentiate themselves from their competitors, whilst maintaining the community and social role that being a small retailer demands. Since collectivism is about developing and maintaining group harmony, one can expect that retailers who possess the cultural value of collectivism will perceive personal communications methods like personal sellings as more important than impersonal promotional tools (Fam and Merrilees, 1998). Small stores are often seen as a contribution to the community or a sense of identity for locals (Smith and Sparks, 2000), and personal selling emphasizes the retailer's commitment to this ideal. This suggests the following hypothesis:

H: *That retailers who are culturally collectivist in nature will perceive personal sellings as more important than other promotional tools.*

METHODOLOGY

Data Collection

The sampling frame for the data set was the cities' Yellow Pages list of clothing and shoes retail stores in these three cities (Pune, Nasik and Aurangabad). Two sets of mailings occurred, three weeks apart. In each mailing, a cover letter with the institution letterhead, a questionnaire and a reply-paid envelope were directed to the manager of each retail store. For large retailers, the questionnaire was mailed to the head office. The sample yielded a response rate of 39% (287 responses).

Research Instruments

The first set of items on the questionnaire relates to retail demographics. The second relates to promotional tool perception (i.e., perception of personal selling, print advertising, broadcast advertising, in-store promotion, direct mail, price mark-downs, public relations, sponsorship and sales promotion). The collectivism variables were measured by three items. They were drawn from studies undertaken by Kirbride and Chaw (1987), and Kelley et al, (1986). Each statement was measured with a seven-point Likert scale. A check item was included in the questionnaire to establish each respondent's job responsibility within the retail firm. The questionnaire was pre-tested.

Sample Characteristics

The respondents were the managers of retail stores because these people (in a smaller store environment) usually have the final say in the choice of promotion. Clothing stores accounted for a larger portion of the responses with 74.2%, 90.6% and 88.7% in Pune, Nasik and Aurangabad respectively. There were 89.2% responses from small and independent retailers in the Pune, whereas 68.3% in Nasik 95.7% in Aurangabad. Small and independent retailers were defined as the ones with between one and five outlets (the majority of the sample having just one outlet) and less than ten employees. The sample choice is similar to that used by Smith and Sparks (2000), in their analyses of the role and function of small firms in Scotland, where they define a small firm as "a retail establishment of any form of organisation (most commonly independently owned)…and having fewer than 10 full time employees".

RESULTS

All three of Maharashtra's cities studied exhibit a collectivist nature in terms of their cultural orientation, with all three sets of respondents also exhibiting a similar level of collectivism. Pune's collectivism scores are slightly lower than those of Nasik and Aurangabad. The comparison of retailers' promotional tool choices and their levels of collectivism support the hypothesis that retailers who are collective in their cultural nature will choose personal selling over other promotional tools. This hypothesis is supported across all three cities to a similar level and the choice of alternative promotional tools is relatively less than that of personal selling.

DISCUSSION

One might question that the very nature of small businesses requires personal selling as a promotional tool. If this were so, then these findings are of little value. We conjecture, however, that the fact that the finding is consistent across all three countries studied proves that there is indeed a linkage between collectivism and choice of personal selling. Whilst it may be true that personal selling is an inherent part of small businesses, the results show that collectivist retailers choose personal selling as a more important tool for their business than other tools. Of the three work-related cultural values, questions two and three were consistently rated most highly by retailers in the three countries studied. Question two, a belief in working sharing responsibilities, helping others and learning from others encapsulates the essence of a good personal selling focus. Sales people should work together, not only with other sales staff, but also with their customers, to achieve and maintain lasting relationships within the retail environment. Question three, the belief in mutual trust and respect also fits well with the essence of personal selling in that the sales person should represent a trustworthy and reliable source of information for the customer and the customer-salesperson relationship should therefore be based on a mutual amount of respect. In terms of promotional tool choice, personal selling best fits the nature of collectivist societies as it reinforces the concept of relationship building (an important concept in marketing at present) and tailoring a promotional package to fit the needs of individual consumers. Relative to the other promotional choices available to retailers in the three cities studied, personal selling, as mentioned previously, was seen to be the most chosen method of promotional communication. This reinforces the link outlined in the literature between personal selling and collectivist cultures, whilst showing that this link indeed holds true across three, somewhat culturally similar cities.

CONCLUSION

It is apparent from this study that small clothing and shoe retailers who exhibit a strong collectivist orientation will favour personal selling as a means of promoting their products and services. This link highlights the fact that, for these collectivist retailers, skills in the personal selling area, as well as competent sales staff, are critical to the success of their business. We suggest then, that small clothing and shoe retailers need to conduct an audit of their abilities in terms of the personal selling communication tool and consider whether the current objectives of their business meet the requirements of a personal selling focus. This may mean that small retailers of this type are forced to learn new skills in terms of using the personal selling tool more effectively in their business and will come to consider personal selling as a means of competitive advantage over their rivals in the clothing and shoe market. It is of no use to a retailer to simply choose a promotional tool over others available without making the best use of this tool possible for their firm. We reinforce the point then, that if small, collectivist clothing and shoe retailers emphasise personal selling so heavily, they need to become aware of the most valuable ways in which it can be used to benefit their business in the long-term.

References

Aaker, J. L. and Maheswaran, D. (1997), The Effect of Cultural Orientation on Persuasion, *Journal of Consumer Research*, 24 (December): 315-328.

Baligh, H. H. (1994), Components of Culture: Nature, Interconnections and Relevance to the Decisions on the Organisation Structure, *Management Science* 40(1): 14-27.

Bond, M. H. (1991), *Beyond the Chinese Face: Insights from Psychology*, Hong Kong: Oxford University Press.

Boone, L. E. and Kurtz, D. L. (1992), *Contemporary Marketing*, 7th Edition, Fort Worth: The Dryden Press.

Brooksbank, R. (1995), "The New Model of Personal Selling: Micromarketing", *Journal of Personal Selling & Sales Management*, XV(2): 61-68.

Burnett, J. (1993), *Promotion Management*, Boston, Houghton Mifflin Co.

Fam, Kim S. and Merrilees, Bill (1998), "Cultural Values and personal Selling: A Comparison of Australian and Hong Kong Retailers Promotion Preferences", *International Marketing Review*, 15(4): 246-256.

Goff, B.G., Boles, J.S., Bellenger, D.N. and Stojack, C. (1997), "The Influence of Salesperson Selling Behaviors on Customer Satisfaction with Products", *Journal of Retailing*, 73(2): 171-183.

Greenley, G. E. and Shipley, D. (1992), "A Comparative Study of Operational Marketing Practices among British Department Stores and Supermarkets", *European Journal of Marketing*, 26(5): 22-35.

Hall, E. T. (1976), *Beyond Culture*, New York: Anchor Press/Doubleday.

Hawes, J. M., Rao, C. P. and Baker, T. L. (1993), "Retail Salesperson Attributes and the Role of Dependability in the Selection of Durable Goods", *Journal of Personal Selling and Sales Management*, 13(4) Fall: 61-71.

Hofstede, G. (1980), *Culture's Consequences*, Beverly Hills. CA: Sage Publications.

Jackson, J.H., Hawes, D.K. and Hertel, F.M. (1979), "Pricing and advertising practices in small retail businesses", *American Journal of Small Business*, 4(2): 22-34.

Kelley, L., Whatley, A., Worthley, R. and Lie, H. (1986), "The Role of the Ideal Organisation in Comparative Management: A Cross-Cultural Perspective of Japan and Korea", *Asia Pacific Journal of Management*, 3 (2): 59-75.

28

Problems faced by Women Entrepreneurs and the Role of Women Entrepreneur Associations to Increase the Profitability of Individual Business – A Study with Reference to Indian Context

Swati Sabale*
Nikita Khatwani**

Gandhiji has acknowledged women as the 'civilizing force in human society'. In spite of being the 'fairer sex' and 'the better-halves', women have always been the disadvantaged sex almost all over the world'. As globalization and the cultural influx came into force, the role and status of women changed. Women are now opening-up and are becoming more and more aware of their identities and their rights.

The paper focuses on understanding Indian women entrepreneur's problems in business and at homes because of their 'woman status'. It also tries to probe into the different woman entrepreneurship associations and their role in solving the problems. An insight into the expectations of women entrepreneurs from such associations and what should be the role of these associations in solving the problems of women is also dealt with in the presentation.

INTRODUCTION

"There is only one way to make a great deal of money; and that is in a business of your own."

—J. Paul Getty
Former oil tycoon and once the richest man in America

The word 'entrepreneur' is derived from the French language and means 'between taker' or 'go-between.'

Entrepreneurship is the process of creating something new with value by devoting the necessary time and efforts, assuming the accompanying financial, psychic and social risks and receiving the resulting rewards of monetary and personal satisfaction and independence.

---

* Asst. Professor, Shri H & G H Mansukhani Institute of Management, Ulhasnagar.
** Lecturer, Shri H & G H Mansukhani Institute of Management, Ulhasnagar.

The characteristics of male and female entrepreneurs are generally similar but female entrepreneurs differ in terms of motivation, personality and occupational backgrounds. Men are motivated by the drive to control their own destinies, to make things happen. Women are motivated by the need of liberation from job frustration. Men are opinionated and persuasive, goal-oriented, innovative and idealistic. Women entrepreneurs are found to be flexible, tolerant, goal-oriented, creative and realistic. Men have more experience in manufacturing, finance and technical areas whereas women tend to have a limited administrative experience often in service related areas.

The development of entrepreneurship in women in India has gone through a paradigm change. Every change in the environmental and social context has been mirrored in women entrepreneurs of that era. Some of the reasons for the changes in the world and subsequently for India are the impact of media, globalization, technology, change in the social mindset and changes in cultural values. Today, women entrepreneurs are symbols of freedom from gender biases who have freed themselves from the centuries-old traditions and social misgivings.

India takes pride in its internationally acclaimed women entrepreneurs like Indra Noori, Kiran Mazumdar Shaw, Tarla Dalal, Ritu Kumar, Ritu Beri, Shahnaz Hussain and many others. But success has not been presented to any of them on a golden platter. They have conquered each challenge meticulously and painstakingly.

Women entrepreneurs in India are increasingly growing in numbers and it is estimated that in another five years, women will comprise 20% of the entrepreneurial force. The industry today is keen to connect and work with businesses run by women, and a multitude of banks and non-governmental organizations are keen to facilitate their development, the time appears to the best for women with vision and enthusiasm to start their own businesses.

Empowered with the powerful sixth sense intuition, women have an intrinsic flair for entrepreneurship. The individual woman entrepreneur single-handedly faces endless problems.

PROBLEMS FACED BY WOMEN ENTREPRENEURS

Women contribute considerably to the running of family businesses mostly in the form of unpaid effort and skills. The value of this effort is underestimated by the families that take her for granted. Also, many of the enterprises defined as being run by women are, in fact, run in their names by men who control operations and decision-making. Families normally provide financial and emotional support to sons rather than their daughters.

An entrepreneur's success cannot be attributed to any single individual. It has and will always be the supporting family and staff that contribute to a major success in business. In the past, families have been more of an impediment to a woman's success. The family of a woman from lower income group would expect her to take up a job with a more stable income. In middle-class families, the woman's success becomes a reason for insecurity, where it is perceived that a successful woman would neglect her family.

The kind of businesses, the women entrepreneurs run are perceived to be largely are women's areas like garments, beauty parlours, interior designing and food production.

It has been observed that at times, it is the women themselves who are to be blamed. They themselves do not try to grow too big, because they want to ensure that they are always one step behind their husbands. Ironically, it is this domestic bliss that has ensured their success at work. It has been a very interesting research finding that the most successful group of women are those who have been married and have two children. Single women do not want to concentrate too much on their businesses because they are worried that, if they get married, they might have to move to a different place. Divorcees or widows are so psychologically affected that they are unable to give everything to their businesses.

Lack of exposure to corporate culture, marketing, lack of professional training and family responsibilities are other problems of women entrepreneurs.

CAN WE CHANGE?

Societal norms are difficult to overcome and gender biases and expectations cannot be changed overnight by a magic wand. What we require is an attitudinal change. It is these women themselves, who need to change, nurture a vision and flourish in their businesses. A woman's dedication to her family should be judged on the basis of quality time she dedicates to her family and not the quantifiable hours that she spends with her family.

Entrepreneurship by definition implies being in command of one's life and activities. It is precisely this liberty that women are denying themselves – to go beyond 'womanhood'.

There are many governmental support schemes that women are not aware of or don't have confidence in. What the government can do to help is build on these schemes and publicize them. Also, some kind of formal training for such women can be organized.

To tackle the major area of difficulty, which is marketing, several initiatives have been started to rectify the shortcoming. At the initial stages, women prefer to be locked into programmes that ensure almost total marketing support, since they seldom have the time or the confidence to seek out and develop markets. Even when they are otherwise in control of an enterprise, they often depend on males of the family in this area.

ASSOCIATIONS AND THEIR ROLES

While women entrepreneurs have demonstrated their potentials, the fact remains that they are capable of contributing much more than what they already are. In order to harness their potentials and for their continued growth and development, it is necessary to formulate appropriate strategies for stimulating, supporting and sustaining their efforts in this direction. Such a strategy needs to be in congruence with field realities, and should especially take cognizance of the problems women entrepreneurs face within the current system.

Several different providers, including governmental, non-governmental, and international organizations, are already providing support to the development of women entrepreneurs in India. The following associations aim to provide an insight into some initiatives to promote women entrepreneurs and professionals in India, in particular as regards providing opportunities for networking, training and support.

FICCI Ladies Organization: Promoting Entrepreneurship and Professional Excellence

The FICCI Ladies Organization (FLO) is a wing of the Federation of Indian Chambers of Commerce and Industry (FICCI), the apex body of Industry and Chambers of Commerce in India. It was established in 1983 with the basic objective of *"women empowerment"*, to encourage women to exploit to the maximum their own human potentials as entrepreneurs, business women and professionals serve the community and nation at large through activities of social welfare on the cultural and social fronts.

As an all-India organization for women, FLO has around 1,000 members comprising entrepreneurs, professionals and executives. It currently has five chapters – in Chennai, Hyderabad, Kolkata, Mumbai and Coimbatore.

FLO works at three levels. At the basic level, it holds entrepreneurship development programmes for women, working with them in advising on how to start a business and following it through with some help in vocational training. At the middle level, it holds seminars and workshops for women who run small-scale businesses, such as computerization and financial management. At the senior level, FLO has sophisticated programmes for women at the helm in areas such as marketing and finance.

Besides undertaking several business-oriented activities for women through entrepreneurship development programmes, workshops and panel discussions, FLO has an active Business Consultancy Cell where free professional guidance is offered and which serves as a single window stop for all information on diversified statutory compliances, procedures and obligations in its Hyderabad chapter. It advises women entrepreneurs on subjects such as company incorporation, registration, preliminary documentation, taxation and policies of the government. In discharge of its functions, FLO has also started giving awards to recognize outstanding women in various walks of life.

Association of Women Entrepreneurs of Karnataka: Entrepreneur Guiding Entrepreneur

AWAKE – Association of Women Entrepreneurs of Karnataka is today one of India's premier institutions for women totally devoted to Entrepreneurship Development. Established in 1983, AWAKE's success has been recognized worldwide. AWAKE was an affiliate of Women's World Banking, New York for Business Development Services.

The Association of Women Entrepreneurs of Karnataka (AWAKE), founded in 1983 in Bangalore, India, is one of the pioneers in the field of providing business development services. AWAKE's mission is *"to empower women through Entrepreneurship Development to improve their economic conditions."* To achieve this mission, AWAKE conducts various activities, such as, business counselling, entrepreneurship awareness, entrepreneurship development training, management development training, business incubator, etc.

With a membership base of about 700 women entrepreneurs, AWAKE promotes women entrepreneurship development to its clients through its various activities. AWAKE's clientele comprise of 90% women, 60% rural, of which 50% belong to low income.

AWAKE provides peer group support and handholds new entrants in various aspects of entrepreneurship. Apart from motivating potential women entrepreneurs, it conducts growth-oriented programmes for sustaining the businesses of existing entrepreneurs. The business ventures of the 700 odd member entrepreneurs of AWAKE ranges from manufacturing of garments, electronic components, printing, machinery manufacturers to services in catering, etc., to using AWAKE' business incubator for food processing. A unique feature of AWAKE is successful entrepreneurs helping potential entrepreneurs. Most women say that AWAKE gives them an identity as an entrepreneur. AWAKE has developed its own 4S module of Stimulus, Start Up, Sustenance and Support.

SEWA Trade Facilitation Centre

Self-Employed Women's Association (SEWA) is a trade union for poor, self-employed women workers, established in 1972. SEWA Trade Facilitation Centre (STFC) is a unique company, owned and managed by more than 15,000 women artisans pursuing craft activities, in particular intricate traditional hand embroidery, in the drought affected and disaster prone districts of Gujarat, India.

The aim of STFC is to strengthen the position of women workers in the informal sector and promote their enterprises in global markets through efficient marketing of their products and services, with a view to provide them economic security and full employment. STFC was established by the artisan members of SEWA to turn their activity into a commercial venture with the main objective of promoting access to national and global markets, through capacity-building and product development. STFC delivers a range of services ranging from marketing support, product development, quality standardization, information systems, access to capital, etc.

Mahakoushal Association of Women Entrepreneurs {MAWE}

Mahakoushal Association of Women Entrepreneurs {MAWE} is a congregation of existing women-entrepreneurs and women aiming at self-employment through entrepreneurship. MAWE aims at empowering women through self-reliance and economic independence.

Through its various Entrepreneurship Development programmes, Management Development programmes, it encourages women and girls from all walks of life towards self-employment and entrepreneurship and also help existing women entrepreneurs to establish their business better.

It also assists the members in marketing their products by organizing various trade fairs throughout the year and facilitating their participation in trade fairs at national and international levels.

MAWE is the only organization in Madhya Pradesh working for women entrepreneurs. MAWE networks at national and international level to provide various opportunities to its members. MAWE's President has been invited for addressing and participating in various international events in the US, Australia, Japan, South Africa, etc.

REVIEW OF LITERATURE

'A reflection of the Indian Women in Entrepreneurial World' by Bharti Kollan and Indira J Parekh W.P. No 2005-08-07 Research and Publication by IIM Ahmedabad.

In this paper, the authors have traced the history of women entrepreneurs since the 15th century.

According to them, women entrepreneurs of the 15th century needed enormous courage to break through the social maps and coding. Women of the sixties accepted the social codings and took small steps to start one woman enterprise at home and from home. In the seventies, women completed their education and were professionals, they not only had aspirations, but also ambitions. For them, entrepreneurship was not out of compulsion but an active choice to take charge of one's lives. The eighties saw highly educated women. This was a decade of breakthrough in many fields for women and they had the courage to stand by their decisions and make new beginnings. But society was hostile and families were non-supportive and women carried the guilt of not playing the traditional and appropriate social goals. The women of the nineties were capable, competent, confident and assertive women. They were clear as to what choices they had and were clear as to what they wanted to do. This was the first time the concept of 'the best' rather than 'male heir' began to be talked about. The woman of 'today' has a new avatar. She is an entrepreneur, who builds an enterprise and discovers her relevance and meaning of her life in herself.

'Home based Women Entrepreneurs in Bombay' by Dr. Pandit

The thesis was based on over 160 personal interviews and discussions with nearly 20 women's organizations in the city.

In her paper, Ms. Pandit finds that the reasons for women to run organized enterprises are their skills and knowledge, their talents and abilities in business and a compelling desire of wanting to do something positive. She discovered that, in many cases, families have been more of a hindrance to a woman's success in business. At the same time, she states that in spite of having proven their competencies, women still have to deal with the worst burden, that of being a 'woman'. It tends to weigh most of them down. The lack of exposure to corporate culture, lack of professional training and family responsibilities are other problems these home-based women entrepreneurs have to cope up with. They try not grow too big because they do not want to hurt the delicate balance of power in their families. They have the vision, but they do not want to expand their businesses. They live with the identity that they are related to someone. They have always been taught to be a woman first. Ironically, it is this domestic bliss that has ensured that these home-based women entrepreneurs are successful at work.

A startling finding of Pandit's research has been the fact that the most successful women are those who have been married and have two children. In contrast, single or divorced women do not seem to do as well in their ventures. "Single women do not want to concentrate too much on their businesses because they are worried that, if they get married, they might have to move to a different place "concludes Dr. Pandit.

'Women Entrepreneurs' by Deepak Walokar Himalaya Publishing House, 2001

In contrast to the Ms. Pandit's findings, in his paper, Mr. Walokar talks about the experiences of women entrepreneurs and concludes that more and more families have started supporting the 'woman entrepreneur'. He also finds that a vast number of entrepreneurs never felt that there was any shortcoming in their role performances as a mother, a wife or a homemaker and neither did their family members feel so.

According to him, participation in entrepreneur activity has had a very positive impact on the families and the woman entrepreneur cannot be said to fit into the stereotype of woman carrying a 'double' or 'triple burden'.

India together: Opportunities and Challenges for Women in Business - November 2001 - Renuka Vishwananthan

In this paper, the researcher opines that women contribute significantly to the running of family businesses mostly in the form of unpaid effort and skills. The value of this effort is underestimated both by the families that take it for granted. On the other hand, many of the enterprises defined as being run by women are in fact run in their names by men who control operations and decision-making. Programmes meant to reach women entrepreneurs can succeed only if they take note of this paradox as well as of the familial and social conditioning that reduces the confidence, independence and mobility of women. Families routinely provide financial and emotional support for sons that they would never extend to daughters. Parents and daughters together need to be convinced that the skills learned in the polytechnics could provide them with profitable occupations.

Her research into the working of polytechnics and NGOs helps her to conclude that "NGOs like RUDSET in Karnataka have succeeded in achieving reasonably high success levels, but others including governmental bodies have still not reached these levels". Continuous monitoring and improvement of training programmes should eventually spread the cult of entrepreneurship among young women according to her.

Women Entrepreneurs: Opportunities, Performance and Problems - S.K. Dhameja, New Delhi, Deep and Deep, 2002, xiv, 210 p.,

The above study was undertaken with a view to find out the entrepreneurial performance and problems of women in business in north-western India.

The author was astonished to see the spectacular performances of some women entrepreneurs. Equally interesting was to find out some of the peculiar problems faced by women entrepreneurs, needed to be addressed by the powers in the right earnest.

The Hindu : Opportunities/Miscellaneous: Women as Entrepreneurs, Online edition of India's National Newspaper, Wednesday, Dec 14, 2005 - Bindu Shridhar

Bindu Shridhar, in his study talks about the special qualities of women entrepreneurs – they are endowed with the famous female intuition that helps them make the right choices even in situations where experience and logic fail, women have innate flair for entrepreneurship. Although men and women may be motivated by different goals and expectations, women entrepreneurs are just as competent, if not better, than their male counterparts. Women are more likely than men to admit when they do not know something and ask for help. They are natural networkers and relationship builders, forging powerful bonds and nurturing relationships with clients and employees alike. They are also more inclined to seek out mentors and develop supportive teams. In business, this translates into establishing rapport with clients and providing great customer service. This perhaps is the reason why many women tend to launch businesses that are client-based or service-oriented.

Factors affecting Women Entrepreneurship in Small and Cottage Industries in India – Dr. S.P. Mishra (November, 1996)

In this study, an attempt has been made to document available information regarding the status of women entrepreneurs, against the backdrop of the socio-economic context and the attendant challenges they face.

The study brings together an extensive amount of information on various entrepreneurship and women's development programmes introduced in India. There is an assessment of the current position of women entrepreneurs, as well as of the existing support programmes such as, credit, training and marketing support, for women to establish their own enterprises.

The study looks at the socio-cultural, educational and legal barriers to women's entrepreneurship in India. It also includes profiles of most of the key agencies involved in promoting women's entrepreneurship and recommendations for policy-makers aimed at enhancing the economic empowerment of women throughout the country.

Objectives of the Study

The study was planned with the following objectives:

1. To study the problems faced by women entrepreneurs.

2. To portray the various women entrepreneurship associations.

3. To explore the role and activities of these associations in the development of women entrepreneurs.

4. To probe into the probable solutions to the problems faced by the women entrepreneurs.

Methodology

Research Design

Exploratory Research

Research Instruments

In-depth open-ended questionnaires and focus group interviews.

Sources of data

Secondary sources: Books, magazines, journals and various web sites.

Primary data: Questionnaires and in-depth interviews.

Sampling method

Random Sampling

Profile of the respondents

Because of time constraint, women entrepreneurs without age, income and nature of business bar were studied.

Coverage of the area

Samples have been collected from Mumbai (Western region) and Thane area.

Sr. No.	Location	Number of samples
1	Mumbai (Western side)	20
2	Thane	20
	TOTAL	**40**

Data collection

Both primary and secondary data were collected for the research. Prior telephonic appointments of the entrepreneurs were taken. Most of the primary data were collected by conducting in-depth interviews of the selected respondents.

The researchers met the respondent face-to-face as fixed earlier. The interview was conducted as per the interview schedule in English as well as in the Marathi and Sindhi.

Data Analysis Stage

Data collected through primary and secondary sources were tabulated and summarized so as to draw logical conclusions.

Presentation of findings conclusions and recommendations: The finding conclusion and recommendation have been discussed later in this paper.

Limitations of the study

The study was confined to Mumbai (Western side) and Thane regions due to cost and time constraints. Detailed discussions with women entrepreneurs only has been taken into consideration for the purpose of study. Other stakeholder's opinions were not taken. The study is based on reported answers in questionnaires and in focus group interviews. Therefore, there is possibility of bias in reported answers there.

FINDINGS

The reported responses have been tabulated as follows:

1. *Time you dedicate to your family.*

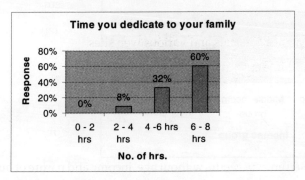

2. *Time you dedicate to your business.*

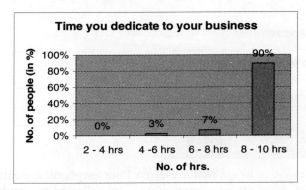

3.   *Number of people working with you in your business.*

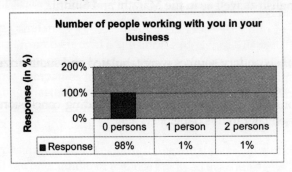

4.   *Number of competitors in your business?*

5.   *How many of them are females?*

6.   *Any big brand is your competitor?*

Most of the women entrepreneurs could not specifically answer the above questions. It implies a lack of environmental knowledge.

7.   *Did you ever feel the need of a mentor?*

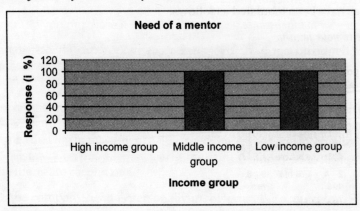

8.   *Why?*

Most of the women have a problem with marketing of their products and procurement of finance.

9.   *Would you like to work with a partner? No.*

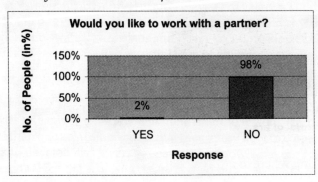

10. *Why or why not?*

   Majority of the respondents said No. The reasons that they quoted were:

   ❖ Danger of partners becoming competitors at a later stage.

   ❖ Lack of trust in partnership

11. *Problems you face in business because you are a woman.*

   Common problems cited were:

   ❖ Marketing

   ❖ Finance

   ❖ Recovery of payments

   ❖ Lack of communication

   ❖ Lack of administrative abilities

   ❖ Lack of technical know-how

   ❖ Completion of the production process on time

12. *Problems you face in your family because you are a woman.*

   Almost all respondents did not have any problem as such; according to them, their families have adjusted to their entrepreneurship status. But on further probe and in-depth interview, the following points were noted by the researchers:

   ❖ They do not have enough time to dedicate to their families.

   ❖ They have guilt of not being able to take the studies of their children.

   ❖ They are skeptical of becoming the major income generator of the family.

13. *Any probable solutions?*

   Almost all respondents did not have a solution.

14. *Would you like to be a member of an Entrepreneur Association?*

   All the respondents said that it would help them be a member of an Entrepreneurship Association.

15. *Your idea of an association:*

   Reported responses were as follows:

   ❖ It should give training in marketing and finance.

   ❖ It should provide consultation services to its members.

   ❖ It should help in improving the network in order to expand the business.

   ❖ It should work on a continuous basis.

   ❖ It should be a platform where the women can display and sell their products.

16.   *Your expectations from the associations.*

Most of the answers were same as above.

17.   *Amount of time that you can dedicate for the association.*

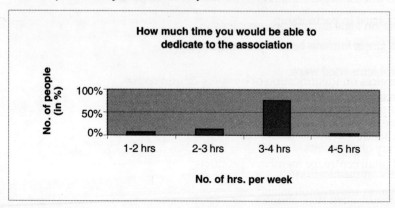

CONCLUSION

The following problems were detected:

- Women consider themselves to be women first and entrepreneurs second. Therefore, precedence is given to the role of a wife, mother, daughter, etc., to business.

- Families which normally support their sons financially and emotionally do not support their daughters.

- Skills required for marketing are lacking.

- In spite of being very good at developing and maintaining relationships, women exhibit low-level management skills. More emphasis on understanding & emotions.

- Women have a low risk-taking attitude.

A few active women entrepreneur associations in India are:

- The FICCI Ladies Organization (FLO)

- AWAKE – Association of Women Entrepreneurs of Karnataka

- Self-Employed Women's Association (SEWA)

- Mahakoushal Association of Women Entrepreneurs MAWE

An ideal association should carry out the following activities for the development of women entrepreneurs:

1.   Technical and managerial services

2.   Seminars and workshops

3.   Business counselling

4. Business consultancy

5. Financial services/access to credit

6. National and international exhibitions (for marketing of products)

7. Free guidance on legal and government liaison

8. Awards

9. Advisory services on identification of business opportunities

10. Business women's directory

11. Information booth

12. Display and retail centre for members' products

13. Financial support for promotion and advertisements

14. Hand-holding new entrants and peer group support

15. Mentoring

The only solution which we suggest is:

Along with all the above-mentioned functions, associations should focus first on attitudinal change and this activity should begin from school days.

In India, this has just begun. There is considerable scope for supporting agencies to establish and also learn from each other. The most common function of these supporting agencies is to provide opportunities for building knowledge and skills and networking with other women entrepreneurs. Policy advocacy and business counselling are also offered by many of the agencies.

Thus, it isn't an easy journey, as any entrepreneur will tell you. But "entrepreneurship is not all that tough if you have the right attitude".

References

Women Entrepreneurs, Deepak Walokar, Himalaya Publishing House, 2001.

Entrepreneurship, Hisrich

Entrepreneurship – Sabu Singh

http://www.sewatfc.org

http://www.awake-india.org.

'A reflection of the Indian Women in Entrepreneurial World' by *Bharti Kollan and Indira J Parekh W.P., No 2005-08-07, Research and Publication by IIM Ahmedabad.*

'Home-based women entrepreneurs in Bombay', *By Dr. Pandit.*

India Together: Opportunities and challenges for women in business – *November 2001, Renuka Vishwananthan.*

Women Entrepreneurs: Opportunities, Performance and Problems, *S.K. Dhameja, New Delhi, Deep and Deep, 2002, xiv, 210 p.*

The Hindu: *Opportunities/Miscellaneous: Women as entrepreneurs Online edition of India's National Newspaper, Wednesday, Dec 14, 2005, Bindu Shridhar.*

Factors affecting Women Entrepreneurship in Small and Cottage Industries in India, *Dr. S.P. Mishra (November 1996).*

29

A Study on Gender and Negotiations in Entrepreneurship

V. Veena Prasad*
Helen Mary Selvaraj*
Dr. Pradip Manjrekar**

Central issue under debate in the study of gender in entrepreneurship is whether there are gender differences between female and male entrepreneurs and their businesses. Findings are mixed and often contradictory. To this end, gender is conceptualised as an ongoing meaning making, as 'doing gender' rather than a sexual division into women and men. "Gender is not a good predictor for negotiations, but an ambiguous situation can trigger different situations by men and women". This article alters the emphasis from examining gender differences per se to analysing how such differences are produced.

Do women negotiate better than men? If yes how much of difference is there? How does gender really matter in entrepreneurship? Are male negotiated salaries higher, on average, than those negotiated by females. In this research paper, an endeavor has been made to see whether men or women are better predictors for negotiations.

In the above background, in this paper, an endeavour has been made to study whether male entrepreneurs or female entrepreneurs are better predictors for negotiations in the upcoming and emerging entrepreneurship industry, in the modern times.

INTRODUCTION

Entrepreneurship is an undertaking, particularly a new business in response to an identified opportunity. Entrepreneurship is often a difficult task, as a vast majority of new businesses vanish at its inception whilst encountering its toothing problems.

Entrepreneurial undertakings or organisations are substantially different, depending on the type of organization that is being started. Entrepreneurship ranges in scale from solo projects (even involving the entrepreneur only part-time) to major undertakings creating many job opportunities. Many "high-profile" entrepreneurial ventures seek venture capital or angel funding in order to raise capital to build the business. Angel investors generally seek returns

* Faculty, S.I.W.S. College, Wadala, Mumbai.
** Professor, Dr. D.Y. Patil Institute of Management Studies, CBD Belapur, Navi Mumbai.

of 20-30% and more extensive involvement in the business. Many kinds of organizations now exist to support "would-be" entrepreneurs, including specialized government agencies, business incubators, science parks, non-governmental organisations, etc.

As compared to olden days, women have given men competition in the modern era of entrepreneurship. Entrepreneurship today is no longer solely dominated by men. It is a win-win situation for men and women in the large industry of entrepreneurship, though apparently not focussed, but brought to forefront issues of gender differences in the industry. This raises a central issue of debate and birth of a study on gender equality or dominance of gender in the emerging entrepreneurship, marking the role of women and their success, surpassing the position of men. Do women negotiate better than men? If yes how much of difference is there? How does gender really matter in Entrepreneurship?, whether Male Entrepreneur looses to a Female Entrepreneur in negotiating cost effective salaries than those negotiated by female or vice-versa. Findings are mixed and often contradictory. To this end, gender is conceptualised as an ongoing meaning making as 'doing gender' rather than a sexual division into women and men. Gender is not a good predictor for negotiations, but an ambiguous situation can trigger different situations by men and women.

Entrepreneurship

The concept of entrepreneurship has been around for a very long time, but its resurgent popularity implies a "sudden discovery", as if we had stumbled onto a new direction for American enterprise. This is a myth, as we shall see, because the American system of free enterprise has always engendered the spirit of entrepreneurship. America was discovered by entrepreneurs, and the United States became a world economic power through entrepreneurial activity. More important, our future rests squarely on entrepreneurial ventures founded by creative individuals. They are inspired people, often adventurers, who can, at once, disrupt a society and instigate progress. They are risk-takers who seize opportunities to harness and use resources in unusual ways, and entrepreneurs will thrust us into the twenty-first century with a thunderous roar.

An Entrepreneurial Perspective

- Entrepreneurship is one of the four mainstream economic factors: land, labor, capital, and entrepreneurship.

- The word itself, derived from 17th-century French *entreprendre*, refers to individuals who were "undertakers", meaning those who "undertook" the risk of new enterprise. They were "contractors" who bore the risks of profit or loss, and many early entrepreneurs were soldiers of fortune, adventurers, builders, merchants and incidentally, funeral directors.

- Early reference to the entrepreneur in the 14th century spoke about tax contractors individuals who paid a foxed sum of money to a government for the license to collect taxes in their region.

- In the 19th century, entrepreneurs were the "captains of industry", the risk takers, the decision makers, the individuals who aspired to wealth and who gathered and managed resources to create new enterprises.

TYPES OF ENTREPRENEURS

According to Schumpeter, there are five basic types of entrepreneurship projects. The introduction of a new good in the market is the first of these. By new product, it means something that has been invented and has never been available in the market. In simple terms, whenever a new invention is made, it is seen as an act of entrepreneurship. The second is the introduction of a new method of production. As we know, it is the production of goods that forms the pillar of the economy. By the new method, it is assumed that the method that is effective and efficient and is able to improve on an existing production method. The third type of entrepreneurship is the opening of a new market. Whenever such resources are provided, it enables the population to benefit, whether it is an economic, education or any other benefit, it establishes a new opportunity that is known as a new market for using that particular resource. The fourth factor is the conquest of a new source of supply. Economists believe that a new supply source allows the industry to increase its productivity. This new source can be in many forms, including the discovery of a natural resource (oil, steel, etc.) or attracting a labour force that hasn't been exposed to that industry. The last, but not the least, is the carrying out the new organization of industry that will increase human welfare.

- The entrepreneur has an enthusiastic vision, the driving force of an enterprise.

- The entrepreneur's vision is usually supported by an interlocked collection of specific ideas not available to the marketplace.

- The overall blueprint to realize the vision is clear, however, details may be incomplete, flexible, and evolving.

- The entrepreneur promotes the vision with enthusiastic passion.

- With persistence and determination, the entrepreneur develops strategies to change the vision into reality.

- The entrepreneur takes the initial responsibility to cause a vision to become a success.

- Risks; entrepreneurs take prudent risks. They assess costs, market/customer needs and persuade others to join and help.

- An entrepreneur is usually a positive thinker and a decision maker.

What is Gender?

Gender is used in this toolkit to refer to the socially constructed roles and socially learnt behaviours and expectations of women and men in a particular society. These relations and the roles that women and men assume are culturally defined and institutionally embedded. Whereas, biological sex (being male or female) is not easily altered, gender as a social identity changes over time (historically) and space (geographically). Gender roles of men or women in one society may differ from another. Gender considers both men and women and the relations between them. It refers to the social differences and relations between women and men which are learned, vary widely among societies and cultures, and change over time. The term "gender" is used to analyze the roles, responsibilities, constraints, opportunities and needs of women and men in all areas and in any given context. (Sex refers exclusively to the biological differences between women and men.)

One of the issues that is under much debate in the study of gender in entrepreneurship today is whether there are gender differences between female and male entrepreneurs and their businesses. The findings are mixed and often contradictory {e.g. Brush (1992); Fischer et al (1993)} identify two theoretical perspectives in gender sensitive entrepreneurship research, i.e., liberal and social feminism. They conclude, first, that research in line with liberal feminist theory assumes women are equally capable of rationality as men (i.e., rationality is seen as a common human essence) and, second, that gender differences observed are explained by reference to discrimination that prevents women from realising their full entrepreneurial potentials. Studies consistent with social feminist theory, in turn, work on the assumption that women's and men's different experiences result in fundamentally different world views, which give rise to differences in entrepreneurial behaviours.

Business people often ask us whether men or women are better negotiators. According to our research, gender is not a reliable predictor of negotiation performance; neither women nor men perform better or worse across all negotiations. However, certain types of negotiation can set the stage for differences in outcomes negotiated by men and by women, particularly, when the opportunities and limits of the negotiation are unclear; and situational cues in these ambiguous situations trigger different behaviors by men and women.

These differences can create huge inequities over time. Awareness of the factors that create gender-related advantages and disadvantages can help you mitigate their consequences—and promote a more egalitarian work .

Why is Gender Equality a Development Issue?

Research has established the business case for gender equality: development projects that take gender relations into account are more likely to achieve their objectives than those that do not (Murphy, 1997). Progress towards gender equality is directly correlated with the alleviation of global poverty. Social considerations, however, are not easily incorporated into policies, laws, markets and organizations. It is particularly difficult to incorporate them into technical projects. The process of incorporating gender equality considerations into development institutions, projects and programmes is often referred to as "gender mainstreaming." Studies confirm that without direct intervention, mainstreaming of gender equality concerns will not occur (Kimani, 2000; IFPRI, 2000).

What are the Key Gender Differentials?

Gender equality and women's empowerment concern structural change in uneven power relations. Development with a gender perspective promotes equitable development methods that take cultural, traditional, and gender stereotyping into account. The use of the concept "gender" is sometimes confused with just improving the status and position of women (as opposed to men). In fact, the "gender" component to development suggests the improvement of women's social and economic status in relation to and alongside men's participation and involvement. It is not an either-or proposition.

Gender Differentials in the MSE Environment

There are distinct differences between men and women in their accesses to resources, information and business support that have direct impacts on their business sustainability and success. Women usually face higher barriers than men to the kinds of training that can make them computer literate or equip them with the skills needed for information and communication technologies-related employment. Women also have less access to collateral and subsequently have less access to finance and affordable capital to invest in ICTs. As well, compared with men, women have less time to balance the tension between earning an income and caring for household members.

Gender Differentials in Value of Economic Output

At the same time, much of women's work remains unpaid. In developing countries, women spent only one third of their time in paid Standard National Accounts (SNA) activities, compared with three quarters of men. If unpaid labour is counted, women do more work than men. In a study of 31 countries, women performed an average of 53 percent of the total work burden in developing countries and 51 per cent in industrial countries. Compared with men, women are more often the shock absorbers of economic stress and uncertainty. Their economic values have been recognized as producers and providers, and more recently as consumers. More and more, however, as creators of wealth, women must also be valued as distributor. Women are both producers and distributors of wealth and this has critical implications if we really want to address poverty in a systemic way.

Gender Differentials in Financial Assistance

Compared with their male counterparts, funding assistance for women's social and economic development is behind the times – it stereo-typically dominates certain sectors such as literacy, health, and fertility programmes for women. Only a few agencies or foundations are beginning to enter the arena of enterprise training for women, and even fewer are investing in ICTs for use by women.

Gender Differentials in access to Business Support

Women are less likely than men to be members of business or employers' associations. This finding provides a great opportunity for representative associations, such as employers' organizations or chambers of commerce, to increase women's membership.

Gender Issues in Negotiation

The Negotiations in the Workplace Project has an abiding interest in gender issues in negotiation. Work on gender issues in negotiation has taken a new direction with the research conducted by Deborah Kolb and her colleagues on feminist theory and negotiations and gender relations in the workplace. Here, Kolb has cast a critical eye on basic assumptions and concepts to see what kinds of behaviors are prominent and which are silenced or left out entirely. Here, they elaborate the concept of the shadow negotiation as the context in which gender issues play out. Contending that existing negotiation theory minimizes the social context in which negotiation occurs, the authors focus on how negotiators tacitly negotiate about how they will negotiate, even though they do not discuss these issues directly. In the shadow negotiation, gender comes into play at personal, expectational and situational levels.

Does Gender matter during Negotiations?

This section summarizes that there are both masculine and feminine factors when talking about entrepreneurship, but here, there are differences that vary for both in nature.

Here, the question arises whether men or women are better negotiators? If yes, how much of difference is there? The research done by Rile says that:

- Women are slightly more co-operative, and men slightly more competitive.

- When there was potential to "expand the pie," the studies found that men were better at claiming the pie. On the other hand, woman – woman dyads were the best at expanding the pie.

- Women have different goals in negotiation, and are maybe more attuned to one-on-one interpersonal relationships while men are more interested in group identity.

- "Women hold back on what they want to claim", which may be a more functional strategy for women. Strong personal relationships may be more important to women's career success than to men.

When parties understand little about the limits of the bargaining range and appropriate standards for agreement, the ambiguity of a negotiation increases. In highly ambiguous negotiations, it becomes more likely that gender triggers—situational cues that prompt male-female differences in preferences, expectations and behaviours—will influence negotiation behaviors and outcomes. By contrast, in situations with low ambiguity, where negotiators understand the range of possible payoffs and agree on standards for distributing value, outcomes are less likely to reflect gender triggers. Some environments are full of triggers that encourage superior performance by women, while others are full of triggers that encourage superior performance by men. Rather than indicating innate differences between men and women, these triggers reflect stereotypes and long-standing behavioural biases.

When Competition is High

Competitive negotiations can act as gender triggers, consistent with societal expectations that men are more likely than women to be competitive and to succeed in competitive environments. Researchers Uri Gneezy of the University of Chicago, Muriel Niederle of Stanford University, and Aldo Rustichini of the University of Minnesota have shown that women and men are equally competent in "piece-rate" situations, in which individuals work to maximize their own payoffs without regard for others' performances.

But men outperform women in competitive environments in which payoffs are determined by comparing relative performances. It's not that the pressure of competition causes women to stumble but, rather, that men step-up their performances in competitive situations.

Workplace, Gender, and Organizational Effectiveness

Gender is used as a lens to analyze work cultures and practices, which typically reflect masculine values and life situations, make it challenging for women (and many men as well) to succeed. But also, analyses demonstrate that these very same cultures and practices can also undermine organization's effectiveness." The group's work with organizations to change these work practices is detailed in the *Harvard Business Review* (January 2000).

Negotiation is basic to this enterprise as individuals use bargaining skills to push back on these cultural assumptions. Individuals caught in double bind around gender issues find that using negotiation skills opens up space for them to be more effective and to have their work recognized as such. Organizational change agents find that negotiation helps them deal with resistance to change over issues that are deeply rooted in gendered assumptions in the workplace.

Competitive negotiations can act as gender triggers...

We found no difference in the salaries negotiated by male and female MBAs hired into low-ambiguity industries, which included 70 per cent of the participants. In high-ambiguity industries, however, male MBAs negotiated salaries that were $ 10,000 higher, on average, than those negotiated by female MBAs. The competitive context cued negotiators to the traditionally "masculine" nature of the interaction, and the ambiguity in certain industries allowed these cues to elicit different negotiating behaviours from men and women. These differences add up over time. Assuming that those 30 per cent of MBAs who take positions in high-ambiguity industries work for thirty-five years and receive a 3 per cent raise per year, the earnings gap grows to more than $ 600,000 over the course of a career—or $ 1.5 million, if those extra earnings are saved at 5 per cent annual interest.

Neutralizing gender differences in negotiation

These suggestions can help prevent gender from becoming a significant factor in negotiations:

1. *Anticipate gender-related triggers:* Some degree of ambiguity is present in all negotiations, so be aware of situations that may trigger gender stereotypes or role expectations. Work to counter gender triggers, or use them to benefit negotiation performance. In highly ambiguous, competitive environments, for example, men may be encouraged to maximize their outcomes by ramping up their competitive drive. Women, on the other hand, may be inspired by reminders that they're representing not just themselves but their colleagues, department, company, or customers.

2. *Do your homework:* Whether you're a man or a woman, learn as much as you can about what is possible or appropriate when heading into a salary negotiation or discussing a contract. Research industry norms, investigate precedent, and talk to others who are already employed at the firm or in the industry. Most important, don't be afraid to ask for whatever you need to remain truly motivated and to get the job done well. You and your organization will be better off in the long-run.

3. *Create transparency surrounding compensation and benefits:* To encourage gender equity regarding compensation and career development, your company should codify and publish opportunities and benefits that it may be willing to offer. This doesn't mean standardizing benefits for all employees but clarifying the range of issues that are up for negotiation and the appropriate criteria on which decisions are based.

4. *Articulate performance expectations:* When sending your employees into competitive bargaining situations, clearly state performance goals. Armed with transparent comparative information and a sense of acceptable targets, both men and women will achieve better outcomes. Setting high but reasonable aspirations is good for all negotiators and may be especially beneficial for women in ambiguous, competitive negotiations.

CONCLUSION

The generally accepted view is that back in early human society, men and women were close to equal. Men and women had separate spheres and did different things, but both were respected. Often, women were gatherers and men were hunters. The total contribution to the group's food was about the same, even though there were some complementary differences.

Nowadays, people do not see any difference in the gender. It is not a reliable predictor of negotiation performance; neither women nor men perform particularly better or worse across all negotiations.

References

Dina W. Pradel, Hannah Riley Bowles, and Kathleen L. McGinn, "When gender changes the negotiations", Harvard Business School, *Working Knowledge Weekly News Letter*, February 13, 2006; http://hbswk.hbs.edu/

See Appendix II of main report for a summary of broad gender differentials in the MSE sector.

www.unifem-eseasia.org/resources/globaleconomy

ILO: *The Knowledge Wedge: Developing the knowledge base on women entrepreneurs; what have we learned.*

United Nations, The World's Women 2000.

Martha Lagace, "Women Negotiating in the New Millennium", Harvard Business School, *Working Knowledge Weekly News Letter*, February 8, 2000.

http://hbswk.hbs.edu

http://go.worldbank.org/X8T0NPX820

www.denisdutton.com

findarticles.com

30

Outsourcing: Growth Opportunities and Constraints for an Entrepreneur

Vinod V. Nayak*
Ravindra Singh*
Dr. Pradip Manjrekar**

The purpose of this paper is to address some aspects of outsourcing with particular emphasis of growth opportunities and constraints that an entrepreneur faces while getting an outsourced business. Outsourcing projects are not always successful, whether they are local, regional or cross border. The paper addresses some of the underlying theoretical fields that should be taken into consideration to make outsourcing successful for both parties, with emphasis on the international aspect. Competitive pressures among firms in High Cost Countries (HCC) have forced them to look for more cost effective ways of operation. An increasingly important source of competitive advantage is buying components, finished goods and services from low cost countries in Asia. Strategic issues for HCC firms concerning growth opportunities and constraints, as well as the growing political concern about lost jobs in the outsourcing countries that are in the lead of this trend. The paper further suggests some underlying requirements for Asian countries to be able to benefit from such outsourced business from high cost companies in the short and long-run. Finally, some areas for research in the field of growth opportunities are suggested.

INTRODUCTION

We are witnessing a major shift in value creation that will have substantial effect both on the HCC and Asian employment and economies. Challenging structural changes will take place in the work forces in the two hemispheres as the outsourcing trend is reinforcing. A period of change creates new opportunities for Asian Small and Medium Enterprises (SMEs), both in Market Expansion and Profit Opportunities. The first is due to improved access to HCC by means of digital technology and improved physical transportation systems. The latter is due to the present cost level differences, making the buyer willing to pay premium prices seen from the suppliers' point of view. Presently, huge savings are apparently possible.

* Faculty, S.I.W.S. College, Wadala (West), Mumbai.
** Professor, Dr. D.Y. Patil Institute of Management Studies, CBD Belapur, Navi Mumbai.

Evidence suggests that cost levels at least 50% lower than in HCCs are common. The actual savings are, however, also dependent on the transaction costs associated with outsourcing. These are unfortunately much harder to quantify.

An understanding of the underlying theories affecting a close relationship between the parties could aid in both interaction with international partners and making the co-operation successful. Surprisingly, little material relating to the principal aspects of international outsourcing has been published in academic journals.

WHAT IS HAPPENING?

External procurement of components as input to manufactured goods and outsourcing of services has become common practice among an increasing number of firms that are under competitive pressures in HCC. Local or regional providers that are specialized and thus, can deliver goods and services at a lower unit cost normally perform the greatest part of delivery of outsourcing activities. That is not unexpected, as that does not require adjusting to a new business environment. The decision to let outside vendors take over some activities is in itself a change in the business model that can be difficult, and many outsourcing projects are reported to be unsuccessful. Lacity and Willcocks (1998), report that the success rate of IT outsourcing is only 56%. Aron and Singh (2005), state, "According to several studies, half the organizations that shifted processes offshore failed to generate the financial benefits they expected to". Considering the fact that IT outsourcing is one of the earliest and most widespread outsourcing activities, the success rate is discouraging. Part of the cause of failures may be lack of understanding of the underlying theories regarding relationships with entities outside own organization, in addition to inadequate execution. Over the past few years, the outsourcing phenomenon is being expanded to include outsourcing of both goods and services, and it is growing at an increasing rate. Suppliers in countries with favourable factor conditions such as access to raw materials, lower priced energy, low labour cost and/or high education level are positioned to benefit from this development. Outsourcing of services (business processes) is becoming increasingly widespread, and there seems to be a tendency to move upward towards higher value creation activities. Asian countries have, in particular, benefited from the trend by offering lower cost; a pool of well-educated personnel and good language skills. To make the transfer of work successful both for the outsourcer and the outsourcing partner (vendor), good understanding of strategic aspects, underlying economies and the required competencies are important. In the following, some aspects of this will be addressed.

Change in strategic thinking

The time of the fully-integrated corporation that makes everything from its inputs to marketing and after sales service of the finished product may be coming to an end. Current thinking suggests that a concentration in the areas of the organization's unique (core) competencies and leaving the other activities to outside specialists increases competitiveness. Numerous authors have in the past addressed the topic core competencies. It has been given several terms, such as invisible assets (Itami, 1987) strategic assets and (Dierickx and Cool, 1988) meta skills (Klein et al., 1991) skills or competencies (Hall, 1992) capabilities (Stalk et al, 1992). The common denominator seems to be that a core competence is a unique organization specific quality. It has value if it gives a customer superior value of whatever is being delivered. There are two ways by which this is expressed: either by lower price or by increased performance for the user. In other words, a core competence has no value unless it can be converted into some form of customer satisfaction. Identifying and nurturing such core competencies is thus, an important issue for the organization as it is through them that a sustainable competitive advantage evolves. Most other value creation activities can be outsourced.

Outsourcing

Outsourcing, i.e., activities that are not considered to represent core competencies of the organization can be bought from specialized vendors outside the organization. Quinn (1992), states that if external vendors can perform the task better, the firm is sacrificing a competitive advantage by carrying it out itself. It may be added: unless the activity is critical to the business strategy.

A definition of the concept of outsourcing could be; "Transfer to an outside entity of responsibility for production of a primary or central support activity that formerly has been carried out by the organization". Strategic aspects of outsourcing care should be taken when deciding on what to outsource. Obviously, activities associated with core competencies should not be outsourced, as they are a very important part of the firm's intellectual property.

OBJECTIVES

- To develop an appreciation and understanding of entrepreneurship and growth opportunities of an entrepreneur.

- To understand, outsourcing as an instrument of success for an entrepreneur.

- To identify and understand the different activities of an enterprise bifurcating the activities into core activities and incidental activities.

- To explore the various constraints that are detrimental for the growth of an outsourced business enterprise.

ENTREPRENEURSHIP

Entrepreneurship has three dimensions: innovation, risk-taking and proactive behaviour. Innovation requires an emphasis on developing new and unique products, services and processes. Risk-taking involves a willingness to pursue opportunities having a chance of costly failure. Proactive behaviour is concerned with implementation and doing whatever is necessary to bring a concept to fruition.

For more and more firms, the issue is not whether they should embrace entrepreneurship, but how they can encourage innovation, risk-taking and proactive behaviour. An entrepreneurial orientation requires employees to think and act in new ways, taking individual responsibility for change while also co-operating with teams. Employees must be more opportunistic, creative and achievement-oriented, yet tolerant of ambiguity and willing to take risks.

ENTREPRENEURSHIP THROUGH THE YEARS

The term 'entrepreneurship' is derived from the French verb 'entreprende' of the twelfth century, though the exact meaning may not be that applicable today. This meaning of the word then was to do something without any link to economic profits, which is the antithesis of what entrepreneurship is all about today. It was only in the early 18th century when French economist, Richard! Cantillon, described an entrepreneur as 'one who bears risks by buying at certain prices and selling at uncertain prices', which is probably closer to the term as applied today.

In the 1776 thought-provoking book, *The Wealth of Nations,* Adam Smith explained clearly that it was not the benevolence of the baker but self-interest that motivated him to provide bread. From Smith's standpoint, entrepreneurs were 'the economic agents who transformed demand into supply for profits'.

In 1848, the famous economist John Stuart Mill described entrepreneurship as 'the founding of a private enterprise. This encompassed the risk-takers, the decision-makers, and the individuals who desire wealth by managing limited resources to create new business ventures'.

Case Study

US contact centers are fast seeing a drop in market share.

More and more jobs are headed around the global outsourcing world to India. Driving this outflow of jobs are tight profit margins and the call for automation. While these spell a shift in the job balance in the American workplace, countries such as, India, Canada and the Philippines stand to benefit. These have also kept the outsourcing companies on their toes, constantly reinventing, partnering, merging, or simply outdoing other companies in the bid to remain alive in the cut-throat outsourcing market. This cut-throat environment is depicted in the Data Monitor Report, "The boundaries between US-based contact center providers and other business process outsourcers are dissolving, and firms are invading each others' territories". A glimpse of US contact center scenario: 90% of jobs lost are outbound telemarketing posts, though this is also due to the Do-Not-Call registry and a higher revenue dangled by the inbound calls field. The Data Monitor Report says, "In addition, the number of agent positions in offshore and near shore countries will continue to grow, due to the growing demand from US and captive market businesses." 2004 saw 37% of the world's outsourced contact center population in the United States. Come 2008, it is expected to dwindle to 25%, with a drop from last year's 315,000 headcount to 291,000 by 2008. This has urged contact center outsourcers to venture beyond call centers and Business Process Outsourcing (BPO) in the name of growth and survival. Companies originally geared towards providing contact center services are now taking on BPO functions, just as the BPO providers are learning the ropes for contact center performance.

Where does all this movement leave American contact centers?

"As the market contracts through to 2009, it will be imperative for outsourcing service providers to choose between competing on the basis of cost or reinventing themselves".

Activities of an Enterprise that can be Outsourced

A strategic evaluation must therefore be made even for all outsourcing proposals. It is of great importance to decide if the outsourced activity could mean loss of future control of processes and know-how. Even by outsourcing non-core activities, the company may facilitate transfer of own discretionary systemic competence to a vendor that will also use these activities.

Supply the Competitors

The outsourcer may also lose uniqueness that in the long-run will reduce the full value proposition to the customers. Porter (2003), suggests that extensive outsourcing also has a tendency to standardize end products and thereby forego a strategic advantage. In the worst case, the outsourcing vendor develops into a full-fledged competitor over time. In case of a badly handled outsourcing process, the outsourcer may even be at ransom if their supplier develops a strong bargaining position. Potential loss of intellectual property consists of the rather obvious items as patents, trademarks and copyrights. But it also extends to trade secrets contained in internal systemic value creation activities such as planning systems and marketing approaches. The intellectual property extends, in fact, to all intangible proprietary information. An HCC firm may be reluctant to enter into an outsourcing agreement with an Asian partner for fear that important intellectual property may be diffused, sometimes, by outright theft, but more likely by inadvertent leakage through employees or by employee attrition. Often, a non-disclosure clause on the part of the goods or service providing firm and its employees is thus required. In addition to the direct cost reduction, outsourcing also reduces the need for investment in plants or personnel, as well as operating capital. Theoretically, it should therefore be rather simple to calculate whether an activity should be carried out internally by the organization, or be outsourced. Unfortunately, costs are difficult to identify clearly, partly due to allocation problems and inadequate accounting systems. The question is further complicated by the fact that human beings are not rational decision-makers. Personal opportunism influences decisions, whether consciously or unconsciously. At best, the decisions are "interdentally rational, but only limited so" (Simon, 1976). A good understanding of the principal-agent theory is therefore useful in connection with an outsourcing decision. A little alliance theory acknowledging the fact that no organization can be outstanding in all fields, one mode for compensating for this is establishing alliances with complementary organizations. An alliance has a greater degree of commitment than for example, a regular supplier-customer relationship.

Hax and Majluf (1991), define a strategic alliance as, "Formal coalitions between two or more firms for short or long-term ventures, borne out of opportunistic or permanent relationships that evolve into a form of partnership among players". Alliances are important instruments in the outsourcing context, as outsourcing is strategic, long-term and requires formalized agreements. An outsourcing relationship is therefore per definition an alliance. Outsourcing decisions can thus, find a good theoretical basis in alliance theory. Alliances can be placed on a scale from full ownership (internal alliances) through part ownership (joint ventures) to no ownership (formalized working relationship or outsourcing). An alliance contains a strategic component, and is therefore, normally a long-term commitment.

A LITTLE RELATIONSHIP THEORY

This theoretical concept focuses on inter-organizational relations and the content of the relationship. A viable relationship is based on exchange of commercial, social and informational activities between organizations. Normally, a contract specifies the rights and obligations of the partners, and a long-term mutual benefit must accrue to both parties to make the relationship work. Three elements of the relationship theory are important to be aware of in an outsourcing context.

Transaction content in a commercial relationship

There is a stream of goods and services between the organizations. The contract that governs these transactions is according to Williamson (1979), established to avoid opportunism by the partners. Such contract clauses in an outsourcing relationship may for example, be non-disclosure and exclusivity in addition to the ordinary price and delivery details.

It may be argued that in the long-run, the contract has diminishing value as the relationship develops organically, and the contract may even be irrelevant as the content of the relationship develops and changes.

Communication and information content

Proper communication with relevant content is essential when developing a lasting relationship. The success of an alliance is dependent on a steady flow of information to reduce transaction costs. Quality of content is part of this effort, so as to eliminate ambiguity and misunderstanding. In an outsourcing situation, communication is of particular importance, as the partners often are expected to work intimately with each other for adjustments, information exchange, queries, etc. For many, a close, external co-operation is a novelty, and particular effort should be placed on establishing proper communication channels and content. The choice of communication medium (face-to-face, group or individual, written or electronic) must be carefully selected for each particular relationship. Social content the qualitative part of a relationship is, according to Mitchell (1973), based on trust, norms and values, expectations, and feelings. The social aspect is in many respects the glue that ties the two partners together, and is of great importance in the outsourcing relationship. Personal relationships can act as a safety valve in case of disagreements that could develop into mistrust, and can to a certain extent substitute parts of the detailed contract that governs the relationship. A prerequisite for the good functional social interaction means a mutual understanding of the partners' cultural setting business ethics and conduct.

OFFSHORING

A big change took place in the latter half of the last century when offshoring, from the HCCs to low cost countries expanded in the 1990s. Sourcing from firms in a totally different culture may yield substantial benefits, but it also requires different competencies in the outsourcing organization. Kotabe and Murray (2004) state, "Sourcing directly from foreign suppliers requires greater purchasing know-how and is riskier than other alternatives that use locally-based wholesalers and representatives".

Fear of the unknown due to lack of knowledge about foreign cultures and business practices can furthermore hold back an otherwise rational decision to initiate international sourcing. On the other hand, the offshoring company can benefit from both their own and their outsourcing partner's core competencies as well as factor condition advantages creating a lower cost. Substantial competitive advantages may therefore obviously be gained from offshoring if it is executed in the right way.

Offshoring of physical input factors

International sourcing of input components for one's own production process has been going on for a number of years, and has been well-developed.

Kotabe and Murray (2004), sum it up, "Today, many companies consider not simply price but also quality, reliability and technology of components and products to be procured. These companies design the sourcing decision on the basis of the interplay between their competitive advantages and the comparative advantages of various sourcing locations for long-term gains".

DISCUSSION

The field of outsourcing initially may seem like an unlikely place for entrepreneurial activities. However, it is a place where various entrepreneurial activities have occurred.

These entrepreneurial activities have resulted in new and better ways to grow opportunities and expansion. Some of these entrepreneurial activities have occurred through classic ways by the development of new firms started by entrepreneurs with expertise in human resource management. Other entrepreneurial activities have occurred through new activities and/or partnerships between existing firms or through entrepreneurial activities by human resource departments.

CONCLUSION

Development of these entrepreneurial activities has reinforced the development of human resource management as a function that adds value to a firm. Like all changing activities, any changes in human resource activities or method delivery must be monitored carefully to guarantee its success. The advantages and disadvantages of encouraging and utilizing the services of specific human resource entrepreneurs must be carefully assessed before deciding to value these entrepreneurs more than human resource professionals who operate in more traditional human resource departments.

In general, the most successful human resource entrepreneurs are found in firms known for quality human resource management. This finding is especially apparent when human resource management is one of the firm's core competencies.

References

Determinants of Entrepreneurship in Europe

I Grilo and Thurik

Motivations and Performance Conditions for Ethnic Entrepreneurship

E Masurel

www.allbusiness.com

www.asiaentrepreneurshipjournal.com

www.sciencedirect.com

31

Organic Growth in Indian SMEs

Suyash Bhatt*
Dr. Pradip Manjrekar**

Acquisition growth is not a common theme in entrepreneurship research. Entrepreneurial growth has traditionally been addressed as 'organic growth', i.e. as internal expansion through the extension of existing operations and internally induced process and product innovations. We contend that acquisition growth may generate entrepreneurial benefits over the long-run, which may not be present in organic growth or green-field establishments. In fact, acquisition can be a way to release entrepreneurial activities in a firm. Acquisitions may revitalize a firm and improve its ability to anticipate or to react adequately to the changing external conditions. We contend that these positive outcomes will only accrue to acquiring organizations when acquisition growth is coupled with the development of acquisition capabilities, i.e., with the accumulation, storage, and exploitation of fresh organizational knowledge.

INTRODUCTION

Acquisition growth is not a common theme in entrepreneurship research. The reason researchers avoid the topic is obviously not grown itself, which is a defining concept of entrepreneurship as a scholarly field. However, entrepreneurial growth has traditionally been addressed as 'organic growth', defined as internal expansion through the extension of existing operations and internally induced process and product innovations. In this paper, we contend that acquisition growth may generate entrepreneurial benefits over the long-run, which may not be present in organic growth or green-field establishments.

Firms that survive the initial formative phases, during which exploration, knowledge, and competence development are key, tend to start promoting the exploitation and fine-tuning of existing organizational routines and practices. Exploitation, defined as the ongoing use of a firm's knowledge base, allows the organization to focus on the knowledge and routines that

*   Ph.D. Scholar, Padmashree Dr. D.Y. Patil University, Navi Mumbai.
** Professor, Padmashree Dr. D.Y. Patil University, Navi Mumbai.

have contributed most to its initial survival and growth phases. However, this gradually reduces variety in the firm's knowledge base and in the set of capabilities it needs for future growth and survival terms, simplicity, i.e., a narrow focus on a single theme, activity, or issue at the expense of all others, coupled with narrowing, increasingly homogeneous managerial "lenses" or world views. However, there is a need to strike a balance between exploration and exploitation. This aim may be achieved by acquisitions.

Under certain conditions, acquisitions may be a response, although obviously not the only one, to resource maturity, ossification, and simplicity. Acquisitions may revitalize a firm and improve its ability to anticipate or to react adequately to changing external conditions. By administering the relatively controlled shocks determined by acquisitions, entrepreneurs can revitalize their organizations and foster their long-term viabilities. The cultural and managerial ferment induced by acquisitions and post-acquisition integration break through the acquirer's rigidities and inertia, and result in an organization that is better suited to pursuing entrepreneurial activities.

We contend that these positive outcomes can only accrue to acquiring organizations when acquisition growth is coupled with the development of acquisition capabilities, i.e., with the accumulation, storage and exploitation of fresh organizational knowledge.

When discussing the potential benefits of acquisitions, a distinction is usually made between value capture and value creation. Value capture is a one-time event that results from features inherent in the transaction itself, e.g., asset stripping and tax benefits. In contrast, value creation is a long-term phenomenon that results from entrepreneurial action and the interaction between firms involved. Value creation embodies the transfer and recombining of capabilities between the two firms, which is commonly referred to as synergy.

How the capabilities for generating value creation through acquisitions evolve in the real world is an open question. We are particularly interested in understanding how "serial" acquirers develop acquisition and integration capabilities over time. We are also interested in investigating how firms that do acquire can report high levels of satisfaction related to the process of external growth, despite the typically dismal record of acquisition performance.

To explore these questions, we perform a longitudinal comparative study of 18 growing Italian Small and Medium-sized Firms (Indian SMEs) from different industries. Indian SMEs represent an ideal context for studying the development of acquisition and integration capabilities, because unlike large market leaders, Indian SMEs are far less likely to engage in acquisitions for the purpose of reducing competition. Instead, the potential synergies are a major reason for acquiring other firms. Over the period of our study, some of these Indian SMEs accomplish impressive growth rates through acquisitions, to the extent that they change from the small, to the medium, and sometimes to the large size category.

METHODOLOGY

Our focus on external growth and related competence development as a process required that we observe and examine a large number of variables that influence growth processes, in particular, the complex relationships among them. The heterogeneity of the phenomenon requires descriptions that are specifically aimed at assessing the abstractions and generalizations that we can meaningfully attempt.

Hence, we conduct a "qualitative" study, targeting a relatively limited number of companies (18) over time, analyzing them in-depth by using many different data sources, and developing insights through a comparative logic.

The unit of analysis in this study is all business activities controlled by the entrepreneur, the entrepreneurial team, or the entrepreneurial family. We are not so much interested in the growth of any individual firm or establishment, but in the overall growth of the whole group of business activities controlled by such individuals or groups of individuals. However, for ease of presentation, we refer to "the firm" or "the organizational entity" in the remainder of this section. We select 18 such cases by sampling on the dependent variable. Our aim is to theoretically sample a number of "cases" that are characterized by different growth rates over the same time period, different attitudes towards acquisitions (eight out of the 18 sampled firms have not acquired), different initial size (see Table 1 and 2 for an overview). We keep industry characteristics relatively constant by selecting only cases of manufacturing firms in relatively mature and traditional contexts (i.e., food, apparel, mechanical, chemical and pharmaceutical products).

We traced the whole acquisition history of each case, which in three cases went back to the early 1990s. However, the comparative analyses focus only on the 1999 to 2007 period.

Table 1 gives an overview of the four phases of the study. For each phase, the table provides the data sources, the tools used for the collection and analysis of data, and the elaborations obtained as the result of each phase. We use certain method precautions to ensure the reliability and validity of our results.

Table 1: The Research Phases, the Tools used, and the Results obtained

Research phases	Main sources of the data used	Data collection and analysis tools	Results obtained
1. Preliminary collection and analysis of secondary data.	Financial statements, articles, books, catalogues, publications, company documents.	Database of secondary data for each case. Analysis of financial statements.	For each case: company history; analysis of financial statements; identification of business areas; description of sector and its evolution; identification of competitors, relevant external events.
2. Semi-structured interviews.	6-7 interviews for each case.	Semi-structured questionnaire (approx. 20 questions per interview of which 8 were common to all interviews).	Completion of data collected in phase 1. Identification of the aspects relevant for the interpretation of the growth path in each of 18 cases.
3. In-depth analysis.	Collection of further secondary data. 2-3 additional interviews, selected on the basis of the results of phase 2.	Unstructured interviews.	In-depth analysis of the relevant aspects arising from phase 2.

Contd...

4.1. Interpretation of individual cases.	All the results of the preceding phases.	Structured company fact sheets. Structured reports for each company.	Understanding of the growth process, its determinants, and its results for each of the 18 cases examined.
4.2. Analysis of the emerging issues.	Structured company and report sheets (phase 4.1).	Centralized database of the collected data.	In-depth transversal analysis of the main issues that proved to be relevant for the interpretation of growth processes.
4.3. Comparative interpretation of the 18 cases.	All the results of the preceding phases.	Centralized database of the collected data.	Comparative interpretation of the growth processes of the 18 cases examined: proposal of shared interpretation keys.

DATA

Growth and Acquisitions

Table 1 classifies companies in terms of final size and historic growth rates. Table 2 details growth and size figures. Out of the eight companies with the highest growth rates (over 100%), three (Telelinks, Ventura, and Temasek Holdings) did not acquire any company and only one (Temasek Holdings) had plans to do so in the near future. Of the remaining companies that grew more than 100%, one carried out six acquisitions, two carried out seven acquisitions, and the other two carried out nine and 19 acquisitions, respectively. We note that the five companies that grew more than 100% and carried out acquisitions combined external growth with significant organic growth processes. They did so mainly by developing new products or by entering into new markets. Among the four companies that grew between 50% and 100%, only one (Alchemist) made more than one acquisition, while two carried out none. The six companies that grew less than 50% made one (Sify), (Zegma) or (SCM) acquisitions, or none at all (Sassa and Cardili). In terms of size reached at the end of the period, the companies in our sample that carried out at least two acquisitions had more than 1,000 employees in 2007.

Table 2: Growth, Corporate Size, and Acquisitions in the 18 firms included in the sample

Sales growth rate (1997-2007)	> 100%	Telelinks (0 – no)	Ventura (0 – no) Saibaba (6 – Yes)	Mapro (9 – Yes) Mala (19 – Yes) Temasek Holdings (0 – Yes) Campani (7 – Yes) Dina(7 – Yes)
	50-100%	Sportsdiva (0 – no)	Frozen (1 – Yes) Alpha (0 – no)	Chilly (6 – Yes)
	< 50%	Sassa (0 – Yes)	Sify (1 – no) Cardili (0 – no)	Zegma (4 – n.a.) Max & Max (n.a.) SCM group (7 – Yes)
	number of employees (2007)	< 250	250-1000	> 1000

Note: we report, in parentheses, for each organizational entity the number of control acquisitions carried out in the company's history; the presence (Yes)/absence (No), as of 2007, of the formal intention to carry out acquisitions in the near future (i.e., within the planning horizon).

Table 3: Relevance of Acquisitions in the Investigated Firms

Firm/Group	Change in Sales since 1997-2007	No. Acquisition	Proposed Acquisition	Sales	Employees
Telelinks	269%	-	No	1231	196
Ventura	141%	-	No	1100	790
Temasek Holding	136%	-	Yes	1000	1440
Saibaba	135%	-	Yes	909	300
Mapro	133%	9	Yes	900	1200
Mala	123%	8	Yes	899	2400
Campani	122%	6	Yes	850	3900
Dina	120%	5	Yes	849	1300
Sassa	100%	7	Yes	835	200
Sify	70%	7	Yes	833	256
Cardili	69%	7	n.a	810	345
Chilly	65%	9	No	800	1856
Frozen	60%	19	Yes	750	323
Max & Max	55%	8	No	650	1444
SCM Group	50%	7	Yes	600	1555
Sportsdiva	45%	7	No	556	161
Zegma	44%	5	Yes	555	1325
Alpha	43%	5	No	106	652

Tables 1 and 2 show that acquisitions are not the only ways for a firm to accomplish substantial growth. Some of the companies grew extensively through internal growth processes. Companies that made acquisitions also did not neglect organic growth. However, the companies that made massive investments in acquisitions had all attained a larger size by the end of the period.

As noted, acquisitions were not necessarily the dominant means of growth. Eight firms did not carry out any acquisition at all, and half of them expressed no intention of doing so in the near future. However, of the companies that made at least one acquisition, only one declared that it had no other acquisitions in mind. Table 3 shows that for these latter companies, acquisitions have gradually become a recurrent, albeit not exclusive, managerial practice in pursuing corporate development. It appears that acquisitions create a sort of "divider" between small firms that have never made an acquisition and have no intention of doing so in the short to medium-term, and those that have acquired other companies and also evaluate further opportunities. Based on our interviews, it seems that this difference is psychological and corporate culture-related in nature.

Motivations underlying the decision to pursue acquisition growth

The firms not engaged in acquisitions gave several reasons for refraining from acquisitions. One rapidly growing company reported that all of its energies and resources were concentrated on organic growth, leaving little room for the evaluation of external growth opportunities. Other companies decided to forgo acquisitions because of their focus on developing a single business niche. In other cases, there were few suitable acquisition targets. Very focused companies or those with a very strong and well-known brand name felt that it was imperative not to alter the perception and the reputation of the trademark.

Our interviews also indicated motivations that stemmed more from the orientation of the entrepreneur and management than from the structural characteristics of the company or sector. One of the entrepreneurs mentioned that the decision not to acquire also reflected strong doubts on the company's ability to integrate an entity that might have a culture very different from theirs. In the following statement, a close collaborator of the entrepreneur of one of the other surveyed companies without acquisition experience makes clear the fear of not being able to bring the integration phase to a successful completion and to manage the acquired companies.

"What held the owners back a bit was the idea: 'if we don't have anybody who can manage it, why should we expand, why acquire?' Even though the owners had always been known to press on, never stopping, improving not only sales but also the results of the company."

The need for having to borrow excessively, the possibility that target companies were overpriced, or, as stated by one respondent, the fear of "biting off more than he could chew" were additional reasons for refraining from acquisitions.

On the other hand, acquiring companies had greater confidence in their abilities to overcome resources constraints. This Noun was summed up by one company, "As far as, I can remember, there has never been a situation in which a really interesting target was excluded for financial reasons." Another one stated that, "Our company has always been perceived for the potential it actually had; even in more difficult times, such as in '95 and '96 when there were the first acquisitions and debt increased, we never feared having real problems in finding financial resources."

Table 4 shows that to a large extent, companies that carried out acquisitions were initially driven by competitive and other contextual conditions.

In Phase 1, we describe how, once a company takes the acquisition path, the learning processes and the consequent accumulation of competencies can significantly reduce the psychological load linked to such operations, making the related strategic decisions less and less difficult and improving the perception of subsequent results.

Phase 1: Learning from experience: the creation of acquisition knowledge.

All the acquiring companies clearly learned from their acquisition experiences. As one of them said:

"The acquisitions were certainly positive. They brought growth and were an opportunity for cultural development, both from the manufacturing and the commercial standpoint, because we also learned from the companies we acquired."

Mistakes and crisis situations, which were greatly feared by the entrepreneurs who did not carry out acquisitions, were the issues on which acquiring firms built their learning paths. Outcomes that failed to meet targets or mistakes and crises during the acquisition process provided learning opportunities.

What emerges with equal clarity is that the learning processes occurred, also thanks to the particular conditions during which the acquisitions were carried out. In the cases we investigated, the majority of acquisitions, both successful and unsuccessful, took place in a context that allowed the consequences of possible errors to be contained, and a "practice field" for the development of competencies for possible use in subsequent operations to be built.

First, firms always made acquisitions with a certain caution and without venturing far beyond the range of the competencies, the company already possessed. A constant characteristic of the acquisitions carried out by our sample companies was that management perceived a high degree of consistency between the activities of themselves and the target firm.

The acquisitions highlighted two other aspects that might have enhanced learning processes. The first was the firm management's perception of its ability to manage the acquired unit, "Our acquisitions were always decided with an eye to our size and to our actual possibility of managing them with the management the company had at that time... ." The second aspect was the presence of very clear and tangible industrial, commercial, or marketing synergies or elements of complementarity. For example, when he discussed his firm's main acquisition, the entrepreneur of a food company declared.

Table 4: An Overview of Acquisition Characteristics in Investigated Firms

Firm/ group	Year	Relevance (size)	Motivation	Related business	Strategic coherence	Integra- tion	Industry Context
Ventura	2000	Low	Product range	YES	YES	Full	Vertical acquisitions
	1999	High	Market share/Product range	YES	YES	Partial	Intense horizontal concentration
	1999	Medium	Market access	YES	YES	Partial	started in the early 1990s
Campani	2002	High	Market access/Products	YES	YES	Minimal	
	2002	Low	Products/Industry	YES	no	Partial	
	2003	Low	Products/Industry	YES	no	Full	
	2003	Medium- high	Market share/Product range	YES	YES	Initial stage	
	1998	High	Geographical market	YES	YES	Full	Presence of strategic opportunities (target firms in geographical markets)
	1999	Medium- low	Geographical market/ Product	YES	YES	Partial	
Chilly	2001	Low	Geographical market/ Product	YES	YES	Minimal	
	2002	Low	Geographical market/ Product	YES	YES	Initial stage	
	2001	high	Product range/new market/Production capacity	YES	YES	Partial	Intense concentration started in the

Contd...

	2000	Medium-low	Brand/Product range	YES	YES	n.a.	1990s
Dina	2000	Low	Product/Market	YES	YES	n.a.	
	2004	Low	Brand/Product range	YES	YES	n.a.	
	2000	Low	Product/Market	YES	YES	n.a.	
	2004	Low	Product range	YES	YES	n.a.	
	2000	High	Complementary	YES	YES	Full	Increasing concen-
			Product/new markets				tration
Cardilini	1999	Medium	Product/niche	YES	n.a.	Partial	Limited concentration
	1999	n.a.	Market	YES	YES	n.a.	n.a.
	2000	Low	Production capacity	YES	YES	Full	High concentration
	2004	Low	Vertical integration	YES	YES	Full	High concentration
Mapro	2004	Low	Vertical integration	YES	YES	Full	High concentration
	2001	n.a.	n.a.	YES	YES	n.a.	n.a.
	2002	High	New market	YES	n.a.	Partial	Limited concentration
Saibaba	2000	Medium-low	Industry	YES	no	Minimal	Segment maturity
SCM	2002	Low	Industry	YES	no	Partial	Segment maturity
Sify	1999	Low	New market	YES	YES	Partial	n.a.
Zegma	1999	Low	Product range	YES	YES	n.a.	Expansion
	2000	Low	Technological know-how	YES	no	n.a.	Expansion

"We feel we took home a mass of quite relevant proportions, exceptional in terms of productivity, because the acquired company is not only a brand, but a factory: we were able to rationalize the different plants and take home a great brand at the same time".

The managers of a chemical-pharmaceutical company also repeatedly underlined how the company's acquisitions were always motivated by the intention to acquire at least one of the following elements: factories with underutilized production capacity; particular technologies; strategic raw materials; strategic geographic positioning; market share; and experienced management.

The lessons learned covered not only the characteristics a target must have, but also the way in which acquisitions should be carried out. Here too, there were only a few, very simple, elements, but they were expressed clearly by the head of a company and the members of his management team.

"First, apart from very rare cases, in which the seller has a particular need, [...] we don't use investments banks [...] The second very important element – and I believe that was our trump card in acquisitions – was our great flexibility in understanding the seller's agenda [...] As long as it is not negative for us, we do anything, we can to facilitate the seller".

The second factor mentioned by this entrepreneur, i.e., the great attention paid to understanding and favouring the needs of the seller, was common in practically all the acquisition stories we heard. In almost all cases, both the acquirer and the target were family businesses. Understanding the mechanisms that drives a family to sell a company branch or an entire business, as well as the mechanisms that influence behaviour in the negotiation phase, were perceived by the acquiring companies as central to determining the success. Companies that carried out more than one deal tried to build future success on such experience.

"We don't believe that who pays 1 Euro more is the winner in acquisitions. There is obviously a minimum amount beneath which you lose. But, once the expectation level of the seller has been met, what really counts is the soft side, except in the case of true auctions where the last dollar wins. The contract, the way of approaching the deal, the way it is structured .... When we were doing our third acquisition, some competitors offered more, but they would have dismantled the organization this 70-year old man had created and wanted to preserve. I realize this may sound strange, but for this 70-year old man without heirs, 400 or 500 million dollars would have been the same because it's only a number written in a bank account. In the end, we won by offering 400 million dollars, coupled with the option of keeping his creation alive and remaining involved in the organization.

In fact, we kept him on board for three years with puts and calls.... . We always try to build something we feel, might be more appealing to the seller."

Finally, further lessons concerned the means of integration. All the companies we surveyed that had made more than one acquisition systematically reported that a "flexible" approach in terms of degree, areas, and tools of integration was preferable to a standardized "cookie cutter" approach. The head of business development of one of the surveyed companies summed this Noun up: "We don't have a recipe for integration, based on which you do 'A, B, C, D' every time you buy a business. We adopt a layman's approach and we see what needs to be done on a case-by-case basis. The factors that play a role are evidently many."

Companies that had made several acquisitions developed advanced acquisition strategies that led them to diversify the degree and means of integration with the target company, instead of following the same modus operandi every time. Although in some cases, acquisitions were managed according to a similar logic, the integration phase was managed in many different ways.

It was precisely for these reasons that almost all of companies in our survey brought in people with previous acquisition experience from larger companies. The managers were typically hired at the time of an important acquisition.

If the knowledge obtained in acquisitions and integration of acquired companies is to become an integral part of the organizational memory and if that knowledge is to be correctly recalled when needed, two additional conditions are necessary: the systematic accumulation of organizational memory linked to acquisitions and the creation of structures and managerial practices aimed at correctly "recalling" organizational memory. Phase 2 discusses the systematic accumulation of organizational memory.

Phase 2: Archiving the lessons learned: the accumulation and the partial formalization of the acquisition competencies matured.

The companies in our survey paid close attention to the organization of the lessons they learnt from their own acquisition experiences. Especially in the case of companies that made more than one acquisition, we observe the gradual emergence of organizational tools that allow companies to archive and accumulate acquisition knowledge. Companies use such managerial tools and practices to gradually organize knowledge on the underlying causes of the success or failure they experience ("know why"), or the operational means that can ensure success in acquisitions ("know how").

A constant element we find is the gradual emergence of simple rules or quantitative parameters that can offer guidance to those involved in acquisitions. The president of one of the companies most active in acquisitions described the lessons he had learnt in the years of deals.

"I believe that in preparing a plan, you first have to identify the critical variables…. For us, a possible acquisition target must have at least one of the following three characteristics: it has to give us a new country, synergies in a country in which we are already present or it has to expand our portfolio and we have to be able to manage it with our current business model. This is what we learned from our business and our acquisition experience. It would be folly to go through with an acquisition that doesn't give you one of these three things; if you did, you would end up with an expensive object you don't know how to manage. It would lose value the minute you purchase it."

An analysis of the competitive characteristics of the targets acquired by this company, and the content of subsequent integration processes, confirmed that acquisitions carried out by this company brought significant progress along all three lines indicated by top management.

These simple rules are always expressed very clearly by the company heads, and are always repeated, with minimal variations, by the other members of the top management team. This indicates that top management has learned the lessons and internalized them homogeneously. A consistency of this sort is clearly the fruit of the managerial practices with which the acquisitions are carried out.

First, the company head is personally involved in the acquisition. Second, all managers are actively involved in each stage of the acquisition process, from the identification and evaluation of the target to the integration and management of the acquired companies: "We have a small, well-integrated team in which we can exchange ideas with perfect frankness and we try to achieve, if not global consensus, at least a substantial global consensus … this allows us to react immediately". In this collective work practice, we can see the presence of interpersonal mechanisms in which mutual respect plays a crucial role. This is rare in most small to medium-sized Italian companies, in which the entrepreneur tends to take over complete responsibility for the main strategic decisions and their execution. He does so for understandable reasons, but it hinders the effective accumulation of knowledge in the entire management team.

Phase 3: Recalling the right concepts at the right time: developing mechanisms to use the acquisition competencies.

Besides, effectively learning and archiving the lessons learned, companies that have made more than one acquisition show that they know how to correctly apply such knowledge. The skills to develop and leverage acquisition knowledge are generated more by the processes through which the acquisitions are carried out than by tools and formal plannings.

The companies in our sample demonstrated the ability to become aware of their mistakes and the reasons of their success. They were also able to modify their own acquisition behaviours over time as a result of the lessons learned. A top executive of one of these companies underlined how past mistakes generated reflection and learning that led top management to change its subsequent behaviour.

"We recently came across some truly unrepeatable opportunities. 10 years ago we wouldn't have thought twice about taking advantage of them. Instead, we decided to forego these acquisitions because experience told us that a growth process must be a 'healthy' growth process that is manageable and within our reach".

The companies in our sample seem to have adopted a very flexible approach, in which the different principles learned from experience are utilized according to the peculiarities of the operation at hand: "It is essential not to start out with dogmas, with the idea that everything necessarily needs to be done like we were accustomed to doing before... you have to approach the issues with an open mindset and not with the conviction that you are the guardian of the truth".

This Noun is also evident in the fact that the people we interviewed highlighted the company's growing "ease" in undertaking and completing acquisition processes.

But how did these companies manage to use the right concept at the right time? Acquisition competencies reside in the team of people who have already experienced acquisitions. Therefore, there are two assumptions to bear in mind. First, that the more a management team is involved in the operations and the more it remains stable over time, the easier it will be for the company to efficiently access its wealth of accumulated knowledge. Second, to correctly utilize this wealth of knowledge, firms build relationships and mechanisms that involve people.

In every one of our cases, identifying potential targets is always the result of spontaneous, rather than planned processes. The firms identify specific opportunities thanks to different inputs. The company head always plays a central role in these processes. During the very first acquisition experiences, if it is not the head of the company managing the acquisition, it is usually an executive that the CEO trusts who follows the acquisition almost entirely.

The direct involvement of the head of the company in the identification and evaluation stages of the acquisition, as well as in the closing of the deal and in the subsequent integration process, is therefore the first guarantee that the lessons learned from the past are correctly utilized in subsequent operations.

However, in general, what guarantees the best results is top executives' openness to receiving suggestions not only from all levels of the organization, but also from outside. The person in charge of business development at one of the companies most active in acquisitions said: "The identification of a target arises from internal intelligence, in which I'd say everybody is involved. Everyone in the company shares the policy of growing through acquisitions. Anyone in the organization, even at the intermediate level, who identifies a potential target, takes it upon him/herself to bring the possibility to the attention of top management."

It is especially in subsequent acquisitions that the gradual development of a dedicated, albeit not full-time, management team that follows the most sensitive stages of each acquisition becomes noticeable. "Once the target company has been identified, the entrepreneur gives the Central Director of Strategic Planning, who's been with the company since 1994, and his daughter, who also works in the Strategic Planning Department, full powers to proceed with the operation. At this point, the two make use of the collaboration of teams created ad hoc, which include professionals involved in virtue of their past experiences or suggested contacts".

Over time, a growing number of people within the company are systematically involved: "In some ways, people grew with the business. People became more interested as the acquisition policy progressed. And certainly, at a certain point, the decision to create a business development function seemed almost natural, precisely because expansion by external lines had already become a structural part of our business."

Involvement usually occurs in periodic meetings, real "organizational routines" of the acquisition process. As the same head of business development specified.

"Of course, once the deal has been closed, we hold periodic meetings at different levels to verify integration, because there is a strategic level and then there are operational levels at which we normally establish integration committees that include our representatives as well as those of the company to be integrated ... . But at the strategic level, right after the acquisition, we have top management meetings twice a month during which we review the progress of integration. Once the acute phase is over, we carry out periodic analyses ... . This has been happening for several years. At least, since our second acquisition."

The integration of the acquired company requires particular involvement by managers at all levels.

Flexibility and speed in decision-making at the top levels of the company certainly aid these executives in correctly recalling the lessons learned at the right time. Flexibility and speed are guaranteed, not only by the management team's mutual trust and ability to work together, but also by the typically concentrated ownership structure of the companies in our survey, and by the role played by the board of directors.

Many of the people interviewed on the subject of integration spontaneously compared the decisional paths the acquisition processes applied by their companies with those of their main competitors, large multinationals with a widespread ownership base.

"We see less flexibility and speed in decision-making in our competitors. We probably see these characteristics less because they're public companies, or because they are larger, and therefore have a more complicated bureaucratic process. Our competitors have longer reaction times. They need to work more on achieving internal consensus and are therefore less reactive and in certain moments you're playing with, I won't say hours, but days".

Tight control over the surveyed companies aided not only the speed of action, but also the quality of the decisions made.

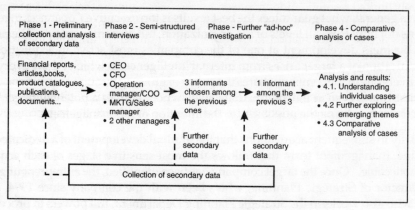

Figure 1: Phases in Data Collection and Analysis

DISCUSSION

Virtuous external growth processes: An emerging model

Understanding the emergence of acquisition capabilities in India SMEs offers a novel perspective for addressing a key question in entrepreneurship research, how and why some growing firms successfully avoid the traps inherent in resource maturity and arising simplicity, while others do not.

The three individual phases in the model are described in previous sections. Along with the knowledge accumulated by carrying out acquisitions and subsequent integration processes, there are other processes such as the development of formal tools that support growth (managerial, financial, accounting and control, operations control, etc.); the internalization of the lessons learned; the internalization of the acquisition/integration model that is gradually developed; the internalization of the new model of company that gradually arises from the acquisition processes (e.g., "we are a company: that grows by external lines; that sticks to certain principles in selecting targets, in deals, in integration, etc."); and the development of routines and mechanisms for correctly recalling accrued capabilities.

The emergence of acquisition absorptive capacity

Our data show that the capabilities and routines that develop during the acquisition and integration processes are of a very special kind. Namely, they are components of an Indian SME's absorptive capacity to gradually learn from early experiences how acquisitions should be carried out, and how such knowledge can be accurately retrieved in subsequent operations.

In the Indian SMEs, we investigate, the configuration of ACAP is that of a set of capabilities by which firms acquire, assimilate, transform, and exploit knowledge to acquire and integrate targets.

Developing and storing acquisition knowledge

The first dimension of ACAP that affects a firm's ability to make acquisitions is given by processes aimed at acquiring and assimilating external knowledge. This process can be seen as comprising the two sub-processes of acquisition (a firm's ability to single out and to access knowledge considered relevant to its purposes), and assimilation (a firm's ability to analyze, process, interpret, and understand knowledge).

The relatively limited resource endowment of Indian SMEs hampers their abilities to recognize the value of acquisitions. Hence, any organizational arrangement aimed at improving an Indian SME's access to acquisition knowledge will significantly improve its prospects of successfully identifying, acquiring, and integrating targets. Acquisition absorptive capacity in the firms we observe developed through a learning process with three characteristics.

First, whether positive or negative, the initial experiences and "crisis" situations determine the gaps between early expectations and actual results, which are the triggering events of capability learning.

Second, such learning is particularly effective when the characteristics of acquired companies are not too dissimilar from those of the acquirer, and when the pace of subsequent acquisitions is manageable by the organizational entity.

We note that acquisition and integration knowledge that is not internally developed by firms through experience is accessed by hiring managers who have the necessary skills and experiences. Here, we observe how some Indian SMEs even hired managers with acquisition and integration experience before such skills became relevant or needed. Such foresight is a characteristic of Indian SMEs that excel in managing rapid growth: they often hire and develop today the managerial team that they will need for tomorrow.

Studies that investigate the characteristics of managers' previous experience within high-growth firms find that "having experience in an industry similar to that of the firm" often discriminates between low and high-growth firms. In contrast, a peculiarity, we observe is that unlike managers of rapid organic growth, managers who are hired to manage future acquisitions do not necessarily come from the same industry. Rather, the skills that the externally growing firm seeks are the skills for using sophisticated managerial tools and for managing complex organizations, regardless of whatever industry and business context they have been developed.

Absorptive capacity is an organizational concept. Hence, potential absorptive capacity (PACAP) will not result only from individual knowledge bases, but also from transfers of knowledge across and within organizational subunits. Hence, organizational arrangements intended to transfer acquisition knowledge within the organization will likely improve absorptive capacity and the firm's ability to successfully carry out acquisitions. Evidence from our case studies suggests that the most effective organizational solutions our firms use to accumulate organizational knowledge linked to acquisitions are documents aimed at archiving "lessons learned"; valuation tools aimed at accessing external knowledge or at making explicit internally developed heuristics; managerial practices and routines that embody both explicit and tacit acquisition and post-acquisition integration knowledge; the development of organizational bodies, such as, an M&A managerial task force, that can provide an organizational arena where cumulated knowledge may reside.

Realizing the potential of cumulated acquisition knowledge

The effects of previous acquisition experiences can be positive or negative, depending on the degree of similarity between previous acquisitions and those underway. Many companies mistakenly apply the lessons learned in previous acquisitions to subsequent operations that involve companies that are too different for the same solutions to be effective.

Even when targets are similar, effective knowledge transfer is not given. Transferring learned solutions to subsequent operations is more than just an objective problem of similarity or difference between past acquisition experiences and present or future experiences. Companies must also have the subjective problem of the managerial team's ability to correctly perceive such similarities or differences.

Only if it has developed this ability can management avoid two mistakes that are apt to reoccur in managing acquisitions. The first mistake is managing acquisitions underway that are similar to operations carried out in the past, as if they required a different approach and responded to a different logic. Thus, it is not uncommon to see companies pay too much for a target, thus, repeating the same mistake, they made in the past; or acquire a company with a very strong, very different culture, when a similar choice had created problems in the not too distant past. The second mistake, unlike the first, consists in using the same approach to manage different kinds of acquisitions, seeing superficial similarities between the past and present operations when there are actually great structural differences.

The transfer of previously developed acquisition knowledge is facilitated by the direct involvement of the entrepreneur in most, if not all, acquisitions, and by the development of dedicated teams of managers, meeting periodically to evaluate new deals, to conclude them, or to manage the post-acquisition integration. Similarly, interlocking directorates within the group facilitates the transfer of resources and competencies. These findings support the results of previous studies on knowledge transfer in international acquisitions.

These organizational arrangements help in overcoming one of the big obstacles to successfully exploiting cumulated knowledge in acquisitions: lack of time. Along with the previously mentioned difficulties, acquisitions, and often, the subsequent integration processes, must be concluded with speed. Due to the time pressures that characterize almost all acquisitions, such operations are almost always identified, evaluated, carried out, and completed exclusively by top management. There is hardly ever time to consult the functional and divisional heads, the directors and managers within the company who could offer valuable knowledge acquired in past operations, important bits of collective information that, due to objective time constraints or pressing reasons of confidentiality, cannot be coordinated and fully exploited. Within most of the firms, we observed, the systematic and often formalized involvement between the entrepreneur and managers at different hierarchical levels offered an effective means to partially overcome this problem. Communication within the acquirer's organization, e.g., by involving business units in the acquisition process or by organizing annual conventions, is a valuable tool in boosting employee morale after mergers. These are all ways of recognizing the need to raise employees' awareness and understanding of the merger and the importance of building commitment to new strategic directions.

Absorptive capacity, external growth and entrepreneurial value creation

As suggested by current studies, ACAP is a dynamic ability to create and deploy knowledge. In turn, such an ability allows firms to build other organizational capabilities, such as the recognition of acquisition opportunities and resource transfers and recombinations that create value out of post-acquisition integration.

Given their nature of specific processes and organizational routines, there will be similarities across different organizations in the ways they access, store, retrieve, and exploit external and internal knowledge to carry out acquisitions and post-acquisition integration. However, given their local and path-dependent evolution, dynamic capabilities are highly idiosyncratic in the specific ways firms pursue, develop, and utilize them. Thus, the concept of ACAP as a dynamic capability that allows firms to improve their chances of successfully carrying out acquisitions may provide a suitable starting point for understanding why and how acquisitions may become value-creating entrepreneurial activities within the organizational entities that carry them out.

To pursue these goals, we have identified the individual components of acquisition ACAP and their organizational determinants, determinants that may be subject to managerial action aimed at improving resulting phenomena.

CONCLUSION AND IMPLICATIONS

Our research identifies lessons that were particularly effective for the companies in our survey, notwithstanding the presence of heterogeneous growth paths in the sample and the different amount of acquisition experience among the various companies.

There is a dominant theme: external growth can either be a source of entrepreneurial opportunities and development, or it can be a threat to the profitability of Indian SMEs. Which path a company takes depends on its ability to build learning paths on this experience. Indian SMEs often see obstacles in acquisitions that are linked to controlling the vigorous growth process; the negative financial consequences of borrowing money for acquisitions; and the difficult and often painful management of integration among organizations that are sometimes very different.

However, the companies that, willingly or reluctantly, decide to embark on acquisitions can draw on the competencies that gradually develop in these situations. This maturation occurs as long as the acquiring companies are able to establish the conditions in which these learning processes can take place, and to develop principles that can be correctly recalled when necessary. Only in this way can the inevitable initial mistakes and the possible crisis situations be transformed into lessons for the future.

These conditions are linked, first of all, to the type of acquisition carried out. Learning is easier when the acquired organizations are not too different from the competitive and production standpoint, but also from that of organizational culture and shared values. The development of competencies is easier when there are clear and tangible potential benefits to both companies. But the learning conditions are linked above all to managerial practices, to operational procedures, and to the tools and logic the companies in our survey used to generate, accumulate, and use the knowledge generated by the acquisition process.

Although none of the sample companies had specific skills before their first acquisitions, our research shows that they were able to gradually learn. This did not prevent difficulties from arising in subsequent acquisitions. However, the lessons learned from previous acquisitions allowed them to interpret external growth processes more as an opportunity than as a threat, thus adding an effective tool to their repertoire of skills for survival and sustainable success.

Emerging "lessons" concern, first of all, the characteristics needed for a potential acquisition target to be interesting. All the companies we analyzed were aware of the characteristics a company must have to be evaluated for the purpose of an acquisition. In other cases, the lessons involved ways of conducting the deal: how to carry out negotiations, the degree of flexibility in meeting the needs of the seller, the decision to take risks that go beyond those already implied in the standard contract, and whether or not to get help from a merchant bank. And last, the internalized experience can relate to the integration process of the acquired companies. Rarely do the lessons learned involve formal rules. More often, they represent principles of flexibility learned from experience.

For owners and managers of small businesses, understanding the process of developing competence in acquisitions can aid in assessing current challenges. It can help in anticipating the key requirements at various points in external growth patterns, from the decision to pursue growth by acquisitions, to the recurrent use of systematically developed and accrued knowledge. These are very specific messages, valid for the managerial team that has gradually distilled them, and they cannot be generalized. However, for the company, they represent a wealth of precious knowledge through which it can continue the external growth path, avoiding many obstacles. This knowledge becomes part of the corporate "genome", and is no longer linked to key-management turnover.

References

Adizes, Ichack (1989), *Corporate lifecycles: How and why corporations grow and die and what to do about it*, Englewood Cliffs, NJ: Prentice Hall.

Aldrich, Howard and Tom Baker (1997), Blinded by the cities? Has there been progress in the entrepreneurship field?, in: Daniel Sexton and Robert Smilor (eds.), *Entrepreneurship 2000*, Chicago, IL: Upstart Publishing Company, 377-400.

Ashby, Ross (1956), *An Introduction to Cybernetics*, London: Chapman & Hall.

Barringer, Bruce R. and Daniel W. Greening (1998), Small business growth through geographic expansion: A comparative case study, *Journal of Business Venturing* 13, 467-492.

Bruton, George D., Benjamin M. Oviatt, and Margaret A. White (1994), Performance of acquisitions of distressed firms, *Academy of Management Journal* 37, 972-989.

Capron, Laurence (1999), The long-term performance of horizontal acquisitions, *Strategic Management Journal* 20, 987-1018.

Cohen, Michael, Roger Burkhart, Giovanni Dosi, Massimo Egidi, Luigi Marengo, Massimo Warglien, and Sidney Winter (1996), Routines and other recurring action patterns of organizations: Contemporary research issues, *Industrial and Corporate Change* 5, 653-98.

Cyert, Richard and James March (1963), *A Behavioral Theory of the Firm*, Oxford: Oxford University Press.

Davidsson, Per (1989), Entrepreneurship – And after? A study of growth willingness in small firms, *Journal of Business Venturing* 4, 211-226.

Davidsson, Per (1991), Continued entrepreneurship: Ability, need, and opportunity as determinants of small firm growth, *Journal of Business Venturing* 6, 405-429.

Delmar, Frédéric, Per Davisson, and William B. Gartner (2003), Arriving at the high-growth firm, *Journal of Business Venturing* 18, 189-216.

Dosi Giovanni, Richard Nelson, and Sidney Winter (2000), *The Nature and Dynamics of Organizational Capabilities*, New York: Oxford University Press.

Eisenhardt, Kathleen (1989), Building theories from case study research, *Academy of Management Review* 14, 532.

550. Eisenhardt, Kathleen and Jeffrey A. Martin (2000), Dynamic capabilities: What are they? *Strategic Management Journal* 21, 1105-1121. Fowler, Karl and Dennis R. Schmidt (1989), Determinants of tender offer post-acquisition financial performance, *Strategic Management Journal* 10, 339-350.

Greiner, Larry (1972), Evolutions and revolutions as organizations grow, *Harvard Business Review* 50, 37-46.

Haleblian, Jerayr and Sydney Finkelstein (1999), The influence of organizational acquisition experience on acquisition performance: A behavioral learning perspective, *Administrative Science Quarterly* 44, 29-56.

Haspeslagh, Philippe and David B. Jemison (1987), Acquisitions: Myths and reality, *Sloan Management Review* 28, 53-58.

Hayward, Mitchell (2002), When Do Firms Learn from Their Acquisition Experience? Evidence from 1990-1995, *Strategic Management Journal* 23, 21-39.

Jemison, David (1988), Value creation and acquisition integration: The role of strategic capability transfer, *Advances in the Study of Entrepreneurship, Innovation, and Economic Growth*, Supplement 1, 191-218.

Jemison, David and Sim B. Sitkin (1986), Corporate Acquisitions: A Process Perspective, *Academy of Management Review* 11, 145-163.

Kim, Linsu (1998), Crisis construction and organizational learning: Capability building in catching-up at Hyundai Motor, *Organization Science* 9, 506-521.

Lubatkin, Michael, Roland Calori, Philippe Very, and John F. Veiga (1998), Managing mergers across borders: A two-nation exploration of a nationally bound administrative heritage, *Organization Science* 9, 670-684.

March, James (1991), Exploration and exploitation in organizational learning, *Organization Science* 2, 71-87.

Marks, Lorenz and Philip Mirvis (2001), Making mergers and acquisitions work: Strategic and psychological preparation, *Academy of Management Executive* 15, 80.

Miller, David (1993), The Architecture of Simplicity, *Academy of Management Review* 18, 116-138.

Mowery, David and Joanne E. Oxley, (1995), Inward technology transfer and competitiveness: The role of national innovation systems, *Cambridge Journal of Economics* 19, 67-93.

Nelson, Richard and Sidney Winter (1974), Neoclassical vs. evolutionary theories of economic growth: Critique and prospectus, *Economic Journal* 84, 886-905.

Park, Sungmoon and Zong-Tae Bae (2002), New venture strategies in a developing country: Identifying a typology and examining growth patterns through case studies, *Journal of Business Venturing* 19, 81-105.

Penrose, Edith (1959), *The Theory of the Growth of the Firm*, Oxford: Oxford University Press.

Schumpeter, Joseph (1934), *The Theory of Economic Development*, Cambridge, MA: Harvard University Press.

Siegel, Robin, Eric Siegel, and Ian C. MacMillan (1993), Characteristics distinguishing high-growth firms, *Journal of Business Venturing* 8, 169-180.

Singh, Harbir, Cynthia A. Montgomery (1987), Corporate acquisition strategies and economic performance, *Strategic Management Journal* 8, 377-386.

Teece, David, Gary Pisano, and Amy Shuen (1997), Dynamic capabilities and strategic management, *Strategic Management Journal* 18, 509-533.

Wiklund, Johan (1998), Small firm growth and performance: Entrepreneurship and beyond, Doctoral Dissertation, Jönköping International Business School, Jönköping.

Wiklund, Johan, Per Davidson, and Frederik Délmar (2003), What do they think and feel about growth? An expectancy-value approach to small business managers' attitudes toward growth, *Entrepreneurship Theory and Practice*, 247-270.

Winter, Sidney (1987), Knowledge and competence as strategic assets, in David J. Teecc (ed.), *The Competitive Challenge: Strategies for Industrial Innovation and Renewal*, New York: Harper & Row, 159-184.

32

An Organisation-level Assessment of Academic Entrepreneurship in Mumbai's Management Institutions: A Conceptual Framework

Amit Aggarwal*
Vaishali Nadkarni**
Dr. Pradip Manjrekar***

Research into the nature, antecedents and effects of university-level entrepreneurial activities has mostly been undertaken in the US and Europe. In Asia, interest on the phenomenon is steadily growing. The main aim of this paper is to develop a conceptual framework to empirically assess the impact of university leadership and organizational climate on academic entrepreneurship in Mumbai's Management Institutions in order to ascertain the extent, these organizations have been effective in fostering entrepreneurship within an academic setting. The study is based on the premise that Management Institutions wanting to be entrepreneurial need to understand how leadership and the internal work environment affect the level of academic entrepreneurship in their organizations. The model presented adopts the corporate entrepreneurship view and measures academic entrepreneurship as an organization level construct.

INTRODUCTION

The literature on entrepreneurial universities, academic entrepreneurship and technology transfer in the US, Europe, Latin America and Asia (Rothaermel *et al*, 2006), allowed this study to form the view that Academic Institutions in developed and developing countries are now asked to play a larger and enhanced role in contributing to international competitiveness of economies particularly via the process of research commercialization and contribute more to local and regional economic and social development. Further, research into the nature, antecedents and effects of Academic Institution-level entrepreneurial activities has mostly been undertaken in the US and Europe. In the Asia Pacific region, interest in the phenomenon is steadily growing (Collin and Wakoh, 2000).

* Sr. Faculty, ITM, Kharghar, Navi Mumbai.
** Principal, BJCC College, Charni Road, Mumbai.
*** Professor, Dr. D.Y. Patil Institute of Management Studies, Navi Mumbai.

The main aim of this paper is to present a conceptual framework that will be used to empirically examine the impact of institutional leadership and organizational climate on academic entrepreneurship in Mumbai's management institutions in order to ascertain the extent, these university organizations have been effective in fostering entrepreneurship within an academic setting. It is actually crucial for universities wanting to be entrepreneurial to understand how leadership and the internal work environment affect the level of academic entrepreneurship in their organizations. Thus, it is important to examine the relationship between these organizational factors and academic entrepreneurship. The model presented adopts the corporate entrepreneurship view and measures academic entrepreneurship as an organization-level construct.

It is argued that the organizational context of the university setting is central in the dynamic for entrepreneurship to take place. Hence, it is viewed that the corporate entrepreneurship perspective better addresses important relationships between academic entrepreneurs, host institution and parent academic discipline (Brennan *et al*, 2005; Brennan and McGowan, 2006). Therefore, academic entrepreneurship shall be defined as:

"Academic entrepreneurship encompasses acts of organizational creation, renewal, or innovation that occur within or outside a higher educational institution".

LITERATURE REVIEW

Several empirical studies which have developed or used an entrepreneurship, academic entrepreneurship or entrepreneurial university framework in examining entrepreneurial activities in a university setting include research by Louis *et al* (1989), Keast (1995), Chrisman *et al* (1995), Clark (1998), Klofsten and Jones-Evan (2000), Louis *et. al.* (2001), Jacob *et al* (2003), Laukkanen (2003), Zhao (2004), Bernasconi (2005), Brennan *et al* (2005), O'Shea *et al* (2005), Powers and McDougall (2005), and, Brennan and McGowan (2006). Keast (1995), studied a single university and interviewed the vice-president and director of research. He found that entrepreneurship activities or initiatives were becoming increasingly important to administrators in the Management Institutions. Chrisman *et al* (1995), also studied a single academic institution and documented the entrepreneurial activities of the Institution's faculties as well as the impact the university had on regional economic and technological development and the impact its budgetary problems might have on such activities. Data were collected through a multi-stage procedure which includes the use of questionnaires to all faculties, interviews with selected faculty members, interviews with entrepreneurs and managers, and secondary data.

It is possible that Louis *et al,* (1989) were among the first to pioneer the use of the academic entrepreneurship label. They studied on the academic entrepreneurial behaviours of life scientists in academic institutions and later extended the study to clinical and non-clinical life sciences faculty in academic institutions in the USA (Louis *et al*, 2001). The study undertaken by Klofsten and Jones-Evans (2000), focused on identifying entrepreneurship activities which had developed in five Irish Academic Institutions and four Swedish Academic Institutions. The study discussed and contrasted the extent to which academic entrepreneurship (i.e. all commercialization activities outside of the normal university duties of basic research and teaching) had developed. Data were collected via a structured questionnaire and statistically analyzed. The results demonstrated that there was considerable entrepreneurial experience among academics in both countries, and that this translated into a high degree of involvement in "soft" activities such as consultancy and contract research, but not into organizational creation via technology spin-offs. A different approach was utilized by Brennan *et al*, (2005) and Brennan and McGowan (2006) in their exploratory study of academic entrepreneurship within a university setting. The overall aim was to understand the enablers and barriers to academic entrepreneurship. The corporate entrepreneurship perspective was synthesized with several other theories to construct a framework of academic processes and five ontological dimensions/knowledge types. In both studies, they used a single case-study method and a purposeful sampling approach. While in-depth interviews were used for both, a questionnaire was developed in the former to assess preferences in academic entrepreneurs. There were also studies that focused on factors that stimulate the creation of spin-off firms from academic institutions. O'Shea *et al*, (2004) and O'Shea *et al*, (2005) argued that existing literature on academic institution spin-off activity can be divided into six distinct research streams or domains. Two studies (O'Shea *et al*, 2005; Powers and McDougall, 2005) used the resource-based view of the firm to investigate the impact of internal determinants i.e. resources, on academic activity spin-off activity. O'Shea *et al*, (2005) collected secondary data and through econometric estimators found history dependence for successful technology transfer to occur other than faculty quality, size, orientation of science and engineering funding, and, commercial capability. On the other hand, Powers and McDougall (2005), ran negative binomial regression analysis on secondary data of 120 academic institutions and found a set of institutional financial, human capital and organizational resources to be significant predictors of institution's commercialization activities. Using semi-structured interviews, direct observation and documentary reviews of five European academic institutions, Clark (1998), identified issues associated with the entrepreneurial transformation of these institutions and found five core elements of entrepreneurial institutions. Bernasconi (2005), used Clark's entrepreneurial institution framework and studied an institution undergoing transformation and privatization. Using secondary data, he concluded that under the pressure of privatization, the institution orientated itself to the market as a means of survival and growth, and used a triple-helix strategy for that purpose. Jacob *et al* (2003), also applied Clark's framework to a single technology academic institution and based on interviews with key personnel involved in the institution's internal transformation process, identified several important elements required for innovation. At the macro level, vision and implementation were crucial while at the micro level, flexibility and diversity were critical. The review of extant literature reveals that there seems to be three differing views on academic entrepreneurship: first, the view that academic entrepreneurship is in conflict with the traditional view of the university; thus, it normally and conveniently occurs outside the university and beyond the traditional role of the academia due to the conflict and tension created thereby (Louis *et al*, 1989; Klofsten and Jones-Evans, 2000; Laukkanen, 2003); secondly, the view that academic entrepreneurship is merely the creation of new business ventures by any of the institution agent, which therefore positions academic entrepreneurship as a mechanism of technology transfer (Chrisman *et al*, 1995; O'Shea *et al*, 2004; O'Shea *et. al.*, 2005; Powers and McDougall, 2005; Kirby, 2006); and thirdly, an integrative view based on corporate entrepreneurship perspective where academic entrepreneurship encompasses organizational creation, innovation and renewal inside and outside the university (Brennan *et al*, 2005; Brennan and McGowan, 2006).

Organizational Climate and Academic Entrepreneurship

In examining six conceptual models or overviews associated with entrepreneurial academic institutions (Clark, 1998; Etzkowitz *et al*, 2000; Sporn, 2001; Etzkowitz, 2004; Kirby, 2006; Rothaermel *et al*, 2006), several key elements demonstrated the impact of the organizational context on institution-level entrepreneurship. In fact, Brennan and McGowan (2006), found that the organization or working climate can profoundly influence the propensity of innovative behaviour. However, they indicated the lack of attention given to the organizational context in past studies on academic entrepreneurship. Some studies (Etzkowitz, 2003; Etzkowitz and Klofsten, 2005) have identified academic institution organizational designs as key construct of interest. The willingness and ability to act upon one's innate entrepreneurial potential is based on a calculated assessment.

Conditions in the internal environment dictate the perceived costs and benefits associated with taking personal risks, challenging current practices, devoting time to unproven approaches, persevering in the face of organizational resistance, and enduring the ambiguity and stress associated with an entrepreneurial initiative.

While organizational climate is defined by an array of elements, four key areas are crucial when it comes to facilitating, nurturing and supporting entrepreneurship. These four elements include *structure, controls, human resource management systems*, and *culture* (Ireland *et al*, 2006a; 2006b).

These four organizational dimensions can inhibit or facilitate entrepreneurial behaviour within organizations. Kirby (2006), reiterated that these organizational factors are barriers to entrepreneurship development in universities due to the inherent nature of educational institutions being large organizations and the lack of enterprise tradition within them. Sadler (2001), argued that it is not the educational institutions themselves which are inimical to entrepreneurship but traditional structures, bureaucracy, values and practices. And, bureaucratic structures and practices can be moulded in such a way as to enable and arguably stimulate entrepreneurial practices.

P1: An organizational climate which is perceived to foster entrepreneurial development is positively related to the level of academic entrepreneurship in the academic institution.

P1a: An organizational structure which is perceived to facilitate entrepreneurial development is positively related to the level of academic entrepreneurship in the university.

P1b: Control systems which are perceived to support entrepreneurial activities are positively related to the level of academic entrepreneurship in the university.

P1c: Human resource management systems which are perceived to encourage entrepreneurial behaviours are positively related to the level of academic entrepreneurship in the university.

P1d: An organizational culture which is perceived to nurture entrepreneurial behaviours is positively related to the level of academic entrepreneurship in the university.

LEADERSHIP AND ACADEMIC ENTREPRENEURSHIP

For internal factors like the organization's structure, control systems, human resource management systems and culture, leadership actually plays a significant role. The importance placed on the role of leadership in supporting academic entrepreneurship in an institution setting results in very different implications for how the university can foster entrepreneurship. In the first perspective, the behaviour of leaders plays a fundamental role in facilitating, nurturing and supporting entrepreneurial activities within the university. One of the critical elements found by Clark (1998), in successful entrepreneurial academic institutions is strong top-down leadership and policies that support and encourage the process of academic entrepreneurship and which merge entrepreneurial orientation objectives with the traditional academic values of the university (O'Shea *et al*, 2004). Guth and Ginsberg (1990), in providing a model for corporate entrepreneurship postulated that entrepreneurial behaviour in organizations is critically dependent on the characteristics, values/beliefs, and visions of their strategic leaders. Bercovitz and Feldman (2004), found a significant leadership effect whereby individual faculty members are more likely to engage in technology transfer activities when the department head is also actively involved in these activities. Hence, P2: The entrepreneurial behaviour of leaders in the academic institution significantly influences the level of academic entrepreneurship in the academic institution. Alternatively, the second perspective suggests that the role of leadership is to create a work environment that is highly conducive to academic entrepreneurship, and when the appropriate conditions are in place, academics and researchers will naturally behave entrepreneurially. Ireland *et al*, (2006b) argued that sustainable entrepreneurship is more likely to exist in organizations that adopt the entrepreneurial mindset. To develop this mindset, the leadership of the academic institution has the responsibility to create a work environment that is highly conducive to entrepreneurship, and when the appropriate conditions are in place, employees of all types will naturally unleash their entrepreneurial potentials (Jain and Yusof, 2007).

P3: The entrepreneurial behaviour of leaders in the university moderates the relationship between organizational climate and the level of academic entrepreneurship in the university.

Methodological Considerations and Research Implication

To date, little research has examined the linkages described in the preceding arguments in the context of universities (Brennan *et al*, 2005; Rothaermel *et al*, 2006). Further, studies have been theoretical, focusing mainly on the description of the phenomenon and testing casually observed relationships without invoking any deductive logic (Rothaermel *et al*, 2006). In fact, these studies were confined to a single academic institution (Keast, 1995; Chrisman *et al*, 1995; Bernasconi, 2005; Brennan *et al*, 2005; Brennan and McGowan, 2006) and varied approaches including surveys, interviews and analyses of secondary data had been used to describe and explain the phenomenon. There were several empirical studies which used a large sample of academicians and researchers, and conducted regression analysis but they were focused on the individual academic entrepreneur as the unit of analysis (Louis *et al*, 2001; Klofsten and Jones-Evans, 2000; Laukkanen, 2003). There is still a paucity of empirical research in this area of inquiry especially in examining the phenomenon at the organization-level (Brennan and McGowan, 2006; Rothaermel *et al*, 2006).

Thus, this study contributes to the literature and advances the research agenda in the area of academic entrepreneurship by making theoretical connection between academic entrepreneurship, organizational climate and leadership. The conceptual model has been constructed on the belief that these organizational factors influence and enable academic entrepreneurship in a university setting.

The research agenda will also encompass rigorous statistical analyses which include hypotheses testing, frequency analysis, chi-square tests, correlation analysis, multiple regression analysis, factor analysis, two-way ANOVA and canonical analysis.

CONCLUSION

The nature of the university evolves through time. Traditionally, universities have been viewed as the "high protecting powers of all knowledge and science, of fact and principle, of inquiry and discovery, of experiment and speculation" (Klofsten and Jones-Evans, 2000). The Industrial

Revolution in Europe and the conception of the modern university in the 19th century had, in fact, changed the nature of the university as the liberator and protector of knowledge to producer of industry-ready workers. In this century, universities are required to evolve again and be important engines of sustainable technological development and economic growth (Klofsten and Jones-Evans, 2000; Jain and Yusof, 2007). Initiating and facilitating change in a university system is a challenging task as universities are bureaucratic organizations traditionally designed to primarily advance their teachings and research missions (Sadler, 2001; Rothaermel *et al*, 2006). Hence, enabling academic entrepreneurship requires a strong conviction especially on the part of the university leadership and essentially on the part of its stakeholders. Creation of an organizational climate in a university environment conducive for the development of an academic entrepreneurship strategy is a complex task that requires the efforts of many committed individuals. These individuals are located in the industry, academia and government and often lack the coordination in their activities. Thus, a concerted effort needs to be organized and through proactive measures and organizational renewal, academics, researchers and scientists should be motivated and encouraged to maximize the potential of their research through entrepreneurial and technology transfer activities and mechanisms including the commercialization of their ideas in order to create value in society.

References

Bercovitz, J. & Feldman, M. (2004), Academic Entrepreneurs: Social Learning and Participation in University Technology Transfer, *Mimeo*, University of Toronto.

Bernasconi, A. (2005), University entrepreneurship in a developing country: The case of the P. Universidad Catolica de Chile, 1985-2000, *Higher Education*, 50(2): 247-274.

Brennan, M.C., Wall, A.P., & McGowan, P. (2005), Academic entrepreneurship: Assessing preferences in nascent entrepreneurs, *Journal of Small Business and Enterprise Development*, 12(3): 307-322.

Brennan, M.C., & McGowan, P. (2006), Academic entrepreneurship: An exploratory case study, *International Journal of Entrepreneurial Behaviour and Research*, 12(3): 144-164.

Chrisman, J.J., Hynes, T., & Fraser, S. (1995), Faculty entrepreneurship and economic development: The case of the University of Calgary, *Journal Business Venturing*, 10(4): 267-281.

Clark, B.R. (1998), *Creating entrepreneurial universities: Organizational pathways of transformation*, New York: Pergamon Press.

Collin, S., & Wakoh, H. (2000), Universities and technology transfer in Japan: Recent reforms in historical perspective, *Journal of Technology Transfer*, 25(2): 213-222.

Etzkowitz, H. (1983), Entrepreneurial scientists and entrepreneurial universities in American academic science, *Minerva*, 31(3): 198-233.

Etzkowitz, H., Webster, A., Gebhardt, C., & Terra, B.R.C. (2000), The future of the university and the university of the future: Evolution of the ivory tower to entrepreneurial paradigm, *Research Policy*, 29: 313-330.

Etzkowitz, H. (2003), Research groups as 'quasi-firms': The invention of the entrepreneurial university, *Research Policy*, 32: 109-121.

Etzkowitz, H. (2004), The evolution of the entrepreneurial university, *International Journal of Technology and Globalization*, 1: 64-77.

Etzkowitz, H., & Klofsten, M. (2005), The innovating region: Toward a theory of knowledge-based regional development, *R & D Management*, 35(3): 243-255.

Guth, W.D. & Ginsberg, A. (1990), Corporate Entrepreneurship, *Strategic Management Journal*, 11: 5-15.

Ireland, R.D., Kuratko, D.F., & Morris, M.H. (2006a), A health audit for corporate entrepreneurship: Innovation at all levels, part I, *Journal of Business Strategy*, 27(1): 10-17.

Ireland, R.D., Kuratko, D.F., & Morris, M.H. (2006b), A health audit for corporate entrepreneurship: Innovation at all levels, part II, *Journal of Business Strategy*, 27(2): 21-30.

Jacob, M., Lundqvist, M., & Hellsmark, H. (2003), Entrepreneurial transformations in Swedish university system: The case of Chalmers University of Technology, *Research Policy*, 32(9): 1555-1568.

Jain, K.K., & Yusof, M. (2007), Leadership challenges in developing an entrepreneurial university, *Proceedings of the International Conference on Leadership in a Changing Landscape*, Hotel Holiday Villa, Subang, Malaysia, 7-8 August.

Keast, D. (1995), Entrepreneurship in universities: Definition, practices and implications, *Higher Education Quarterly*, 49(3): 248-266.

Kirby, D.A. (2006), Creating entrepreneurial universities in the UK: Applying entrepreneurship theory to practice, *Journal of Technology Transfer*, 31(5): 599-603.

Klofsten, M., & Jones-Evans, D. (2000), Comparing academic entrepreneurship in Europe – The case of Sweden and Ireland, *Small Business Economics*, 14(4): 299-309.

Laukkanen, M. (2003), Exploring academic entrepreneurship: Drivers and tensions of university-based business, *Journal of Small Business and Enterprise Development*, 10(4): 372-382.

Louis, K.S., Blumenthal, D., Gluck, M.E., & Stoto, M.A. (1989), Entrepreneurs in academe: An exploration of behaviors among life scientists, *Administrative Science Quarterly*, 34(1): 110-131.

Louis, K.S., Jones, L.M., Anderson, M.S., Blumenthal, D., & Campbell, E.G. (2001), Entrepreneurship, secrecy and productivity: A comparison of clinical and non-clinical life sciences faculty, *Journal of Technology Transfer*, 26(3): 233-245.

O'Shea, R.P., Allen, T.J., O'Gorman, C., & Roche, F. (2004), Universities technology transfer: A review of academic entrepreneurship literature, *Irish Journal of Management*, 25(2): 11-29.

O'Shea, R.P., Allen, T.J., Chevalier, A., & Roche, F. (2005), Entrepreneurial orientation, technology transfer and spinoff performance of U.S. universities, *Research Policy*, 34(7): 994-1009.

Powers, J.B., & McDougall, P.P. (2005), Universities start-up formation and technology licensing with firms that go public: A resource-based view of academic entrepreneurship, *Journal of Business Venturing*, 20(3): 291-311.

Rothaermel, F.T., Agung, S.D., & Jiang, L. (2006), University entrepreneurship: A taxonomy of the literature, *Special Issue of Industrial and Corporate Change: The Rise of Entrepreneurial Activity at Universities: Organizational and Societal Implication*, Retrieved April 26, 2007 from http://www.cherry.gatech.edu/t2s2006/papers/rothaermel-4002-3-T.pdf

Sadler, R. (2001), A framework for the emergence of entrepreneurship and innovation in education, Conference paper for the Centre for the Economics of Education and Training. Retrieved June 20, 2007 from http://www.education.monash.edu.au/centres/ceet/docs/conference papers/2001confpapersadler.pdf

Sporn, B. (2001), Building adaptive universities: Emerging organizational forms based on experiences of European and US universities, *Tertiary Education and Management*, 7(2): 121-134.

Zhao, F. (2004), Academic entrepreneurship: Case study of Australian universities, *The International Journal of Entrepreneurship and Innovation*, 5(2): 91-97.

33

Why are Reality TV Programmes so Popular? Entrepreneur Creative Marketing Idea

GOI Chai Lee*

After the first reality TV programme created by Allen Funt in 1948, a lot of reality programmes were created to satisfy the viewers' needs. The reality programmes can be categorised into documentary-style, elimination/game shows, self-improvement/ makeover, renovation, dating shows, talk shows, hidden cameras, and hoaxes. This study tries to review the reality TV programmes currently viewed by TV channels and to explore why reality TV programmes are so popular to entrepreneurs. Finally, this study also tries to review the perception of reality TV programme and provide criticism of reality TV programmes available in Malaysia.

INTRODUCTION

Reality TV programme is a TV programming that offers unscripted dramatic and featured by ordinary people without any paid actors or actresses (Reality TV Online, n.d.). The first and longest running reality-based comedy programme, *Candid Camera* premiered on ABC 10 August 1948 under its original radio title Candid Microphone. The format of the programme featured footage taken by a hidden camera of everyday people caught in hoaxes devised by the show's host Allen Funt (Loomis, n.d.). Debuting in the 1950s, game shows *Beat the Clock* and *Truth or Consequences*, involved contestants in wacky competitions, stunts, and practical jokes. In 1948, talent search shows *Ted Mack's Original Amateur Hour* and *Arthur Godfrey's Talent Scouts* featured amateur competitors and audience voting (Rowan, 2000; Wikipedia, 2007a). First broadcast in the United Kingdom in 1964, the *Granada Television* series *Seven Up!*, broadcast interviews with a dozen ordinary seven-year old children from a broad cross-section of society and inquired about their reactions to everyday life. The first reality show in the modern sense was the 12-part 1973 PBS series *An American Family*, which showed a nuclear family going through a divorce (Wikipedia, 2007a). In year 1992, reality TV shows started to begin very popular in when the broadcast of *The Real World* by MTV. However, on the time, the show was not yet known as reality show. It was more known as TV series. Until year 2002, when CBS's air the show which was called *Survivor*, it was then finally given reality a name (Reality TV Online, n.d.).

* Faculty, Department of Marketing and Management, School of Business, Curtin University of Technology, Sarawak Campus, CDT 250 98009 Miri Sarawak, Malaysia.

TYPE OF REALITY PROGRAMMES

There are a number of sub-categories of reality TV programme (Wikipedia, 2007a):

i.   Documentary-style: Within documentary-style, reality televisions are of several subcategories or variants:

  ❖ Special living environment: *The Real World* is the originator of this style.

  ❖ Celebrity reality: These show a celebrity going about their everyday lives, examples, *The Anna Nicole Show*, *The Osbournes*, *Newlyweds: Nick and Jessica* and *Hogan Knows Best*.

  ❖ Professional activities: Documentary-style shows, example, *COPS* portray professionals about day-to-day business or performing an entire project over the course of a series.

ii. Elimination/Game shows: This type of reality TV is reality-competition or so-called reality game shows.

  ❖ Dating-based competition: Dating-based competition shows follow a contestant choosing one out of a group of suitors, examples, *The Bachelor*, *The Bachelorette*, *Temptation Island*, *For Love or Money*, *Average Joe*, *Flavor of Love*, *I Love New York* and *Rock of Love*.

  ❖ Job search: The competition revolves around a skill that contestants were pre-screened for examples: *The Apprentice*, *America's Next Top Model*, the *Idol* series, *Hell's Kitchen*, *Project Runway*, *Top Design*, *Last Comic Standing*, *The Starlet*, *On the Lot* and the *MuchMusic VJ Search*.

  ❖ Fear-centric: Introduced in 2000 by *MTV's Fear*.

  ❖ Sports: These programmes create a sporting competition among athletes attempting to establish their names in that sport, examples: *The Club*, *The Big Break*, *The Contender* and *The Ultimate Fighter*.

iii. Self-improvement/makeover: The shows cover a person or group of people improving their lives, examples: *The Swan*, *Celebrity Fit Club The Biggest Loser*, *Extreme Makeover*, *Queer Eye For The Straight Guy*, *Supernanny*, *Made*, *What Not to Wear*, *Trinny & Susannah Undress* and *Flavor of Love Girls: Charm School*.

iv. Renovation: It makes over part or all of a person's living space, work space or vehicle, examples being *Changing Rooms*, *Trading Spaces*, *Extreme Makeover: Home Edition*, *Debbie Travis' Facelift*, *Designed to Sell*, *While You Were Out* and *Holmes on Homes*.

v.   Dating shows: Unlike the aforementioned dating competition shows, some shows feature all new contestants each episode. This format was first used in the 1960s show *The Dating Game*.

vi. Talk shows: A talk show is that of a host interviewing a featured guest or discussing a chosen topic, examples, *Ricki Lake* and The *Jerry Springer Show*.

vii. Hidden cameras: This type of reality programming features hidden cameras rolling when random passers-by encounter a staged situation, examples *Candid Camera*, *Punk'd* and *Trigger Happy TV*, *Scare Tactics* and *Room 401*.

viii. Hoaxes: The show is focusing on pranks, although in these shows the hoax is more elaborate (lasting an entire season), the participants know they are appearing in a TV show (it is the true nature of the show that is kept secret from them), the cameras are out in the open and to parody the conventions of the reality TV genre, *The Joe Schmo Show*, My *Big Fat Obnoxious Boss*, *My Big Fat Obnoxious Fiance*, *Space Cadets* and *Invasion Iowa*.

There are a number of reality TV programme series available in Malaysia, examples, Akademi Fantasia (singing competition), The Firm (job interviewing competition), Ikon Malaysia (singing competition), Malaysian Idol (singing competition), One in a Million (singing competition), Please Give Me a Job! (job interviewing competition), Project Runway (fashion design competition), So You Think You Can Dance (dancing competition), Star Idol (reality drama competition), The Top Kid (kid talent competition), The Ultimate Prom Nite (ultimate prom king and queen), and What Women Want (Wikipedia, 2007b).

Objective

The objective of this study is to review the reality TV programmes currently viewed by TV channels. The study also tries to explore why reality TV programmes are so popular to entrepreneurs. Finally, this study tries to review the perception of reality TV programme and provide criticism of reality TV programmes available in Malaysia.

Why are Reality TV Programmes so Popular to Entrepreneurs?

According to Zona Latina (n.d), there are several reasons that reality TV programmes have become popular today. Entrepreneurs not only think of providing a creative idea of programme, but focus on the concepts of money, instant fame, and the guilty pleasure phenomenon. The first catalyst for reality TV programmes being popular today is money. Today's shows offer huge sums of money to people who do not necessarily possess the career skills that would make them a productive enough member of society to amass such wealth through honest work. Simplified, dumb people get lots of cash. Second, it takes ordinary people, sets them up in extraordinary situations on a world stage with other similarly commonplace individuals, and makes them the focus of a nation's attention. Obviously, the majority of the population has no chance of ever being picked as a participant for the show itself, but again the concept of vicarious living kicks in and the audience is hooked. The members of the show are satisfactorily every-day individuals for fans to wilfully suspend their disbeliefs. The third reason is guilty pleasure syndrome. It means taking delight in the misfortunes of others. It is a guilty pleasure.

The current concept of reality TV programmes is 'regardless of how people vote, letting the public dictate the outcome is a critical element of the show's success formula' (Sloan, 2004). Entrepreneurs use reality TV programmes to portray the reality situations in the shows. Reality is a more commercial version of what documentaries are (Keveney, 2007). Reality TV programmes are known for their lengthy, sometimes limiting contracts (Arnett, 2007). The main concept of this programme is to be so popular that the thrill of guessing who will be eliminated and who will ultimately win, followed by imagination of oneself in that similar situation (Findarticles, 2001).

It grew across the world last year to represent around 18% of top entertainment shows. It also revealed a jump in average Asia-Pacific viewing hours, adding 47 minutes a day to reach three hours and 23 minutes (Considine, 2004). Even, there is no need of an amount of money to generate the kind of buzz that these reality TV programmes can attract (Caristi, 2000).

In the entrepreneur point of view, reality TV programmes shows are the ultimate profit generating products that are intangible in nature.

The reality TV programmes are relatively cheaper because there is no need to pay writers or actors, no endless rehearsals, no need for elaborate sets, or even no need for rights clearance for music. Using ordinary people and later minor and declining celebrities is a cheap way to make television. Reality programming provides a cheap alternative to a drama. Typically, an hour-long drama can cost approximately US $1.5m per hour, whereas reality programmes can cost as little as US $ 200,000 per hour (Hill, 2005; *International Socialism*, 2007).

Reality TV shows were named as 20 of 25 highest rated shows in 2002 earned millions of dollars in advertising (Reality TV Introduction, n.d). the cost of the commercials of Fox Network for 30 second advertising spot on American Idol 3 were US $ 415 000 in year 2004, while CBS Network was able to sell US $ 428 000 just for 30 second advertising in Survivor (Patsuris, 2004). According to Howard (2004), only 16% of the viewers will watch the advertising when viewing live TV. In order to solve this problem, advertisers are increasingly integrating their sponsorship and their products or product placement into the reality TV programmes, rather than limiting their presence to commercials (Carter, 2003).

The popularity of such programmes is located in the shifting economics of broadcasting, which involves increasing competition and a move from the search for a mass audience to a niche audience. Television began as a technology that could only sustain a small number of channels. The imperative was to try to attract the largest possible number of people to a channel and programme types. The variety shows were developed precisely to generate mass audience (International Socialism, 2007). Reality TV programmes have the largest reach of any independently operated reality television and are the Internet's leading resource for reality television news and information. It provides coverage of nearly 300 reality television programmes and it has been featured and cited by countless print, electronic and online media (Reality TV World, n.d).

Reality TV programmes allow viewers to actively participate, empowering viewers through the voting process. The very common SMS contests being organised usually as a collaborated effort between the telecom carrier, the broadcaster and sponsors are essential in helping these media to generate strengthened public relations. These SMS contests build into the business model in a way that adds profits the more people cast votes. The charge is at RM0.50 for Malaysia, SGD $ 0.50 for Singapore, THB $ 6.00 for Thailand, PHP $ 2.50 for Philippine, NT $ 10 for Taiwan and HKD $ 2 for Hong Kong (StarTV, 2006). During the five months of American Idol show period, the audiences helped to generate 64.5 million text messages by using wireless mobile phones to votes for their favourite participators (AT&T, 2007).

Criticism of Current Reality TV Programmes in Malaysia

Tan (2006), in Citizen's Blog, The Star Online commented: are we becoming a nation of copycats and why is everything similar to the West? Reality shows, in fact, are embarrassing to the audience. Nevertheless, it is facing criticism by religious and government leaders who say the foreign-inspired fare threatens traditional values and steers viewers towards moral and cultural corruption. We're supposed to be modest Asian people, but we risk our heritage when we borrow from the West's lifestyle. U.S. reality shows including Survivor and American Idol have been big hits here, making Malaysian adaptations inevitable. And just as inevitably, such spin-offs are upsetting detractors who insist Malaysians should not take part in such shameful shenanigans (*The Associated Press*, 2005). Astro, NTV7, TV3, TV8, TV1 and TV2 today have moved away from presenting a cultural picture of the people in Malaysia. One of the sources of moral decline among youth, as it published articles and photos which were partly explicit and unbeneficial (BBC Monitoring Media, 2005). According to the psychologist, Professor Phillip Zimbardo, the programmes are misleading. He said, "The thing I hate about Survivor is that it promotes the worst aspects of human behaviour and wrong values" (Mason, 2001).

For the talent competition, example, singing competition, the quality of the winner sometimes is doubtful. By paying RM $ 0.50 per vote, viewers are given the power to choose their favourite contestant as winner. They are given the power to eliminate the contestants whom they do not like. For the second session Malaysian Idol finale, 1.6 million votes were received by the TV station (Elber, 2006).

Many people start wondering how real the reality TV programme is. Certain producers even admit that the situation of the reality TV programmes may not always to be real (Barry, 2005). Though everything seems spontaneous to TV viewers, certain scenes or occurrences are often recorded repeatedly over several takes to ensure that the camera angle, lighting and staging are the best possible (Arnett, 2007). Roger Graef a Britain's leading film-maker and broadcaster has revealed a litany of dishonour among reality shows. In some reality programmes, he had producers come to him and say, "I can't do this any more, I have been told to change the ending to conform to the script. They were told to force children to cry on Supernanny. They were told to change things on Wife Swap. If what you are producing is entertainment and you are using real people to do it, the truth is, there is a long tradition of illusions. That is the reality behind it" (Roberts, 2007).

CONCLUSION

The world reality itself has already drawn a lot of attraction throughout the world. The reality of reality TV programmes are not just, all about the competition, but also about the different human behaviours. To win the competition, each participant will be using different tactics, either sympathy, conspiracy and betrayal. This is what the audiences like to watch. Due to the high demand for these programmes, it is booming with tremendous growth of differentiated reality TV programmes which cater to the interests of different target markets.

References

Arnett, L. (2007), *The Real Deal*, Dance Spirit, Vol. 11, Iss. 9.

AT&T (2007), American Idol-AT&T Returns this Session as the Official Telecom Sponsor of the Popular Television Program, http://www.att.com/gen/press-room?pid=9674.

Barry, J. (2001), Reality Television: Does Anything Go?, Speakout.com, http://www.speakout.com/activism/issue_briefs/1275b-1.html.

BBC *Monitoring Media* (2005), Malaysia: Islamic Party Youth Wing Condemns "Disgraceful" TV Programmes, 27 March.

Caristi, D. (2001), Reality Shows to the Networks' Rescue – Prove Financial Boon for Television Networks, Findarticles, http://www.findarticles.com/p/articles/mi_m1272/is_2674_130/ai_76550709.

Considine, P. (2004), *Reality in Asia*, Campaign, 21 May, p. 35.

Elber, L. (2006), American Idol, Proves Global Reach, CBS News, http://www.cbsnews.com/stories/2006/05/23/ap/entertainment/mainD8HP5RV00.shtml.

Findarticles (2001), The Tribe has Spoken – Nearly Half of Americans are Faithful Viewers of Reality Television – Statistical Data Included, American Demographics, http://www.findarticles.com/p/articles/mi_m4021/is_2001_Sept_1/ai_78426786.

Hill, A. (2005), Reality TV, *London, p. 6.*

International Socialism (2007), Reality TV: The Big Brother Phenomenon, 9 April, http://www.isj.org.uk/index.php4?id=314&issue=114.

Keveney, B. (2007), "How TV started getting Real; for Good or Bad, 'The Real World' Revolutionized TV", *USA Today, 10 October.*

Loomis, A. (n.d), Candid Camera, The Museum of Broadcast Communications, http://www.museum.tv/archives/etv/C/htmlC/candidcamera/candidcamera.htm.

Mason, B. (2001), Psychologist Puts the 'Real' into Reality TV, Stamford Report, http://www.news-service.stamford.edu/news/2001/may2/zimbardo-52.html.

Patsuris, P. (2004), The Most Profitable Reality TV Shows, Forbes.com, http://www.forbes.com/home/business/2004/09/07/cx_pp_0907realitytv.html.

Reality TV Online (n.d), History of Reality TV, http://www.reality-tc-online.com/articles/history-reality-tv.html.

Reality TV World (n.d), Advertise on Reality TV World, http://www.realitytvworld.com/realitytvworld/advertise.shtml.

Roberts, L. (2007), "Reality Show Toddlers forced into Tears to push up Ratings", *The Daily Telegraph,* 28 September.

Reality TV Introduction (n.d), http://www.enotes.com/reality-tv-article.

Rowan, B. (2000), Reality TV takes Hold, Infoplease.com, 21 July.

Sloan, P. (2004), The Reality Factory Fremantle: Media Didn't Invent Reality TV, But It's Minting Money with 263 Shows in 37 Countries, Including Megahits like American Idol and The Apprentice. Here's How the U.K. Media Power came to Rule the World's Airwaves, http://money.cnn.com/magazines/business2/business2_archive/2004/08/01/377373/index.htm.

StarTV (2006), Miss World 2006, http://www.startv.com/missworld/faq.htm.

Tan, Z. (2006), Malaysia's Most Beautiful????!!!!!!!!, Citizen's Blog, The Star Online, 27 January, http://blog.thestar.com.my/permalink.asp?id=805.

The Associated Press (2000), Reality TV in Malaysia stirs Controversy, ABC Inc., 9 September, http://abc13.com.

Wikipedia (2007a), Reality Television, 7 November, http://en.wikipedia.org/wiki/Reality_tv.

Wikipedia (2007b), Category: Malaysian Reality Television Series, 2 June, http://en.wikipedia.org/wiki/Category:Malaysian_reality_television_series.

Zona Latina (n.d), Reality Television, http://www.zonalatina.com/Zldata302.htm.